This bold and unabashedly utopian book advances the thesis that Marx's notion of communism is a defensible, normative ideal. However, unlike many others who have written in this area Levine applies the tools and techniques of analytic philosophy to formulate and defend his radical political program.

The argument proceeds by filtering the ideals and institutions of Marxism through Rousseau's notion of the "general will." Once Rousseau's ideas are properly understood it is possible to construct a community of equals who share some vision of a common good that can be achieved and maintained through cooperation or coordination that is at once both voluntary and authoritative. The book engages with liberal theory in order to establish its differences from Rousseauean-Marxian political theory.

This provocative book will be of particular interest to political philosophers and political scientists concerned with Marxism, socialist theory, and democratic theory.

" . . . unrelentingly intelligent and innovative. . . . What gives this book its particular quality is the author's consistently sensible dealing with important and controversial questions, his ability to shape difficult claims persuasively to the argument in hand."

Alan Gilbert, *University of Denver*

The general will

The general will

Rousseau, Marx, communism

ANDREW LEVINE
UNIVERSITY OF WISCONSIN – MADISON

CAMBRIDGE
UNIVERSITY PRESS

Published by the Press Syndicate of the University of Cambridge
The Pitt Building, Trumpington Street, Cambridge CB2 1RP
40 West 20th Street, New York, NY 10011-4211, USA
10 Stamford Road, Oakleigh, Melbourne 3166, Australia

First published 1993

Printed in the United States of America

Library of Congress Cataloging-in-Publication Data

Levine, Andrew, 1944–
The general will : Rousseau, Marx, communism / Andrew Levine.
p.   cm.
Includes bibliographical references (p.   ) and index.
ISBN 0-521-44322-9
1. General will.   2. State, The.   3. Communist state.
4. Democracy.   5. Rousseau, Jean-Jacques, 1712–1778 – Contributions
in political science.   6. Marx, Karl, 1818–1883 – Contributions in
political science. I. Title.
JC328.2.L48   1993
320'.01'1 – dc20   93-2768
CIP

A catalog record for this book is available from the British Library.

ISBN 0-521-44322-9 hardback

Contents

Preface   *page* ix

Introduction   1

The end of the state   3
Exculpations   7
An overview   15

CHAPTER 1
The general will in theory   18

Are all wills private?   20
Nonwelfarist interests   22
Individuals   25
A free-rider problem?   30
Internal relations   33
The reality of the general will   34

CHAPTER 2
The "origin" of the private will   36

The original state of nature   38
Before the private will   41
From self-love to *amour propre*   44
De facto states   50
Freedom   54
Ephemeral Hobbesianism   57

CHAPTER 3
Solidarity   60

A point of departure   60
What is solidarity?   63
The practice of solidarity   66
Beyond solidarity   68
Solidarity forever?   73

Contents

CHAPTER 4
Democracy in the Age of States   75

Democracy   76
Modeling democracy   80
Democracy in a world of states   85
Limits to decentralization   88
Representation   90
Representation versus delegation   94
Elections   98
Democratization   99

CHAPTER 5
The last state   101

Democracy and dictatorship   102
Relative autonomy   106
Beyond liberal democracy?   112
The ideological state apparatus   115
Cultural revolution   120

CHAPTER 6
The liberal state and/versus the last state   123

Romanticism/Careerism   128
Enhancing autonomy   133
Self-realization and the good   136
Higher and lower pleasures   138
Experimentalism   141
The liberal state and the last state   142

CHAPTER 7
Rousseauean Marxism and/versus liberalism   147

What do liberals want?   152
Autonomy   159
Harmony   162
Community   165

CHAPTER 8
Communism   168

Beyond scarcity?   169
Beyond self-interest?   173
Liberalism and the general will   175
Virtue   179
From virtue to justice   182
Equality and "bourgeois right"   185
Basic liberties   188

Contents

Justice internalized   190
Responsibility   191
Justice and the general will   193
The exercise of the general will   196
Aggregating autonomy   198

CHAPTER 9
After Communism, communism?   203

Small-*c* communism   206
Socialism   209
Marxism today   210
Historical materialism   214
Must we bring social democracy back in?   217

Index of names   221

Preface

In the spring of 1988, when I formed the intention to write this book, (big-C) Communism reigned over more than a third of the world's population, the Cold War still simmered, and the prospect of nuclear annihilation continued to threaten. Then, in a remarkably short time, Communism was overthrown as an economic system and mode of governance in Eastern Europe and the former Soviet Union, the Cold War ended, and the threat of nuclear war receded dramatically. It is not at all clear what impact these events ought to have on philosophical reflections on politics or on social theory. But, by accelerating a process evident for some time and in varying degrees throughout the world, they have had a definite effect on our intellectual culture. By 1992, as I write these words, forms of theorizing linked, however tenuously, with the Bolshevik Revolution and its continuations, with Marxism, and even with socialism have fallen into greater disrepute than at any time in this century.

To set out to defend (small-c) communism at a time when the Gorbachev Revolution was unfolding was already to go against the current. In the present conjuncture, it may seem incomprehensible. I maintain, however, that doing so is reasonable, timely, and even urgent. The discussions of Rousseauean political philosophy and Marxian communism that ensue will, I hope, partly vindicate this contention. However, the reader should be aware at the outset that what I shall try to defend has at least two interconnected dimensions that I have purposely confounded. It was, in part, to signal this intention that I have made Rousseau the central figure in the chapters that follow, even more than Marx himself, and that I have made the *general will* its organizing concept.

At one level, I argue that Marx's notion of communism or, more precisely, his core idea bereft of some of the unrealistic (and

ix

undesirable) claims he made in its behalf is a defensible normative ideal and that some ideas of Rousseau's about rational cooperation – understood in a way that renders them inoffensive to mainstream, liberal "individualism" – help to elaborate Marx's idea. Were I to have framed my positions exclusively in these terms, what I would go on to argue would be *politically* out of line with the current consensus but *theoretically* consistent with it. Then the general will, far from being central to my argument, would be, at most, an intriguing but inapt concept – from which a few useful insights could be teased out and reconstructed. For several years, in the course of an interminable and (for me) always illuminating debate, Erik Wright has urged me repeatedly to adopt this framework. He has convinced me, despite considerable resistance on my part, that most of what I have to say about Marxian communism can be accommodated within it.

However, in the end, I have not followed his advice. No doubt, in making the general will central, I do throw an extrapolitical obstacle in the way of acceptance of my principal claims, at least for some readers. Nevertheless, I believe that the advantages that follow from according the general will pride of place more than offset this loss. It will emerge that mainstream theorizing – which, in Rousseauean terms, acknowledges only *private* volition – is inhospitable to Marxian communism. It is so, I shall argue, in consequence of its tacit reliance on an underlying metaphor that depicts individuals, like atoms, as radically independent of each other. On the other hand, the general will, as Rousseau conceived it, rests on a different metaphor, according to which, as I shall go on to explain, individuals are related "internally." It may indeed be possible to translate, more or less "without remainder," from a theoretical framework based on one of these metaphors to one based on the other. But in political philosophy forms of expression matter – not least for what they suggest heuristically and, above all, for the kind of politics they promote, for what we might call their "political tendency." This is why I think it worthwhile to dislodge a metaphor that tends, as it were, in the wrong direction and to adopt, when appropriate, a more felicitous idiom, resting on a different metaphor, in its stead. Thus, at the same time that I offer a brief in defense of Marxian communism, I also argue for the coherence and possible applicability of Rousseau's notion of the general will.

It is, in the main, readers influenced by contemporary forms of economic modeling who will find the general will problematic. Others may feel that I pay too much attention to defending Rousseau's idea and wonder if what I say is not, in consequence, overly defensive. I shall go on to argue, however, that individualist challenges to Rousseauean political philosophy and Marxian political theory have merit and that no defender of Marxian communism can neglect them without peril. In the end, however, the general will withstands critical scrutiny and has a crucial if not strictly indispensable role to play in the normative theory of communism.

There is a sense in which the debate with mainstream "individualism" that runs throughout the following pages resembles the dispute between atheists and those liberal theologians who effectively concede the atheists' case against traditional believers but who nevertheless represent their views in a theistic idiom. It could be said that what is at issue between them is only a form of expression. But both sides would agree that this difference has momentous consequences – for both theory and practice – and that their respective positions can only be assessed in light of these consequences. Similarly, my quarrel with individualists who would dispute the coherence or applicability of the general will revolves ultimately on the consequences of taking up one or another form of expression. It is, in short, because I think the case for communism compelling that I opt for the idiom I do. The analogy, however, is not perfect – unless one believes, as some "postmodern" relativists do, that scientific naturalism is just one form of discourse among others with no particular purchase on truth. If we reject this account of science, as I think we should, a nontheistic construal of what, by hypothesis, both the atheists and the theologians believe has a clear mark in its favor. For reasons that I will not attempt to elaborate, I do not believe that the kinds of normative discourse deployed here can track truth with the authority that science does. In this instance, therefore, neither governing metaphor can be defended on a priori grounds; their heuristic implications and political tendencies are decisive.

I conceived the idea for this book in 1988, but it continues a line of inquiry that I have pursued intermittently since 1965 when, as an undergraduate at Columbia University, I attended a remarkable course on Rousseau and Marx taught by Professor Robert Paul Wolff. In the time that has elapsed since then, political philosophy has changed almost as dramatically as the political climate in which it operates. Until well into the 1970s, Marxism, for American philosophers, was still a barely naturalized European immigrant. With the rise of "analytical Marxism," that situation has altered beyond recognition.[1] What follows here attests to these transformations. Twenty-five years ago, before *A Theory of Justice*[2] and all that has followed in its wake, the liberal egalitarianism that figures so prominently in some of the chapters that follow was more implicit than self-conscious. This too has changed profoundly; today, liberal egalitarian social philosophy is a flourishing and ongoing concern. Only Rousseau studies exhibit a certain continuity. However, in recent years Rousseau has not much engaged political philosophers, in contrast to scholars interested mainly in the history of political thought. It should be obvious that I consider this neglect unwise, and I will be pleased if what follows here helps in some small way to rectify it. In any case, I would note that, despite all the changes of the past quarter century, my thinking on Rousseau has remained remarkably constant. My lodestars remain Wolff's own investigations of Rousseauean political philosophy[3] and what seems to me, in retrospect, a European import that has held up remarkably well over the years, Louis Althusser's still little-known lectures on *The Social Contract*.[4]

I have not hesitated to draw on earlier work of mine on Rousseau, Marx, and Marxian communism. However, so far as possible, I have relegated references to my previously published writings to footnotes, and then only when assertions made in the text call for extensive argumentation that would be off-putting to rehearse in the present context. I trust that readers unfamiliar with what I have written elsewhere will find that what I shall go on to discuss here stands well enough on its own.

I cannot begin to thank everyone who has helped in one way or another to shape my views on the themes of this book. In addition

1 Cf. Erik Olin Wright, Andrew Levine, and Elliott Sober, *Reconstructing Marxism* (London: Verso, 1992), Chapter 1.
2 John Rawls, *A Theory of Justice* (Cambridge, Mass.: Harvard University Press, 1971).
3 Unfortunately, very little of this has found its way into print; but see Robert Paul Wolff, *In Defense of Anarchism* (New York: Harper, 1970).
4 Louis Althusser, "Sur le *Contrat Social* (Les Décalages)," in *Cahiers pour l'analyse*, no. 8, *L'Impensée de Jean-Jacques Rousseau* (Paris, n.d.), translated as "Rousseau: The Social Contract," in Louis Althusser, *Politics and History* (London: New Left Books, 1972). In my first sustained investigation of Rousseau's political philosophy, I attempted, in effect, to deploy Althusserian positions on Rousseau to some of the theoretical problems identified by Wolff; see *The Politics of Autonomy: A Kantian Reading of Rousseau's "Social Contract"* (Amherst: University of Massachusetts Press, 1976).

to countless conversations, Erik Wright has read and commented in heroic detail on drafts of this manuscript. Daniel Hausman has also provided extensive and insightful comments at various stages of its composition. Others who have provided comments on particular chapters or on talks that have eventually become chapters include Richard Arneson, G. A. Cohen, Gerald Doppelt, Jane Mansbridge, Debra Satz, Elliott Sober, Robert Ware, and Daniel Wikler. I must note that few if any of these friends and colleagues would want to sign on to all or even very much of what I shall go on to maintain. A version of Chapter 1 was read at a conference on Biology, Behaviour, and Society at the University of Alberta, Edmonton, in May 1991; an article based on that talk will appear in a special supplement of the *Canadian Journal of Philosophy*. What follows also draws on talks I have given at the University of Wisconsin – Madison, the University of Massachusetts – Amherst, the University of California – San Diego, the University of British Columbia, the University of Turin, Iowa State University, and the University of Chicago, and at the 1989 International Meeting of the Conference for the Study of Political Thought in Williamstown, Massachusetts. I have benefited greatly from discussions at these events. I would also like to thank my students at the University of Wisconsin – Madison, some of whom helped enormously in the gestation of my thinking on Rousseau and Marx. Finally, special thanks are due to Terence Moore at Cambridge University Press for his assistance in seeing this book through to publication.

Introduction

For nearly four centuries, a principal concern of political philosophers has been to justify the coordination of the activities of
radically independent *individuals* by the state, a complex of institutions that monopolize the right to compel compliance by the use
of threat of force. In what follows, I will challenge aspects of this
project – the better to accommodate a way of thinking about society and politics that, following Marx's lead, envisions a social order, communism, constituted by people who have substantially
overcome a need for state-compelled coordination. My aim is to
defend a nonutopian but still Marxian version of this idea.

In an intellectual culture as prone to historicism as ours now is,
it should be widely acknowledged that such major historical transformations as the expansion of (individualizing) market relations
and the emergence of the nation-state have profoundly affected
philosophical reflections on politics and society. Nevertheless, the
extent to which prevailing understandings of the individual and
the state depend upon transitory real-world phenomena is commonly overlooked. For many purposes, the coexistence of a widespread awareness of the historicity of these concepts with their
ahistorical treatment in contemporary political theory has been benign. But in order to defend Marxian communism, it is especially
important to bear in mind how marked political philosophy today
is by the historical specificity of its fundamental concepts.

The individualistic aspect of modern political philosophy is at
variance with earlier understandings of politics and also, to some degree, with political currents, whether of the Left or Right, that privilege *communal* values and perspectives. A case in point is Marxism
itself. Since its inception, Marxism has developed partly in opposition to, partly in isolation from mainstream, "bourgeois" social science and philosophy. According to each side's self-representations

and in their polemics against each other, bourgeois theorists endorse and Marxists oppose "individualism." However, recent work in the social sciences and philosophy and new styles of Marxist theorizing have transformed this shared understanding irreversibly. Partly in consequence, many of the methodological and substantive positions that were once thought to distinguish Marxism from mainstream views have come to seem less salient and many alleged differences now appear illusory.[1] Indeed, so many of the old certainties have given way that it has become apt to ask what, if anything, remains that is distinctively Marxist. In the chapters that follow I investigate this question – with a focus on normative concerns. It will become evident that Marxist positions in political theory and philosophical accounts of the state are not nearly so orthogonal as they formerly appeared. But it will also emerge that there remain fundamental differences with far-reaching implications that distinguish Marxist political theory from mainstream positions.

I shall assume as a working hypothesis that an idea introduced by Rousseau, the general will, bears importantly on the possibility and desirability of Marx's notion of statelessness. Rousseau's idea, very generally, is that in some contexts individuals *can* and *should* coordinate their activities by seeking to advance their interests as integral members of the collective entities they freely constitute. In particular, Rousseau maintained that it is reasonable for individuals in a "state of nature" to subordinate their "private wills," which aim at "private interests," to the "general will," which aims at the "general interest," the interest of "the whole community" – in order to become the autonomous agents they potentially are.

My intent in representing this idea in Rousseauean terms is partly reflationary, partly deflationary. Rousseau is a central figure in today's "canon" of political philosophers, yet his notion of the general will, surely his principal contribution to Western political thought, plays virtually no role in contemporary political philosophy. This situation is not nearly so odd as may at first appear. Rousseau's account of the general will invites misunderstandings, and much of what he used the concept to express can be represented in more familiar terms. Nevertheless, it will become evident that there are good reasons for taking Rousseau's account of

---

1 Facets of this thesis are defended, implicitly and explicitly, in Erik Olin Wright, Andrew Levine, and Elliott Sober, *Reconstructing Marxism* (London: Verso, 1992).

the general will seriously and for attempting to retrieve the conceptual insights and empirical speculations that constitute its "rational kernel." It is therefore worth attempting to reflate this currently defunct idea. However, at the same time, if the general will is to be put to use in defense of statelessness, it is crucial that the misunderstandings it elicits be dissipated. Doing so will deflate the apparent novelty of Rousseau's idea and recast its function in political arguments. But it will not render the idea otiose. What I shall say about Rousseau is relevant to the defense of communism, and what I shall say in behalf of communism bears on the case I shall make for the pertinence of Rousseau's idea to philosophical and political concerns. Thus I shall enlist Rousseau in defense of communism and communism in defense of the cogency and timeliness of the general will. The principal justification for bringing the general will to center stage in the chapters that follow is to facilitate these mutually reinforcing objectives.

In addition to Rousseau and Marx there will be a third point of reference in several of the chapters that follow: liberalism. Not long ago, Marxists were eager to deride liberalism's defects. However, in one of the more ironical turns of recent political and intellectual history, many progressive philosophers today find in liberalism a vehicle for waging the struggle for equality associated historically with Marxian socialism. I believe that in the present conjuncture it is important not to forsake Marxian insights but also to acknowledge Marxism's flaws in contrast to aspects of liberal theory and practice. My contention – modest in comparison with what many on the left once believed, outrageous in light of today's received wisdom – is just that communism, understood generally as Marx intended, implements a sounder normative vision than anything liberalism can contemplate and that general will coordination, an idea liberalism resists, has an important role to play in Marxian communism.

THE END OF THE STATE

Rousseau's aim in *The Social Contract* can be succinctly put: "[T]aking men as they are and laws as they might be," he sets out to demonstrate the possibility of legitimate political authority and obligation.[2] In his terminology, supreme authority over a given

---

2 *The Social Contract*, Book I, Introductory Note. Rousseau's *Social Contract* is divided into relatively brief chapters and is available in English in many editions,

3

territory or population is "sovereignty"; what the sovereign rules is a "state."[3] Rousseau then contends that "sovereignty is nothing but the exercise of the general will"[4] or, equivalently, that a state is established when individuals place themselves "under the supreme direction of the general will."[5] Since the general will is the true will of each of the state's members, the sovereign and its subjects are one.[6] Rousseau succeeds in demonstrating, at least to his own satisfaction, that the general will is real and therefore that political authority and obligation are possible – in short, that the idea of a just state is coherent and applicable under human conditions. But it is one thing for a just state to be possible and something else for it to be a feasible political objective. Rousseau was deeply pessimistic about the latter prospect. The world is divided into de facto states; authority is everywhere asserted and acknowledged. A coercive apparatus superintends and reinforces a civil society based on political and material inequalities. In consequence, human mentalities have become corrupted, perhaps irreversibly, and the de jure state, where legitimate authority and obligation exist, may never be realizable anywhere.

Thus, in Rousseau's political thought, the exercise of the general will is more nearly a regulative idea than a plausible political aspiration. Sovereignty is possible in principle but almost certainly not in real history. Already in the *Discourse on the Sciences and Arts*, *The First Discourse*, Rousseau faulted "progress" for corrupting human nature and burdening the human race with institutions detrimental to its well-being. *The Second Discourse* extended this diagnosis by attributing the detrimental effects of progress to the emergence of inequalities within human communities. In *The Social Contract*, the toll exacted by these developments is depicted in an even more devastating light. Identifying essential humanity with freedom of the will (autonomy) and arguing that the exercise of the general will is a necessary condition for actualizing this es-

none of which is standard. For the convenience of the reader, therefore, I shall not cite a particular edition in referring to it but will instead indicate the chapter in question. All translations from *The Social Contract* are my own and are based on the text edited by Bernard Gagnebin and Marcel Raymond, published in Jean-Jacques Rousseau, *Oeuvres complètes*, vol. 3 (Paris: Gallimard, Bibliothèque de la Pléiade, 1964). The English translation that I have consulted most frequently is by Donald Cress. It may be found in Jean-Jacques Rousseau, *The Basic Political Writings* (Indianapolis and Cambridge, Mass.: Hackett, 1987).

3 Ibid., Chapter 6.   4 Ibid., Book II, Chapter 1.   5 Ibid., Book I, Chapter 6.
6 Ibid.

sential trait, he contends that obstacles in the way of realizing a just state are mortal dangers to humanity itself.[7]

Several years ago, in *The End of the State*, I argued that, in conditions of material abundance and under socialist property relations, Rousseau's regulative idea or some close approximation actually is historically feasible.[8] I maintained that communism in Marx's sense is Rousseauean sovereignty attained or rather overcome, since what Rousseau's social contract establishes is not, in the end, a state at all but, as Kant would have it, a "republic of ends." To be sure, without considerable uncoerced compliance, no de facto state could long endure. But, ultimately, states coordinate individuals' behaviors "externally" – through force. On the other hand, in republics of ends, behaviors are "internally" coordinated by what Kant called a harmony of rational wills.[9] The use or threat of force may sometimes be necessary even in a republic of ends, just as uncoerced compliance is indispensable in states. "The administration of things" that, according to Engels (and, before him, Saint-Simon), replaces "the governance of men" after the demise of class society may still need to use force to overcome collective "weaknesses of will." Thus public coercive force is unlikely to disappear entirely under communism. But the use of force in genuinely communist societies would be, as it were, an administrative imperative, not an exercise of *state* power. I argued that the difference is not merely definitional. The idea that the state under communism would "wither away" is distinct from other claims that

7 Ibid., Chapters 4 and 6. See also Andrew Levine, *The Politics of Autonomy:* A
  Kantian Reading of Rousseau's "Social Contract" (Amherst: University of Massachusetts Press, 1976), passim.
8 Andrew Levine, *The End of the State* (London: Verso, 1987).
9 There is reason to think that what Kant intended by a "harmony of rational wills" is, at least in part, the ideal of rational cooperation implicit in Rousseau's account of legitimate political association. A historical and conceptual connection between Rousseau and Kant has long been acknowledged. Hegel discerned it in *The Phenomenology of Mind* in the section entitled "The Moral View of the World." In this century, the idea that an important motivation for Kant's work in moral philosophy was precisely to provide foundations for Rousseauean political philosophy has been pressed most forcefully by Ernst Cassirer; see especially, *The Question of Jean-Jacques Rousseau*, trans. and ed. Peter Gay (Bloomington: Indiana University Press, 1954), and *Rousseau, Kant, Goethe*, trans. James Gutmann, P. O. Kristeller, and J. H. Randall (Princeton: Princeton University Press, 1945). I argue in support of Cassirer's thesis by exhibiting conceptual affinities joining Rousseau's political philosophy with Kantian moral philosophy in *The Politics of Autonomy*.

can be made for Marxian communism – and less susceptible to disputation than many of them.

These claims depend on the plausibility of the core theses of Marx's theory of history, historical materialism. In the historical materialist scheme, communism is the end of a determinate process of historical change. In *The End of the State*, I argued that a defensible historical materialism implies only that the material conditions for a communist economic structure can come into being.[10] I also argued that there are reasons for thinking communism more than just materially possible. In addition to "discovering" the model of rational cooperation communism supposes, Rousseau, despite himself, provided support for the conclusion that communism actually is feasible. The aspects of Rousseau's political philosophy that encourage faith in the transformative effects of political institutions – above all, in the institutions that implement democratic deliberation and collective choice – support the idea that the motivations of citizens in genuinely radical democracies can change; that individuals can become less self-interested, more solidary – in short, more inclined to support general over particular interests. I maintained that a similar faith in democracy is evident in Marxist political theory or, at least, in an important strain of it, and that this conviction plays a pivotal role in Marx's case for communism. Thus the idea that the state can and should wither away is underwritten by venerable and persuasive, though hardly incontrovertible, arguments.

In an era of diminished expectations, when ideas of this sort are everywhere dismissed as utopian, this conclusion will seem anachronistic, if not quaint. Nevertheless, "the withering away of the state" merits serious consideration. In Chapters 8 and 9, in reflecting on communism and on the significance of continuing to uphold the idea at a time when leftist politics has devolved into a motley of good causes devoid of any unifying vision or aim, I will try to show why this conclusion is of more than passing theoretical interest. I concede, however, that a study in political philosophy can only issue in tentative conclusions about these matters. The prospects for organizing political communities as republics of ends depend on speculations about human nature and the likely outcomes of institutional arrangements that theoretical considerations

10 See Levine, *The End of the State*, Chapter 5. See also Wright, Levine, and Sober, *Reconstructing Marxism*, Chapters 3 and 5. The claims that follow in this paragraph are supported in *The End of the State*, Chapters 6–8.

can never finally resolve. It remains for real-world political developments themselves to establish or refute the claim that communism, in something like the sense Rousseau anticipated and Marx intended, is a realistic and desirable political objective. However, if communism is to be brought back into political theory, as I will contend it ought to be, there is no choice but to proceed in the face of vulnerability to empirical confutation.

It is now clear that the most sustained attempt to date to move humanity toward communism, the Bolshevik Revolution, ended in failure. Partly in consequence of this historic defeat, political initiatives with similar ambitions have effectively vanished from the popular imagination. However, capitalism and the state system remain in place. Can the aspiration to replace them with a communist order remain suppressed indefinitely? If, as I shall argue, these core features of our civilization are impediments to autonomy and self-realization, and if communism is a feasible and desirable alternative to them, this question answers itself. I would therefore venture that, before long, the communist project will resume – not just in economically backward and politically underdeveloped countries but in the vastly more propitious conditions Marx himself envisioned. It will be of some help in this endeavor if, when the time again comes, philosophy is not caught unawares.

EXCULPATIONS

I remarked at the outset that contemporary political philosophers generally fail to take due account of the historical specificity of currently dominant notions of the individual and the state. The case I will go on to construct in behalf of Marxian communism will in fact appeal to different understandings of these and other political concepts. Nevertheless, there is a sense in which what follows here is itself ahistorical in the manner of contemporary political philosophy. In this section, I shall advance a brief comment on this feature of the ensuring discussion. Then, still in an exculpatory spirit, I shall excuse my neglect of two important issues – the metaphysics of volition and the "post-Marxist" challenge to communism – that some readers might expect to see addressed in a book on the general will that defends key Marxian positions.

Philosophy outside history

Rousseau, Marx, Hobbes, Locke, Mill, and others figure prominently throughout the discussions that follow. However, this book is not a study in the history of ideas. It is intended instead as a contribution to contemporary political theory. From a historical point of view, its use of past philosophy therefore requires comment and justification.

It is commonplace for philosophers to approach the history of philosophy by focusing only on major figures, abstracted from their historical contexts and inserted into an imaginary moment in which they somehow join in dialogue with one another and with philosophers today. In this way, most of philosophy's past is excluded from the history of philosophy: Only a handful of philosophers – indeed, only a handful of these philosophers' writings – are accorded legitimacy; everything else is ignored. Curiously too, the words of these co-investigators are then in varying degrees venerated – like oracles from whose writings Truths can be teased out or, more precisely, read in. To account for this unlikely configuration of attitudes, it is well to recall the peculiar position of philosophy – as a traditional, humanistic discipline but also as a component of an emerging scientific culture. Many philosophers treat the history of philosophy – or at least the fragment of it they recognize – in much the way that Renaissance scholars and their successors treated the writings they recovered from the Greek and Latin traditions. At the same time, like scientists, most philosophers believe in the growth of understanding and knowledge. Practicing scientists characteristically have little use for the history of science. In philosophy, where progress has proven more elusive, the history of philosophy, reduced to some major works of a few master thinkers, is a more timely source of insight. From this point of view, the philosophical canon is not so much something to be studied for its own sake as it is a resource among others. With progress sufficiently slow, past philosophy remains contemporary for as long as it continues to be relevant to issues still in dispute.

Humanistic and scientific attitudes toward the history of philosophy hardly cohere and, together or separately, they offend a genuinely historical sensibility. From a historical point of view, ideas, like everything else, should be understood in context. It is this requirement that motivates some contemporary investigators to read past philosophers, "great" and minor alike, against the background of their time and place and to focus on the ways in which their positions are addressed to their own contemporaries, rather than to philosophical giants of different times and places or to issues of contemporary concern.

8

As noted, my treatment of historical figures, Rousseau especially, is more in line with contemporary philosophical practice
than with "contextualist" historical research. Thus I identify Rousseau's "private will" with the wills of individuals in a Hobbesian
state of nature, and I represent Rousseau as if he were engaged in
a protracted dialogue with contemporary understandings of Hobbesian moral and political philosophy. This picture is plainly at
odds with a contextualist account of the (major) texts I discuss.
Hobbesian philosophy was not in fact a central concern of Rousseau's, especially in the form I shall present it.[11] Indeed, from a
more historical point of view, a discussion of the "general will"
would have to engage theological disputes about sin and the nature of grace as much as Hobbes's attempt to extricate hypothetical
individuals from a devastating "war of all against all." It would focus on theological controversies aroused by the Jansenist revival of
the doctrine of predestination – in particular, on attempts to join a
belief in God's "general will" that humanity be saved with the
"particular" salvation of the elect.[12] But French theological and political theory in the century before Rousseau will hardly intrude on
the discussions that follow. Along with Rousseau, Hobbes, Locke,
Mill, and, above all, Marx are the figures that matter for my purpose, not Pascal, Malebranche, Bossuet, Fénelon, Bayle, Montesquieu, or Diderot.

In short, what follows is not intended as a historical study. It is
instead an investigation of the historical possibility of the general
will, and of the forms and limits of its desirability. To this end, the
odd and even contradictory attitude philosophers assume toward
the history of their subject actually is appropriate. I would readily
acknowledge that humanist postures are of dubious value in the
modern world, especially when they encourage the veneration of
authors and texts. However, I shall maintain that it is reasonable at
the present time to continue to identify with the tradition Marx inaugurated, and especially with that strain of Marxism that bears a

11 The Hobbes who figures in the following pages is very much a creature of con-
    temporary political philosophy. For a trenchant attack on what she calls "the
    standard philosophical interpretation" of Hobbes, see S. A. Lloyd, *Ideals as In-
    terests in Hobbes's "Leviathan": The Power of Mind over Matter* (Cambridge: Cam-
    bridge University Press, 1992).
12 Cf. Judith N. Shklar, "General Will," in Philip P. Wiener (ed.), *Dictionary of the
    History of Ideas* (New York: Charles Scribner's Sons, 1973), vol. 2, pp. 275 ff.;
    and Patrick Riley, *The General Will before Rousseau: The Transformation of the Divine
    into the Civic* (Princeton: Princeton University Press, 1986).

conceptual affinity with Rousseauean political philosophy.[13] In addition and more importantly, Rousseau and Marx and the other figures I discuss still do speak to us instructively on the issues in contention here. If it is conceded that a philosophical investigation of the general will is worth undertaking, then even a committed contextualist should concede that there is no harm in using historical figures ahistorically for this purpose. This is not to say that historical sensibilities can justifiably be set aside. Misrepresentations, deliberate or not, are unlikely to be helpful or even benign. It is therefore advisable to be scrupulous in respecting the results of historical research. But within this constraint, so long as there is no pretense of advancing intellectual history, the noncontextual use of the writings of the "immortals" is surely unobjectionable and even wise.

In any case, I have tried to treat the writings I discuss as more than suggestive inkblots in a philosophical Rorschach test. What I extract from them may not be quite what their authors intended or what contemporary readers saw. But the texts still constrain what there is to see. So understood, these writings advance theses and contain arguments that cast light on the topics they address. This, I think, is what explains the exclusion of most of philosophy's past from the history of philosophy as philosophers typically construe the subject. Some philosophical writings remain sources of insight even in circumstances remote from their conditions of origin. Others, the vast majority, are of interest today primarily as artifacts of their time and place.[14] Thus a properly historical history of philosophy frequently will diverge from a philosophical use of philosophy's past. Again, it is well for the sake of good work in both domains that historical and philosophical investigations inform one another as much as possible; and it is crucial that the two not be at odds. But good intellectual history is not always good philosophy or vice versa.

It is frequently the case, for both historians and philosophers, that God, as the saying goes, is in the details. But sometimes, especially in philosophical uses of the history of philosophy, the insights that underlie particular theses and arguments are more important than the formulations through which they are ex-

13 See Chapter 9 herein.
14 Cf. Ian Hacking, "Five Parables," in Richard Rorty, J. B. Schneewind, and Quentin Skinner (eds.), *Philosophy in History: Essays on the Historiography of Philosophy* (Cambridge: Cambridge University Press, 1984).

pressed. For the present purpose, it will often be useful to distinguish the core ideas of the writers I discuss from their actual positions, even supposing that they can be uncontroversially ascertained. I register this observation not so much to excuse what might otherwise be considered a cavalier disregard of the facts of the matter but to signal the reader that, throughout much of what follows, it is Hobbesian, Rousseauean, Millean, and Marxian positions that are at issue, rather than the versions of these positions actually developed by Hobbes, Rousseau, Mill, or Marx.

An ahistorical use of the history of philosophy is, of course, at odds with the spirit and letter of Marx's writings. But it is definitely in accord with Rousseau's self-conscious practice. "Let us therefore begin by putting aside all the facts," Rousseau declared at the beginning of *The Second Discourse*, "for they have no bearing on the question." To be sure, Rousseau exaggerated his disregard of the facts. But, in truth, he was not a speculative anthropologist or historian. He sought not to advance understanding of what actually happened in the past but to develop a philosophical account of inequality and its consequences for moral, social, and political life. In view of what is now known, many of the ostensibly historical claims made in *The Second Discourse* are false. But from his own vantage point, the story Rousseau told was as plausible as any other. It respected accepted views about the first human beings without worrying over their accuracy. A similar attitude will be assumed here with respect to Rousseau himself and the other philosophers, including Marx, whose ideas I shall deploy. To advance reflection on the general will – indeed, to insert the idea back into its real historical context – I consider the general will ahistorically, much as Rousseau removed his reflections on the development of inequality from the real history of the human race. Like Rousseau, I will doubtless fail to add anything to what is already known of the historical facts. But, again like Rousseau, I shall try to respect what the best histories tell us and to take advantage of the understandings gained through historical research, whenever they can be put to philosophical use.

The will

The distinction Rousseau drew between the private and the general will is central to his political philosophy and to his politics – conceived as an eternal struggle, waged in and over institutions, to bring about the supremacy of the general will within each citizen of a just state.[15] But, in Rousseau's writings, the concept of the *will* is taken over from received ways of thinking without much scrutiny or elaboration. In this respect, I shall follow Rousseau's lead.

The will figures in many everyday reflections and philosophical explanations, but especially in attempts to conceive the difference between actions and other events, including *mere* behaviors. Some events are also actions, executed by *agents* who are in pertinent senses *responsible* for what they do. Agency is then held to involve volition essentially. How agency is possible, what its forms and limits might be, and what its implications are for a host of metaphysical, moral, and legal concerns are matters Rousseau ignores. Perhaps, as already suggested, his political philosophy implicitly assumes an account of volition, supplied retrospectively by Kant. But Rousseau himself had little if any interest in these issues, and neither did Marx. What follows here will suppose, as they did, that human agency is a fact and that the standard view of it, according to which volition plays an essential role, is sound. I trust that these assumptions are uncontroversial. However, should they eventually prove faulty, the case for general will coordination will likely not be impugned. Where the general will is in question, very little weight is borne by whatever the term "will" suggests to philosophers with more directly metaphysical concerns.

There are perhaps accounts of volition that would be incompatible with Rousseau's idea. I would venture, though, that general will coordination is compatible with any *plausible* metaphysical view. But I shall not attempt to defend this claim here. Many positions in moral, social, and political philosophy rest on notions of freedom, agency, and the self about which sensible people can reasonably disagree. However, in doing moral, social, or political philosophy it is usually unnecessary to focus on underlying metaphysical assumptions or even to make them explicit. There is no reason to expect otherwise in this case.

For the present purpose, it is enough to hold that wills are distinguished by their objects – by the interests toward which they aim. The private will aims at private or particular interests; the general will aims at general interests. I shall try to provide an account of these interests, and of their role in normative social and political theory. This task is sufficiently daunting – and suffi-

15 See Levine, *The Politics of Autonomy*, Chapters 4 and 5.

ciently independent of metaphysical worries about volition – to be taken up independently. My subject is "the general *will*" because Rousseau introduced the idea into political philosophy in these terms, not because I have anything metaphysically contentious to say about the will.

Post-Marxism

Neither will I directly engage challenges to the positions advanced here by "post-Marxists," including some feminists, who maintain that power relations not grounded in class divisions obstruct autonomy and self-realization in the way that Marxists think class divisions do.[16] I shall, however, venture two brief and speculative comments intended partly to excuse this absence and partly to indicate how objections of this sort might be met.

My first comment depends upon a conclusion that will emerge from the chapters that follow. It will become evident that what makes general will coordination *materially possible* at the level of "whole communities" is not the elimination of interindividual conflicts per se but the removal of *systemic* factors that set individuals at odds, conflicts inherent in social structures themselves. For Marx, class divisions are systemic in this sense. Although he never directly addressed the issue, it is plain that, in his view, nothing else is. I will go on to argue that, if Marx was right, the elimination of class divisions is necessary (though not sufficient) for a society to be directed, when appropriate, by a general will.

If there are other obstacles to "the exercise of the general will" that are systemic in character, whether in addition to the one Marx identified or instead of it, then they too would have to be removed for general will coordination to become materially possible. Could this "correction" be accommodated without fundamentally changing the case for Marxian communism? It is not possible to answer this question in general; we would need to assess particular

16 Despite the risk of concocting a "straw man," I have characterized "post-Marxism" with a broad brush in order to encompass a wide range of views. On this characterization, the designation "post-Marxist" would aptly describe, among others, Richard Wolfe and Steven Resnick, *Knowledge and Class* (Chicago: University of Chicago Press, 1988); Barry Hindess and Paul Q. Hirst, *Marx's "Capital" and Capitalism Today* (London: Routledge and Kegan Paul, 1977); Heidi Hartman, "The Unhappy Marriage of Marxism and Feminism," in Lydia Sargent (ed.), *Women and Revolution* (Boston: South End Press, 1981); and Anthony Giddens, *A Contemporary Critique of Historical Materialism* (Berkeley: University of California Press, 1981).

claims. But it is plain, even in the absence of an exhaustive investigation, that there is no obvious reason why basic changes in the account that follows would be necessary. Post-Marxists only add to or alter the one-item list of systemic impediments to autonomy and self-realization that Marxists proffer. However, we shall find that what matters for communism is more the existence of such a list than its content. I would therefore suggest, tentatively but in the absence of a good reason for thinking otherwise, that the case to be developed here in communism's behalf would still generally hold even if a post-Marxist challenge to Marxism could somehow be sustained. Perhaps in those circumstances it would not quite be *Marxian* communism that would realize Rousseau's ideal. But something very much like it would.

How likely is it, though, that there are systemic obstacles in the way of general will coordination other than class divisions? Needless to say, this too is an empirical question that cannot be settled by philosophical speculation. But it is surely reasonable to demand, before we admit the existence of systemic oppositions, that there be *something* that underwrites claims for their systematicity. Liberals effectively deny the systematicity of any interindividual oppositions because they do not acknowledge a theoretical basis for privileging some social divisions over others or for according special weight to any of the particular oppressions they generate. On the other hand, the Marxist conviction that class divisions are systemic and that nothing else is follows from Marx's theory of history. It is because of the role class divisions play in the historical materialist account of history's structure and direction that the end of class oppression is indispensable for the realization of the normative vision communism embodies.[17]

In contrast to liberals who deny that any oppositions are systemic and to Marxists who hold that class divisions alone are, post-Marxists assert a plurality of systemic oppositions. But is there any warrant for this claim? Again, this question cannot be answered in the absence of a careful study of particular cases. However, it is fair to lay the burden of proof on the post-Marxists. For if there is a "functional equivalent" to historical materialism, it is not at all clear what it might be. It appears, in fact, that post-Marxists infer

17 Thus it will be argued in Chapter 7 that Marxists and liberals disagree more about social theory than about normative concerns. On the connection between Marxism as an explanatory project and its emancipatory objectives, and on some fissures in the assumed connection between these aspects of Marxist theory, see Wright, Levine, and Sober, *Reconstructing Marxism*, Chapter 8.

the existence of systemic oppressions from the very beliefs that lead liberals to deny their existence altogether. If this observation is correct, it is plainly the liberals, not the post-Marxists, who draw the right conclusion.

My second comment, then, is that post-Marxists typically advert to the kinds of social theories that liberals do and then deploy them in a confused and misleading way. If I am right, instead of altering or adding to the Marxists' one-item list of systemic oppressions, they should, like the liberals, deny that there is any list at all. But then this challenge to Marxian communism would effectively devolve into the liberal challenge. Of course, post-Marxists might still differ from liberals in other respects. They might even be justified in concentrating on particular social divisions and the oppressions to which they give rise. But no social or historical theory would ground this focus. It would be determined instead by political agendas or extrapolitical interests or perhaps by the empirical salience of one or another opposition in particular instances. These factors figure too in explaining Marxists' recourse to class analysis. But Marxists also have a theory of history that warrants their privileging class divisions. For what will follow, this reason makes all the difference.

To be sure, these very brief and speculative assertions are unlikely, separately or together, to allay the qualms of readers inclined to take post-Marxist positions seriously. I offer them here only to account for my own neglect of this currently influential strain of theorizing and to alert the reader to the "old-fashioned" but, I think, more than ever timely nature of the chapters that follow.

AN OVERVIEW

This book consists of essays on a variety of topics that bear on the general will and communism – moving from a focus on Rousseau to a focus on Marx.

As remarked, general will coordination is difficult to reconcile with current ways of thinking about individual and group interests. Therefore some readers are likely to find the idea problematic if not incoherent. Chapter 1 addresses this issue directly by distinguishing general from private will coordination in a way that accommodates many contemporary misgivings but that nevertheless accords with the intuition that led Rousseau to draw the distinction initially. Chapter 2, an essay on Rousseau's *Second Discourse*, argues indirectly for the cogency of general will coordination by underscoring some peculiar aspects of its putatively unproblematic rival, the private will. Chapter 3, "Solidarity," probes the limits of general will coordination by analyzing *different* forms of social interaction that resemble it in crucial respects. A focus on solidarity effectively historicizes Rousseau's treatment of general will coordination, a consequence of some moment for the normative assessment of this model of rational cooperation. In Chapter 4, the state, the distinctively modern political form described at the end of *The Second Discourse* and throughout modern political philosophy, is faulted in light of the expressly political value of democracy. Since this political form instantiates private will coordination at the level of "the whole community," a demonstration of its shortcomings with respect to a defensible and widely acknowledged standard provides a further reason for reflecting on social orders that do not assume the ineluctability of private volition. Then, in Chapter 5, an essay on the state that superintends the transition to communist statelessness in Marxist political theory, I show how Marxism's "last state" fares better with respect to democratic values than do actually existing states.

To investigate these issues is to put the nature and limits of liberal and Marxist moral philosophy in question and therefore to reflect on their affinities and differences. I have already suggested that received understandings of the differences separating Marxists from liberals cannot be sustained. Nevertheless, there are respects in which Marxist political theory is non- or extraliberal and therefore at odds with what has become the dominant political ideology. Much of what follows is *about* Marxism, liberalism serving mainly as a point of reference. But it is not always the case that Marxist positions are preferable to liberal ones. Chapter 6, an essay on the state liberals endorse, identifies elements of liberal theory that appear indispensable in any defensible normative account of social and political arrangements. I argue there that, despite a surfeit of opinion to the contrary, the form of the state Marxist political theory envisions need not offend defensible liberal values. Chapter 7 then investigates affinities and differences between liberalism and Marxism – focusing on their respective understandings of autonomy, human flourishing, and equality – and their differing accounts of the role(s) political institutions can rightfully play in realizing these objectives.

After identifying some real differences distinguishing liberalism from Marxism, it will be appropriate finally to investigate communism as a normative ideal. Chapter 8 presents and defends crucial elements of Marx's idea, focusing directly on the role of general will coordination and on its limits. What I defend there will seem pale in comparison with traditional Marxist accounts. To some degree, traditionally unacknowledged affinities between Marxism and liberalism explain this divergence from standard expectations. Indeed, throughout what follows, a number of the positions I take concede a great deal to liberal views widely considered incompatible with Marxism. In Chapter 9, an essay on "communism after Communism," after the self-destruction of the Communist system in the Soviet Union and Eastern Europe, I offer some reflections on this situation.

At a time when liberalism is virtually hegemonic, Marxism in crisis, and communism in disrepute even among those who continue to call themselves Marxists, I do not expect the case I shall present to alleviate many doubts about communism as a feasible project and worthwhile ideal. I will be content if I can convince skeptical readers that this ostensibly defunct idea, an inspiration for so many generations of socialist militants, is worth taking seriously again. I do so with the understanding that political conjunctures and intellectual climates change, sometimes with astonishing rapidity, and that what today appears anachronistic may soon seem timely again. What follows is an essay in political theory, motivated by the conviction that it is important, perhaps now more than at any time in the recent history of the Left, to defend hope in a communist future.

Chapter 1

The general will in theory

The Social Contract contrasts *general* wills with *private* or *particular* wills. A general will is said to be the will of "the whole community"; private wills are ascribed paradigmatically to individuals in a state of nature. Genuine authority exists only when laws are made by individuals expressing their opinions about what the general will is, rather than their private wills as registered in their preferences. Collective choices that aggregate preferences represent "the will of all," not the general will. The distinction is exhaustive: Any will that is not general is private. Thus the wills of groups less than the whole community and even the will of all are assimilated conceptually to the category defined by the primordial condition that motivates the establishment of de jure states. Practical politics, in Rousseau's view, is a struggle for supremacy of the general over the private will, a struggle waged at the level of "opinion" for the character and judgment of each individual.

However, despite the centrality of this distinction for his political theory, Rousseau's account of the difference between general and private willing is poorly elaborated and easily misconstrued. Like other eighteenth-century contractarian formulations, Rousseau's appears to suggest that the state of nature and the political community that succeeds it designate real historical conditions. This construal implies the actuality of general will coordination in existing political communities – obscuring the distinction, implicit in *The Social Contract*, between de jure and de facto authority and conveying a misleading sense of the obstacles in the way of general will coordination for modern states. More seriously, Rousseau's formulations support the idea that the general will is somehow borne by a supraindividual entity, the whole community, rather than by the individuals who constitute that *social* entity. It need hardly be said that neither understanding is correct. The contrac-

18

tarian story, even in its eighteenth-century versions, is only metaphorically temporal: Legitimacy is established not by an event occurring at a determinate time or place but by a "contract," ascribed by way of a rational reconstruction, that undergirds particular institutional arrangements. And, whatever Rousseau's language may imply, the bearers of the general will, as of the private will, are always and only individuals. If the distinction Rousseau intends is unsustainable, it is not because it implies implausible ontological commitments or otherwise violates sound individualist intuitions.

Wills, as Rousseau understands them, are distinguished not by their bearers but by their objects or, more precisely, by the interests toward which they aim. Private wills aim at private interests; general wills aim at general interests. Thus Rousseau is committed to the idea that these interests are qualitatively distinct.

Rousseau's express formulation suggests that an individual who aims at a private interest seeks what is individually best; an individual seeking to realize a general interest aims at what is best for "the whole community." But even if it is conceded that there always is some outcome that is unequivocally best for the whole community, this way of distinguishing general from private interests admits of two distinct understandings, neither of them adequate for marking off a genuinely qualitative difference. On one reading, what is best for the whole community just *is* what is individually best. But, then, general interests would be "private" in the sense that they are supposed not to be. Rousseau's account of individuals' interests would differ from other theorists' only insofar as he identifies what is individually best with what is best for the collective entities individuals constitute, whereas others tend to endorse more "individualistic" understandings of the individually best. Undoubtedly, this is an important difference separating Rousseau from Hobbes and his successors in the liberal tradition. But it is not a difference in kind that would constitute a departure from mainstream normative individualism. Moreover, on this construal, Rousseau's position is extremely implausible. To defend his view, one would have to show, not just for the social contract itself but also for the issues that arise in the popular assemblies of the state, that the interest of the whole community actually is individually best for each citizen. It seems unlikely that such a claim could be sustained. Certainly, Rousseau made no attempt to do so.

The second reading identifies "individually best" with "best for oneself as an individual" and therefore regards general and private interests as proper subsets of an individual's interest all things considered. The general interest would then be the individual's interest *qua* citizen; the private interest would be his or her interest *qua* individual or, what comes to the same thing, the individual's interest all things considered with the general interest, as previously defined, abstracted out. Were general interests only proper subsets of individuals' interests all things considered, it could still be argued that it is reasonable, under some conditions, to privilege this proper subset over others. Arguably, Rousseau's account of the establishment of de jure states by a social contract in which each individual "puts his person and all his powers in common under the supreme direction of the general will"[1] could be interpreted this way. It is arguable too that, whatever Rousseau intended, he ought to have had this understanding in mind. But, again, on this reading, general will coordination would not differ in kind from the now standard understanding of rational cooperation.

For reasons that will become apparent shortly, I shall call theorists who deny a qualitative difference between private and general interests *substantive atomic individualists*. Substantive atomic individualism is pervasive in our intellectual culture. But it is not a core conviction in the sense that its abandonment would render other, more defensible, intuitions about moral and political life untenable. Rather, substantive atomic individualism is a dogma that blocks progress in political philosophy. Ultimately, the power of this dogma rests on the appeal of a metaphor of very doubtful pertinence.

ARE ALL WILLS PRIVATE?

It is plain that only individuals bear interests. But it does not follow from this fact of nature that interests can only be predicated of individuals and not of sub- or supraindividual entities of animals or even of things. But the wills that aim at such interests are individuals' wills. It is tempting to conclude from this truism that all interests are, in Rousseau's terms, private – in one or the other of the senses just sketched. Whoever values the interest of his kidneys over his body altogether or of her political community over her own well-being or whoever accords preeminence to the interests of whales or trees is either seeking to realize an objective that,

---

1 *The Social Contract*, Book I, Chapter 6.

for whatever reason, he or she considers individually best or else is privileging some proper subset of what is individually best over other subsets and even over what is individually best tout court.

To dispute this claim for the ineluctability of private volition it is well to reflect on the intuition that motivates the idea of general will coordination. Consider, therefore, situations in which it is natural not to expect reasonable individuals always to do what is *individually* best. Small group interactions and deliberations among persons involved in intimate relationships provide ready examples. Imagine, for example, a couple deciding where it is best for them to reside. John wants to live in X. Mary prefers to live in Y. However, both can perhaps agree that, insofar as what matters is the endurance and quality of their relationship, it would be best for them to live in W. W, by hypothesis, is not where either John or Mary, conceived individually, wants to live all things considered, nor is it in any obvious sense a compromise between X and Y. However, there is a sense in which W is best for both John and Mary conceived as "indivisible" parts of a "moral and collective body," the couple John–Mary. If we add that John and Mary are equal in morally relevant senses, this John–Mary interest, irreducible to the interests of John and Mary respectively, is paradigmatically a general interest.[2]

To make sense of the intuition upon which this paradigm rests, it will be helpful to realize that each of the construals of Rousseau's position that I have sketched assumes that individuals' interests have to do exclusively (or, at least, mainly) with personal well-being or, in contemporary terms, *welfare*. "Welfarism," the conviction that only welfare need be taken into account in "rational choice" explanations, or in normative assessments, is nowadays widely assumed. But it is hardly a position that bears careful

2 In attempting to make sense of Rousseau's idea, Kant recognized the importance of what has come to be called "the moral equality of persons" for implementing a genuine "republic of ends." Following Kant, we can say that persons must be equal *as* moral agents. But equality in this sense is unlikely to be realized in real-world situations unless there is considerable equality of status and condition among the deliberating parties. Thus the distinction between private and general willing, despite Rousseau's insistence to the contrary, is not exhaustive. There can be deliberations that are not private will deliberations that are also not general will deliberations in Rousseau's sense. Parents, for example, can privilege the interests of the family of which they are an integral part over their own well-being and even over the well-being of their children without deliberating in accord with the Rousseauean model, because of the inequalities of status and condition that the parent–child relationship entails.

21

scrutiny even in the limited contexts in which it typically figures.[3] If nothing else, it is plain that welfare is not the only basis for the interests people actually act upon. Thus personal integrity and commitment to principles can also motivate human behavior, along with a host of other factors. It is plainly not irrational for people to act, say, for the sake of their own integrity or for principles to which they are committed, and no plausible moral theory could maintain that individuals ought not to act in these ways.

Welfarism is insidious precisely because, having become so pervasive, "welfare" tends to be confounded with value generally. In consequence, it frequently serves as a placeholder, standing in for whatever individuals happen to value. But when the idea is actually deployed, as in the unsuccessful attempts just sketched to depict general will coordination as a distinct kind of rational cooperation, more particular understandings of welfare are effectively assumed.

Historically, there exist at least two different accounts of what welfare is. For the first utilitarians and other early welfarists, but also for some utilitarians today, welfare is identified with states of mind – specifically, with pleasure or happiness. More recently, some writers have come to identify welfare with preference satisfaction.[4] It is plain that, on either view, welfare hardly includes everything that people value or ought to value. But for individuals directed by *private wills*, it *is* fair, though anachronistic, to identify rationality with welfare maximization and value with personal well-being in the sense(s) the welfarist tradition provides.

NONWELFARIST INTERESTS

The preceding account of John's and Mary's deliberations appealed implicitly to considerations that are distinct from interests in personal well-being. When John or Mary privileges a John–Mary interest over their John or Mary interests respectively, they evince a *commitment* to the couple John–Mary that is distinct from their concern with their own or even each other's welfare. When

3 Cf. Amartya K. Sen, "Rational Fools: A Critique of the Behavioral Foundations of Economic Theory," in Jane J. Mansbridge (ed.), *Beyond Self-Interest* (Chicago: University of Chicago Press, 1990).
4 Cf. Richard B. Brandt, "Two Concepts of Utility," in Harlan B. Miller and William H. Williams (eds.), *The Limits of Utilitarianism* (Minneapolis: University of Minnesota Press, 1982).

John or Mary acts out of a commitment to the collective entity John–Mary, they are acting in a way that is, as it were, welfare-indifferent. But then what is it that John or Mary seeks to advance when they privilege their John–Mary interests?

Some purchase on the nature of general interests can be gained by asking what it is to be a nonwelfarist interest. Supra- and sub-individual entities as well as things and (most) animals, inasmuch as they are incapable of having states of mind or desires that can be satisfied, can only have nonwelfarist interests. Therefore the general interest, the interest of the supraindividual entity "the whole community," must be nonwelfarist.[5] In this respect, it differs from the interests registered in "the will of all" – the aggregated private interests of the individuals who constitute "the whole community." The will of all may be a combination of welfarist interests. But the will of all is not the general will, a point Rousseau insisted upon repeatedly.[6]

At the very least, we can say that x is in the (nonwelfarist) interest of y, where x is a state of affairs and y is anything of which an interest can be predicated, if x contributes to the survival of y. Thus, if John and Mary are committed to their relationship even at the expense, if need be, of their own welfares, they evidently want, above all, that their relationship should endure. It is difficult to imagine why mere survival should be a paramount concern in this case. But no matter how unwise it might be, there would be nothing incoherent in John or Mary making the survival of their relationship their overriding interest. Arguably, "deep ecologists" evince commitments of this sort for endangered species,[7] as do opponents of "cultural genocide" and some nationalists.

In order to impute more likely motives to John and Mary, and in most other cases in which nonwelfarist interests figure, we can say that for x to be in the interest of y, x must do more than contribute to y's survival; x must also be good for y. But good in what sense? This question cannot be answered in general. It depends on the nature of the entity y of which x is predicated. Thus it is premature, at this point, to specify more precisely what a general interest

5 With respect to the nature of (nonwelfarist) interests, nothing of consequence hinges on how large communities are or on how they are individuated. Thus, for the present purpose, the couple John–Mary counts as a "whole community" in just the way that Rousseau's de jure state does.
6 See, for example, *The Social Contract*, Book II, Chapter 3, and Book IV, Chapter 2.
7 Ecologists of this sort are more likely to invoke rights than interests, but their ideas would seem to lend themselves more naturally to the idiom just proposed.

is. Perhaps this is also why Rousseau himself was reticent on this topic. If, as I maintain, his model of rational cooperation has specifically political applications only under material conditions that he never imagined, he could hardly have had more than the barest intimations of the good for such communities. In any case, for now, it will suffice to say that x is in the (nonwelfarist) interest of y if it contributes to y's survival and also (usually) if it is in some appropriate sense good for y.

Needless to say, for purposes of normative theory, reasons must be given for according weight to the interests people have. In this respect, welfarist interests are no less problematic than interests of any other kind. Even supposing that more than the survival of their relationship is at stake, it is not at all obvious in the case of John and Mary that it is wise for either of them to privilege their John–Mary interests over their interests as John or Mary.[8] But the reality – that is, the coherence and possible applicability – of John–Mary interests should be clear enough to anyone not blinded by welfarist assumptions. Tentatively, we can regard the general will at the level of the whole community as a John–Mary interest writ large. It may be doubted whether such interests actually exist in collectivities larger than intimate associations or small groups. Perhaps individuals' abilities to commit to collective entities cannot extend to communities that include nonintimates and strangers. It may seem even more doubtful whether commitments to "whole communities," even if they can be made, ought ever to govern individuals' deliberations. But the idea is surely cogent. We can imagine what a John–Mary interest writ large would be even if, *pace* Rousseau, we doubt its relevance for political life or its role in normative political philosophy.

However, those who are skeptical about general will coordination could concede that interests can be predicated of supraindividual entities or of anything else and still maintain that all interests are private. They could argue that when John or Mary gives precedence to a John–Mary interest over their own or each other's well-being, they seek to realize what, in the circumstances,

---

8 In this case, it is not even plain that only the interests of John and Mary and John–Mary bear on their choice of domicile. If their place of residence appropriately affects the interests, however construed, of individuals other than John and Mary, these other persons ought presumably to have a role in the decision too. Arguably, even the judgments of individuals not directly affected may also be relevant.

they take to be individually best; or else that they privilege a proper subset of what they take to be individually best over other subsets and over what is individually best tout court. Thus they aim at private interests, albeit of a nonwelfarist kind.

But this rejoinder is inadequate. It fails because it supposes, incorrectly, that the notion "individually best" is unequivocal. It assumes, in fact, an understanding of "individually best" that supports, without quite implying, welfarism and that, even more than welfarism itself, has come to pervade our political culture and its theory. To expose this assumption, it will be well to acknowledge that the expressions "individually best" and its equivalents like "best all things considered" are ambiguous, depending, as it were, on how the individual is conceived. As already remarked, this ambiguity is obscured by a metaphor, deployed throughout the past three centuries with varying degrees of explicitness by political philosophers including Rousseau, that describes the fundamental constituents of social and political life in a peculiarly tendentious way.

INDIVIDUALS

According to the ancient atomists, matter consisted of indivisible parts or atoms bearing only external relations to one another. Therefore, to account for matter at higher levels of organization, atoms – or, according to the refinement introduced after Galileo's revolution in physical theory, atoms in motion – are all investigators need to countenance. Of course we now know that the atoms scientists eventually identified are not, in fact, the ultimate constituents of matter. But this discovery does not impugn the atomists' guiding idea; it only betokens a mistake in the original execution of their project. In any case, what matters for our purpose is not the viability of atomism in physical theory but the lesson social and political theorists have taken from the atomists' program.

For atomists, science is about atoms in motion. But it does not follow from this tenet that scientific explanations must refer to atoms in motion only. The problem, for atomists, is not that physicalism is conceptually flawed. It is that the human mind is incapable of processing accounts of the complexity that physicalist explanations would require. This pragmatic consideration suffices to justify explanations that make reference to matter at higher levels of organization. Were our minds more like God's is supposed to be, it would be feasible to explain everything atomistically. But in view of human limitations, scientific explanations cannot always be framed at the level of the ontology they propose.[9]

However, political philosophers are free from this pragmatic constraint and can therefore be more atomistic than the atomists themselves. Insofar as political philosophy purports not to explain phenomena but only to justify institutional arrangements, there is nothing that stands in the way of full-fledged atomistic accounts. For philosophers captivated by the atomists' program, it is therefore natural to take the individual conceived atomistically as a point of departure for moral, social, and political theory. It has long been recognized that Hobbes's political philosophy assumes a view of individuals conceived by analogy with atoms in motion. We will see in Chapter 2 how Rousseau arrived at a similar position. For Hobbes and Rousseau and for the majority of theorists after them, political philosophy is about forms of association entered into by *atomic individuals*.

Before atomizing market relations came to structure economic and social life in early modern Europe, it could hardly have seemed intuitive to make the individual a point of departure in accounts of social order or institutional arrangements. When, as throughout most of human history before the triumph of capitalism, more solidary, distinctively social entities – villages, clans, estates – actually were the fundamental constituents of social life, they, not atomic individuals, must have seemed a more natural basis for reflecting philosophically on social and political arrangements.

In view of the historical particularity of the intuitions that nowadays seem commonsensical to us, it is wise to be cautious in acceding to them. However, I shall not question them or their implications here. It is important, though, to distinguish what I shall call *methodological* atomic individualism, the idea that social and political philosophy starts from a conception of the individual and his or her interests, from *substantive* atomic individualism, the view that individuals are radically independent centers of volition. It is substantive atomic individualism not methodological atomic individualism, that blocks recognition of the cogency of general will coordination. Therefore it is substantive not methodological atomic individualism that must be dislodged in order to find a place for the general will.

9 Some nonpragmatic reasons for eschewing the atomists' inclination to explain everything in terms of atoms in motion are provided in Wright, Levine, and Sober, *Reconstructing Marxism*, Chapter 6.

Unfortunately, the name "methodological atomic individualism" invites confusion with "methodological individualism," a well-known position in the philosophy of the social sciences according to which social facts are explained by facts about individuals, not social groups.[10] I have chosen to use it nevertheless because the designation is apt in a way that its near namesake is not. Methodological individualism is a thesis about social scientific explanation. Properly understood, it is not a methodological thesis at all but a claim about what is, as a matter of fact, explanatory. Methodological atomic individualism, on the other hand, genuinely is a methodological thesis – about the nature of normative theory.

It is compatible with methodological atomic individualism that an individual can will anything on any basis whatsoever, welfarist or not. An individual can even will outcomes that fail to represent the radical independence of atomic individuals. Thus one might seek to maximize some value distributed across a social group, regardless of its distribution among the individuals who constitute that group. Atomic individualist philosophers typically suppose that individuals seek to advance their own *welfare* interests. In this regard, Hobbes's case is exemplary. But, as Hobbes's example attests, self-interestedness follows from what is supposed to be true of human nature, not from atomic individualism per se.[11] Methodological atomic individualism can coexist with any conception of individuals' interests.

I would venture that, for those who are not wedded to welfarism, it is methodological atomic individualism that covertly sustains the conviction that all wills are private. Since only particular or "private" individuals bear wills, and since this fact is registered as a methodological tenet, whatever one wills, for whatever reason, is private by definition. However, if atomic individualism is understood as a claim for the volitional independence of individuals, for the substantive reality of an atomic individualist methodology, the universality of *private* willing is anything but assured.

It is one thing for a radically independent "atom," bearing only external relations to other atomic individuals, to seek to advance

10 For a critical assessment of methodological individualism, see ibid.
11 Thus, in the *Leviathan* (see, especially, Chapter 13), Hobbes depicts individuals as "diffident," "vainglorious," and "competitive" and therefore inclined to seek security, domination of others, and untrammeled acquisition of resources. It is these aspects of human nature, not the fact that individuals' wills are radically independent of one another, that motivate Hobbes's claims about the nature of individuals' wants.

its own interests (welfarist or not); and it is something else for an integral part of a supraindividual entity to seek to advance its interests as an "indivisible part" of that entity. Each of these cases can be conceived to accord with the requirements of *methodological* atomic individualism. But only in the former case is an individual's will *substantively* independent of the wills of other individuals.

This difference in willing is easily overlooked because it need not be evident in the *content* of the ends individuals seek to bring about. An atomic individual in the substantive sense can will any outcome whatsoever. Therefore a story can always be told that explains individuals' choices which accords with substantive atomic individualist assumptions. Thus even paradigmatic examples of general will coordination, like John and Mary's deliberations over a choice of domicile, can be construed in a substantively atomic individualist way. In view of what is usually supposed true of human nature and the human condition, there is reason not to expect individuals to take anything other than their own well-beings into account in their practical deliberations or normative assessments. But substantive atomic individualism does not preclude this prospect a priori.

Similarly, general will deliberations can result in outcomes indistinguishable from those undertaken by individuals intent on promoting their own welfare. A person concerned to advance the interests of a "moral and collective body" of which he is an integral part might aim to realize precisely what he would seek to bring about were he deliberating as a substantive atomic individualist. The general interest can coincide with the welfare interests of particular constituents of "the whole community." In fact, since there is an evident (causal) connection between what is best for the whole community and what is best for the individuals in it conceived independently, it is fair to expect that the general interest frequently will coincide with the welfare interests of many of the individual members of the whole community.

Substantive atomic individualism is a claim about the self and its relation to other selves in the context of individual and collective deliberations. A substantive atomic individual assesses alternatives *as if* she bears no internal relations to other individuals; *as if* her valorization of others' well-being, whenever her preferences do involve the well-being of others, is strictly contingent. Substantive atomic individualism is suggested by methodological atomic individualism. But it is not entailed by it. Similarly, it suggests welfarism, but it does not imply it.

Welfarism, in turn, suggests but does not imply egoism, the idea that, in deliberating on what is to be done, one ought to take only one's own welfare into account. Even dedicated welfarists, if they are not also amoralists, would deny that individuals ought to be concerned with their *own* well-being exclusively. They would at least concede that nonegoistic willing is reasonable and even commonplace in moral contexts. Utilitarianism, for example, enjoins an attitude of benevolence – according to which individuals take their own welfares into account, while according equal weight to the welfares of all relevant others. Utilitarianism is therefore not egoistic. But it is substantively atomic individualist and also welfarist; its fundamental principle, to maximize (aggregate or average) utility, requires agents to assess the consequences of their actions for their welfare effects on substantively independent individuals whose respective utilities are then added together.

Implicitly, four senses of individualism in normative contexts have now been distinguished: (1) methodological atomic individualism, (2) substantive atomic individualism, (3) welfarism, and (4) egoism. According to (1), the individual, conceived atomistically, is the point of departure for moral, social, and political theory. For adherents of (2), individuals assess alternatives *as if* they are related to other individuals only externally, though from within that perspective they may seek to bring about any state of affairs whatsoever. Proponents of (3) acknowledge only welfare interests. According to (4), individuals take only their own welfare interests into account. (1) requires that social and political institutions accommodate individuals' interests; (2) holds that individuals' interests are radically independent; (3) asserts that these radically independent interests are always only welfare interests; and (4) maintains that these welfare interests are always self-regarding. For Hobbes and Rousseau, self-regarding welfare interests are mortally antagonistic in the "state of nature"; for philosophers, liberals especially, who follow Hobbes but not Rousseau, interests remain in competition even after the state of nature is laid to rest. (4) is therefore nowadays widely assumed. But support for (4) is easily shaken. (3) is more secure; at least it can be maintained without abandoning the moral point of view. However, it too is eminently vulnerable. Support for (1) is very deeply entrenched, perhaps for good reason. But (1) tends to be conflated with (2). In this respect, the liberals and Rousseau are of one mind. In Chapter 2, we will find that Rousseau assumes (1), conflates (1) with (2), and then recounts the emergence of (4) and implicitly therefore also of (3). His notion of general will coordination in *The Social Contract* is expressly a "solution" to a problem (4) generates. Fortunately, Rousseau's account – or rather the idea it expresses – stands independently of the problem it purports to solve.

Individuals who coordinate their behaviors according to the Rousseauean model advance their interests *qua* methodological atomic individualists. In this sense, they aim at what is individually best. But what is individually best in cases like the ones Rousseau depicts is what is best for individuals conceived as integral parts of the "moral and collective bodies" they form. To advance their own interests, they therefore advance the interests of the collective entities that join them together. It is this idea that suggests itself intuitively when we think about (some) deliberations in small groups or intimate associations. Thus, when John or Mary accords priority to their John–Mary interest over their interests considered atomistically, they do what is best for themselves as members of an entity they relationally comprise. When they place themselves "under the supreme direction of the general will," it is the interests of the couple – not of the individuals who constitute it, conceived independently – that matters for their deliberations. The couple John–Mary is an internal relation formed by John and Mary. It cannot be decomposed into two radically independent entities, the (atomic) individuals John and Mary, because in this case it is the relation itself, not the parties related, that is fundamental for the proposed deliberation.

For substantive atomic individualists, on the other hand, it is inconceivable that individuals could be related internally. Their picture of the atomic individual precludes this conception. But we shall need to (re)introduce precisely this idea into political philosophy in order to put to use the insights implicit in Rousseau's account of legitimate political arrangements and in Marxian communism.

A FREE-RIDER PROBLEM?

Altering or, in this case, restricting the scope of a governing metaphor can have consequences for more than just the language with which the situations it represents are described. In this instance, doing so affects the way conflicts between (putative) general and private interests are conceived, and the way resolutions of these conflicts figure in normative theories.

Since the difference between general and private volition is not unequivocally evident in the content of the ends agents will, a substantive atomic individualist could in principle account for the same phenomena as proponents of general will coordination. At issue is the reality of general interests, not the content of individuals' choices. Consider, then, how a substantive atomic individualist would describe a conflict between an (alleged) general interest and a private interest. An extreme case will put the matter into focus. Imagine an individual who would give up her life in the interest of some "whole community" – a family, a tribe, a nation, a people, or a (de jure) state. It is plain that there are imaginable instances of such behavior that substantive atomic individualists would consider rational (or not irrational) and even morally praiseworthy. How can they reconcile these assessments with the individualism they profess?

One way would be to construe the individual's self-sacrifice as an act of altruism undertaken to benefit particular others. However, this interpretation becomes increasingly unlikely the larger "the whole community" involved. It is one thing to sacrifice one's life for one's children and something else to do so for (unknown) compatriots or (unborn) future generations. In any case, imagine an act of self-sacrifice – perhaps an act of exceptional bravery undertaken in time of war – that cannot plausibly be interpreted altruistically. It would seem that the only way to maintain a substantive atomic individualist perspective in cases of this sort is to suppose that the self-sacrificing individual is intent on not becoming a "free rider."

People have interests in their own well-being. But individual well-being may depend upon the existence – and perhaps also the good (however conceived) – of one's family, tribe, nation, people, or state. A substantive atomic individualist might then claim that each individual would be best off not making sacrifices for these collective entities but letting others do whatever is necessary to sustain them and make them flourish. Individuals would do best, in other words, if they "free-ride" on the efforts of others. But, by nearly all accounts, free riding is reprehensible, and a refusal to free-ride is correspondingly praiseworthy. Thus it could be argued that the esteem accorded those who make sacrifices for collective entities is nothing more than the esteem that attaches to those who refuse to obtain benefits without incurring the costs required to produce them.

This construal of self-sacrifice, like the interpretation that as-similated self-sacrifice to altruism, assumes a welfarist under-standing of individuals' interests. But this is not the principal reason why, in imaginable examples, an individual who would give up her life for "the whole community" evinces something distinct from a reluctance to free-ride. In the cases in question, she would not free-ride, even if she could somehow be released from her (acknowledged) duty to contribute toward "public goods," because, by hypothesis, her true interest is the interest of "the whole community" of which she is an "indivisible part."[12] She has, in other words, made the general interest her own. Therefore, even in giving up her life, she does what she truly wants, not what she feels she must do despite her desires.[13] If she feels conflicted, it is not because she faces a free-rider prob-lem. What she faces is an intrapersonal conflict in which her interests *qua* atomic individual and her interests *qua* part of the irreducibly collective entity for which she would give up her life vie for control.

Rousseaueans are not alone in advancing a notion of internal conflict that resists a free-rider construal. The deep ecologist who would have the interest of a forest take precedence over his own welfare interests is, in this respect, in the same situation as the in-dividual who would sacrifice her life for the state. If his position is flawed, it is in virtue of the cogency of his reasons for favoring the forest's interests over his private interests, not because it is inco-herent to make a forest's interests one's own.

Needless to say, a case must be made for adopting a general interest or a forest's interest or indeed any interest whatever. The reasonableness of acting on welfare interests is relatively uncontroversial. On the other hand, persuasive reasons for mak-ing the interests of supra- or subindividual entities – or of animals or plants or inanimate objects – one's own are more difficult to defend in an intellectual culture in which substantive atomic indi-vidualism, welfarism, and even egoism predominate. But the co-herence of these nonegoistic, nonwelfarist, and substantively nonindividualistic interests and their possible applicability should be beyond dispute. In this (Kantian) sense, the general will is real,

12 For the same reason, the social contract Rousseau envisions is not the outcome of a protracted negotiation. It is, as it were, each individual's initial negotiating position, the outcome desired most by each contracting party.
13 A similar argument is provided by Rousseau in *The Social Contract*, Book II, Chapter 5.

whether or not it has an important role to play in political philosophy or normative theory generally.

INTERNAL RELATIONS

It was to draw a contrast with the atomic individual that I invoked the idea of internal relations. Historically, the term has designated a variety of positions, but its role here is straightforward and uncontroversial. A property is *essential* to some entity if the entity would not be what it is in the absence of that property. Relations can be essential properties. Thus being the day after Sunday is essential for being Monday. When entities are related in a way that is essential for their being what they are, they are related *internally;* relations that are not internal are *external.* Intermittently since the eighteenth century, internal relations loomed large in metaphysical discussions – intersecting debates about universals, analyticity, essentialism, and the theory of truth. The idea has proven particularly useful in attempts at rendering Hegelian insights clear. Thus it was widely invoked in Britain and America from the 1890s until the First World War – in the work of Bradley, Royce, Bosanquet, and other neo-Hegelians. For much the same reason, it has also figured in some recent attempts at Hegelian reconstructions of Marxist positions, for example in Bertell Ollman's analysis of alienation.[14]

However this may be, the notion deployed here is innocent of portentous methodological or metaphysical implications. The term is intended only to signal an alternative to atomism in normative theory. The idea is that, in thinking about how social and political arrangements ought to be, it is sometimes appropriate to consider

14 See Bertell Ollman, *Alienation: Marx's Conception of Man in Capitalist Society* (Cambridge: Cambridge University Press, 1971). In Ollman's use, the notion bears an affinity with and arguably clarifies the Althusserian concept of "expressive totality," ascribed by Althusser to Hegel and the young Marx and then, in Althusser's view, abandoned by Marx after his "epistemological break" with the "problematic" of his early writings. See Louis Althusser, *For Marx* (London: Allen Lane, 1969); Louis Althusser and Etienne Balibar, *Reading "Capital"* (London: New Left Books, 1970). On this understanding, each part of a social totality somehow contains within it ("expresses") the essential properties of the whole. On the Ollman–Althusser view, the universe can in principle be apprehended in a grain of sand. However, in practice, as Ollman concedes, it is necessary to know a great deal about a social system in order to ascertain precisely what a particular case expresses. Indeed, it is far from clear what this doctrine, so understood, adds to standard accounts of social scientific practice – beyond an obscure metaphysical redescription.

33

individuals to be related internally. Thus John and Mary, in the couple John–Mary, are what they are in virtue of their role in that relation. The John and Mary who exist independently of the John–Mary couple are not *essentially* the John and Mary related internally. Needless to say, the names designate the same human beings, and the independent spatiotemporal existence of John and Mary is not in dispute. What is at issue is how their interests are conceived – whether atomistically or as integral parts of "the whole community" they constitute. For the larger communities pertinent to political philosophy, the same consideration applies.

THE REALITY OF THE GENERAL WILL

I first described general interests as nonwelfarist and communal. That characterization was apt but incomplete inasmuch as private interests can be nonwelfarist and communal too. I therefore proposed a characterization that more incisively differentiates general from private willing. Private interests are individuals' interests *qua* atomic individuals; general interests are individuals' interests *qua* members of collective entities in which they are related internally.

To hold that there can be "moral and collective bodies" within which individuals are internally related is to maintain that collectivities can have interests irreducible to the interests of their constituent parts conceived atomistically. General will coordination exists whenever individuals deliberate and act with a view to realizing such interests. I have noted that within intimate associations and in small groups there exist phenomena that Rousseau's idea plainly models, and I have argued for the superiority of the Rousseauean account of these phenomena over the most likely substantive atomic individualist descriptions. But, so far, I have said nothing in defense of its applicability to "the whole communities" of interest to political philosophy. Neither have I yet addressed the question of its desirability.

Liberals have always argued for principled limitations on the rightful use of state power.[15] Because "the exercise of the general will" seems inimical to individuals' sovereignty over themselves, people with liberal sensibilities are likely to question the desirability of general will coordination in the political arena, even if they concede its feasibility. Similar hesitations, though for different reasons, are likely to resonate for anyone influenced by Marx. Marx

15 See Chapter 6 herein.

34

believed that true general interests cannot exist in class-divided societies even notionally, and he thought that appeals to the general interest are always veiled invocations of private interests – typically of those who benefit from the prevailing system of class domination.[16] But, as I have already claimed, we shall find that Marx's assessment is different for societies that have overcome class divisions. Not unrelatedly, we shall also find that liberalism is not quite so inhospitable to general will coordination as liberals are inclined to believe.

Questions about the reality and desirability of general will coordination are conceptually distinct. However, treatments of these questions intersect – in part because the exercise of the general will at the level of whole communities is desirable just in those material conditions and under those social relations in which it becomes feasible; in short, in the conditions that define communism in the Marxian sense. Of course, Rousseau hardly envisioned this implication of his model of rational cooperation. Nevertheless, it will emerge that in crucial respects he was an important, if unwitting, contributor to its defense.

16 See, for example, the essay *On the Jewish Question* in Karl Marx and Friedrich Engels, *Collected Works* (New York: International Publishers, 1975), vol. 3, pp. 146–174. A similar claim is advanced by Rousseau in *The Second Discourse*; see Chapter 2 herein.

Chapter 2

The "origin" of the private will

The term "private will" is rarely used nowadays except in scholarly discussions of Rousseau. Nevertheless, what it designates pervades moral, social, and political theory. As remarked, even those who would concede the existence of the general will, the private will's rival in the Rousseauean scheme, believe that it has little, if any, applicability in political contexts. On the other hand, the reality and applicability of private volition are beyond dispute. I have suggested that this understanding is partly a consequence of a lingering inclination to consider individuals to be relevantly like radically independent atoms. But the idea that the private will is unproblematic and ubiquitous is also encouraged by more direct confusions.

Individuals moved by private wills seek, insofar as they are rational, to do as well for themselves as they can. This claim appears innocuous. But we have seen that it is ambiguous and potentially misleading. It is also contrary to the views of virtually all moral philosophers before Hobbes. Practical reason, on the formerly dominant view, was substantive, not just instrumental; rationality concerned the ends individuals' willed much more than the adequacy of the means they adopted. To be sure, some philosophers along with theologians and moralists continue to resist instrumentalist accounts of practical reason. Still, the idea that rationality is a matter of advancing one's own interests (where "interest" is a placeholder term, awaiting substantive elaboration) is so seldom disputed nowadays – and so integral to the tradition of economic modeling in contemporary social and political theory – that it has effectively become part of common sense.

However, the common-sense view does not fare well under scrutiny. On the most natural interpretation of it, value is utility, and rational agency is utility maximization.[1] But it is doubtful whether, even for purposes of normative theory, individuals can be said to have well-defined utility functions. It is also plain that the rationality of straightforward utility maximizing can be challenged, particularly in contexts of interdependent action, where the "payoffs" to agents depend, in part, on what other agents do. In recent years, insights adapted from the mathematical theory of games and from decision theory have shed light on the nature and limits of this notion of rational choice. But it has been known at least since Hobbes's account of the "state of nature" (in which instrumentally rational agents pursue their own ends without constraint) as a "war of all against all" that unconstrained utility maximization can be problematic. In any case, whatever we conclude about the dominant view of rational agency, what matters, for now, is that it is neutral with respect to claims about the content of individuals' interests. It is one thing to hold that rational agents seek to advance their own interests and something else to say what their interests are.

Nevertheless, the complex of ideas included in current notions of private volition – and in Rousseau's earlier elaboration of the idea – includes claims about interests. Thus it has become commonplace to construe individuals as *economic agents* intent on maximizing their shares of resources, including leisure. To join this view of interests to the utility-maximizing view of rational agency, it need only be supposed that individuals' utility yields rise with increasing amounts of material resources and diminishing labor inputs. But this causal connection is not implied by the theory of rational agency with which it is historically associated. To say that rational agents maximize utility is not to say anything about the utility consequences of particular states of the world. So far as the received view of practical reason is concerned, individuals *could* be acting rationally when they seek to increase the shares of others, to implement particular distributive outcomes, or even to diminish their own resource bundles while maximizing their labor inputs. If actions of these kinds seem "irrational," it is because standard economic models are so taken for granted that it affronts common sense to call their predictions into question.

1 A forceful statement of this position is provided by David Gauthier in "Reason and Maximization," *Canadian Journal of Philosophy*, vol. 4, no. 3 (1975), pp. 411–433.

These observations will be developed in the reflections on Rousseau's *Discourse on the Origin of Inequality among Men* or *Second Discourse* that follow. The lesson I shall draw is that, despite what is widely believed, the private will – especially but not only as Rousseau conceived it – is problematic too. What is of continuing philosophical importance in *The Second Discourse* is obscured if we assume, as readers today are wont to do, that Rousseau's aim was only to describe the genesis of a form of volition that no one can reasonably fault. In fact, it was Rousseau's contention that the emergence of the private will and then its exclusive reign is a transitory episode in human history. My aim in this chapter is to bring this claim into focus and to strengthen it by disentangling some of the ideas about practical reason and human interests that Rousseau inadvertently confounded.

THE ORIGINAL STATE OF NATURE

According to Rousseau's express declaration, *The Second Discourse*, in its first part, aims to provide an account of "the natural state of man." However, what Rousseau intended by this expression is easily misunderstood. Perhaps it was obscure even to Rousseau himself. At the risk of overlooking some facets of the story *The Second Discourse* tells, I shall here provide a clarifying sketch of this natural state, the original "state of nature," that is faithful to most of what Rousseau says. Since there is no familiar category into which the concept fits, it will be helpful, at the outset, to distinguish it from other notions with which it might be confused.

Despite references to indigenous peoples in the Pacific islands and the Americas, Rousseau's account of "the natural state of man" is not a composite picture of primitive societies. His depiction of human beings' natural state is based largely on his own imagination, constrained only by a few, widely accepted "facts." As speculative anthropology, therefore, the state of nature that Rousseau describes hardly warrants serious attention even in comparison to the travelers' journals and tales of exotic customs and places that appeared in Rousseau's time. In short, *The Second Discourse* is not a *history* of the origins of inequality.

For readers today, Rousseau's state of nature may suggest the "original position" deployed by contemporary contractarian theorists.[2] Within this genre of theorizing, the idea figures in

2 This designation was first deployed by John Rawls in *A Theory of Justice* (Cam-

thought experiments in which institutional arrangements are justified by demonstrating that they would be chosen by rational individuals in a setting, the original position, in which all vestiges of these arrangements have been abstracted away. In its account of the establishment of sovereignty by contract, *The Social Contract* arguably does depict the state of nature as an original position. Thus Rousseau maintained that just political arrangements are constructed by rational individuals at the point at which the state of nature has become a Hobbesian "war of all against all" – where "obstacles that are harmful to [each individual's] maintenance" come into mortal contradiction with "the forces that each individual can bring to bear to maintain himself."[3] But we shall see that this unfortunate condition is, in fact, the culmination of a process that *The Second Discourse* recounts. In *The Second Discourse*, therefore, "the state of nature" refers to more than the original position of *The Social Contract*.

Unlike the prototypical "war of all against all" in the *Leviathan*, the original position of *The Social Contract* is not an eternal condition lurking beneath the fragile surface of political order. It is socially produced. The state of nature that the social contract ends is therefore not a description of human nature and the human condition per se. It is an account relativized to particular circumstances – specifically, to conditions that develop *after* the introduction of private property in land, the principal nonhuman productive asset in preindustrial economies. This monumental event and the ineluctable transformations that follow in its wake are recounted in Part 2 of *The Second Discourse*. For political philosophers focused on *The Social Contract*, *The Second Discourse* can therefore be read as a prologue. From this perspective, it is natural to construe Part 1, Rousseau's account of the time *before* the introduction of private property, as stage setting. However this

bridge, Mass.: Harvard University Press, 1971). It aptly characterizes only one of the uses to which Rousseau and other earlier contractarians put "the state of nature."

3 *The Social Contract*, Book I, Chapter 6. Rousseau expressly denied that this condition is a state of *war*, insisting that only states, not individuals, can be at war. But the universal opposition among individuals that Rousseau describes is precisely what Hobbes's expression designates. Since "the war of all against all" is a widely known and well-understood description of the idea Hobbes and Rousseau share, I shall, where appropriate, use the Hobbesian term despite Rousseau's objections to it. For further discussion, see Levine, *The Politics of Autonomy*, Chapter 1, esp. pp. 20–28.

impression is misguided; Rousseau's depiction of the original state of nature bears considerable philosophical interest.

Thus it is well to reflect on Rousseau's contention that, in those first days, human life was solitary but happy and secure. What he evidently intended to convey was the idea that human nature and the human condition are as compatible with peace as with a war of all against all or, more precisely, that "the natural state of man" is too indeterminate to generate any conclusions about war or peace. To arrive at a precise determination, the social conditions that pertain must be specified.

Rousseau's aim in describing "the natural state" of the first human beings was precisely to characterize human nature and the human condition apart from any particular social conditions. Hence the solitude of the first men and women. According to Rousseau's story, in those first days individuals encountered each other infrequently and by accident. There was no language; therefore there were no linguistic communities. Families did not exist. Of course, there was sexual intercourse, but men and women stayed together only long enough to copulate; then they parted, perhaps never to see each other again. Children stayed with their mothers only until they were old enough to fend for themselves. At that moment, the mother–child bond dissolved. In short, in their natural state, "with neither a fixed dwelling nor any need for one another, [people] hardly encountered one another twice in their lives."[4]

This graphically atomistic picture might be motivated by a conviction that human beings really are disposed to be solitary; that communities of any sort, even the most intimate, are at odds with human nature. But Rousseau believed nothing of the sort. The state of *The Social Contract* is a community united by a general will, and a sense of community on the part of its citizens is necessary for its maintenance and well-being. Unless we suppose that the capacity to join together in this way arose out of nothing, its roots must lie in human beings' innate capacities. Thus Rousseau claimed that pity (*pitié*), empathy, and compassion for the suffering of one's fellows moved even the first human beings. Pity is the root from which the sociability that makes general will coordination possible grows. Inasmuch as pity, by Rousseau's account, is a

---

4 J.-J. Rousseau, *Oeuvres complètes*, vol. 3 (Paris: Pléiade, 1964), p. 146. Subsequent references to *The Second Discourse*, hereafter *SD*, will be to this edition. In all cases, the translations are my own.

sentiment human beings share with the higher animals, its introduction is not quite ad hoc. But its inclusion in a socially unmediated state of nature is certainly fortuitous. It is because human beings are capable of pity that, though naturally solitary, they can eventually join together to form a just state.

Thus Rousseau abstracted society away, while allowing for its (re)constitution. His aim was to examine the will under natural – that is, pre- or nonsocial – conditions. One of the conclusions he derived from this exercise is even more startling today than it was in his own time: that the private will is not a direct expression of human nature. It is a consequence of very particular social circumstances.

BEFORE THE PRIVATE WILL

Individuals moved by private wills seek to realize their private interests as "efficiently" as possible. As already noted, this idea includes distinct claims about rational agency and individuals' interests. Perhaps one could not succeed in realizing private interests, except capriciously or by accident, without being an instrumentally rational agent. But one can be a rational agent without aiming at private interests.

Rationality, in the sense in question, is tantamount to consistency or, more strictly, transitivity. Suppose, as is commonplace today, that interests are represented by preferences for alternative outcomes.[5] Then, for any rational agent, if x is preferred to y and y is preferred to z, x is preferred to z. Since reason does not rule on the content of our ends, a preference for x over y or y over z is in itself neither rational nor irrational. But, given these preferences, x must be preferred to z. If we require in addition that preferences be complete – that, for any agent and for all x and y, either x is preferred to y or y is preferred to x – preferences can be represented by ordinal numbers. Additional conditions must be satisfied for preferences to be represented by cardinal numbers. Unless cardinal numbers can be assigned to utilities in a theoretically meaningful way, individuals' utilities cannot be added together as, for instance, utilitarianism requires. But even ordinal rankings are beyond the capacities of individuals in the original state of nature.

5 For greater verisimilitude in modeling actual choice situations, it would be better to describe the indicated relation not as "preference" but as "preference or indifference." However, to simplify the exposition, I have omitted this precision.

Rousseau did not conceive the problem of rational agency so abstractly; he therefore never quite impugned the rationality of the first human beings in these terms. But he was eloquent in describing the absence of arts and sciences in the original state of nature and in ascribing this (for him) mixed blessing to the underdevelopment of peoples' intellectual capacities. "The progress of the mind [is] precisely proportionate to the needs received by peoples from nature or to those needs to which circumstances have subjected them."[6] In the original state of nature, desires are so limited that they can only be satisfied directly and immediately. Thus circumstances militated against the development of individuals' (innate) abilities to adapt means to ends. Even ranking alternatives was beyond the capabilities of the first men and women.

To seek to do as well for oneself as one can is to seek to advance the well-being of a unitary entity enduring across some span of time. Rational agents may have time preferences, represented by the rate at which their utility functions discount future outcomes.[7] But reason itself is indifferent to temporal stages. This view of rationality therefore presupposes that persons are capable *psychologically* of conceiving of themselves as beings who exist continuously over time (though not necessarily for entire lifetimes).[8] Thus agents must have minds sufficiently integrated to join particular actions into coherent projects. But, in Rousseau's view, for an inhabitant of the original state of nature, this capacity does not yet exist. Of this benighted individual, Rousseau writes:

His soul, agitated by nothing, is given over to the single feeling of his own present existence, without any idea of the future, however near it may be, and his projects, as limited as his views, hardly extend to the end of the day. Such is, even today, the extent of the Carib's foresight. In the morning he sells his bed of cotton and in the evening he returns in tears to buy it back, for want of having foreseen that he would need it that night.[9]

In other words, in the original state of nature, human beings lacked the very capacity to will coherently. Their "wills," if they

---

6 *SD*, p. 144.
7 A minority current within the mainstream, represented most famously by Sidgwick, denies even the rationality of time preferences. See Henry Sidgwick, *Methods of Ethics* (New York: Dover, 1966), Book III, Chapter 13, section 3.
8 This position has been contested by a number of writers recently, most famously by Derek Parfit in *Reasons and Persons* (Oxford: Clarendon Press, 1984). A similar objection was, of course, raised long ago by David Hume; cf. *A Treatise of Human Nature*, Part 4, Chapter 6.
9 *SD*, p. 144.

can be so designated, were merely successions of impulses. The first men and women could therefore act only out of immediate inclination, never in a calculated way. Thus their wills were not yet fully private, if only because they were not rational agents in the requisite sense.

Like other living things, the inhabitants of the original state of nature were moved by "self-love" (*amour de soi*), by a concern for their own well-being. But lacking the capacity to plan for an ever-receding future, they could only act unreflectively – to protect themselves and to satisfy their wants. They were incapable of forbearance or planning or strategizing. Therefore their "interests," if the term properly applies to the objects of the impulses that constitute their "wills," were more ephemeral than those toward which true private willers aim. This fact has important implications for the nature of their interests. Prior to the social contract, competition gives rise to a war of all against all because bearers of private wills, according to Rousseau's account, are accumulators, not just consumers; and accumulators, unlike consumers, can pursue their passion indefinitely without encountering natural limits to mitigate their conflicts. Lacking means to coordinate their activities, competition among rational accumulators therefore takes on the deadly aspect Rousseau imputes. On the other hand, inasmuch as their interests did not extend beyond what they were immediately able to grasp, the first men and women were not accumulators – nor could they be. For these primordial human beings, the motivational principle that so many today consider universal was literally inconceivable.

Bereft of rationality and of desires beyond their immediate horizons, the first men and women differed in nearly all respects from the individuals who end the state of nature by a social contract. In each case, the people depicted are substantive *atomic* individuals. But their dispositions differ, and therefore their social interactions differ too. In the original state of nature, lacking the capacities necessary for protracted antagonisms, individuals were necessarily at peace. In the circumstances that make the social contract necessary, individuals' wills are opposed and conflict is universal. But, *pace* Hobbes, this situation is not a consequence of human nature and the human condition after everything distinctively social is subtracted away. In fact, universal conflict is unthinkable for men and women in their truly natural condition.

Nevertheless, a Hobbesian war of all against all is humanly possible in certain conditions, and so too is the harmonious, internally coordinated order that the social contract establishes. It is the burden of *The Second Discourse* to demonstrate the social conditions necessary for realizing these supposedly exhaustive possibilities. But the conditions Rousseau adduces are not equally attainable at all moments of the history he recounts. General will coordination becomes possible only after private volition has worked its effects.

FROM SELF-LOVE TO AMOUR PROPRE

The private will emerged in consequence of a process begun by a singular event. According to Rousseau's account, "the first man who, having enclosed a plot of land, took it into his head to say *this is mine* and found people simple enough to believe him, was the true founder of civil society."[10] It was this act that inaugurated a historical dynamic culminating in a war of all against all waged by bearers of full-fledged private wills.

From primitive times through Rousseau's day, land was, along with labor, the principal means of production. Of course, in the original state of nature neither labor nor land is owned. But there is an important difference. Labor cannot be separated from the individuals who deploy it; land is attached to no one by nature. Therefore, even without private property, people effectively controlled their own labor and appropriated its product. A successful assertion of self-ownership in the original state of nature would only formalize what was already the case. On the other hand, the private appropriation of land marked a profound departure from "the natural state of man." It is not just that a social relation – private property in alienable means of production – was then introduced into an otherwise nonsocial condition. What is crucial is the nature of this social relation. Making a plot of land one's own poses a revolutionary challenge to the *ancien régime* of Rousseau's story. The revolution succeeded according to Rousseau, and the consequence was an epochal transformation in the condition human beings confront.

In Rousseau's view, the successful enclosure of plots of land – or, more generally, the private appropriation of alienable means of production – might not have occurred. In contrast to what was to come, the original state of nature, like the social orders of nonhuman species, was reproducible indefinitely. But there were potentially destabilizing aspects of this condition that distinguished it

10 *SD*, p. 164.

from the situation of other animals. To a degree unprecedented in the animal kingdom, the first humans beings were potentially rational in the Hobbesian sense and intelligent. Without language or other means for cultivating innate capacities, rationality and intelligence were undeveloped and might have remained so forever. But, as a matter of fact, "progress" did occur. Needing to compensate for physical shortcomings, people fashioned tools to aid in hunting and gathering. With means for transmitting knowledge lacking, what was invented was usually lost only to be reinvented by others elsewhere. But some imitation took place. With so little social interaction, imitation served the accumulation of knowledge poorly. Still, over time, a few advances came to be widely shared. Above all, knowledge of metallurgy became part of the technological legacy of humankind. Through gradual accretion, these advances eventually made settled agricultural production materially possible. But this technology could not be productively deployed. Without private ownership of land, the products of agricultural labor are available for anyone to seize. Therefore, despite its potential for augmenting yields per unit of land, agricultural technology in the absence of property relations would probably be less productive than hunting and gathering; it would certainly be less productive than it could otherwise be. In short, in the conditions Rousseau described, settled agriculture was impossible; the technology was "fettered." It remained so until it was liberated by "the true founder of civil society."

In Marxist terms, this change in *social relations of production* facilitated the development of *productive forces*. Labor power became more productive, the product of labor increased, and scarcity – understood in absolute terms, as an inverse measure of socially desired things – diminished. Marx's theory of history purports to explain epochal social transformations by appeal to a universal human interest in diminishing scarcity. However, this is not quite the interest that explains the demise of the original state of nature. Since the first men and women lacked the capacity to desire anything that was not immediately present, they made no demands on nature that nature could not fulfill. For them, the miserliness of nature passed unnoticed. Scarcity was neither a spur to development nor a source of social instability. It is not absolute but *relative* scarcity, the supply of socially desired things relative to the demand for them, that unleashes the dynamic process Marx identified. Absolute scarcity was never more acute than in the original state of nature. But in those first days, relative scarcity did not

45

exist at all. Paradoxically, it was development itself or, more precisely, development under the property relations introduced by "the true founder of civil society" that made scarcity a salient and causally efficacious aspect of the human condition. Once relative scarcity was *socially* introduced, history became invested with a determinate structure and directionality. The subsequent course of human affairs then became inevitable.

Those who succeeded in turning plots of land into private property and who farmed their plots successfully were, of course, better off than their neighbors who continued to hunt and gather on unowned land. They became models to imitate. Those who failed to follow their example became even worse off than they were before, if only because they had less land upon which to roam in search of food. Insofar as the remaining hunters and gatherers had, by that time, become somewhat intelligent and (instrumentally) rational, they were moved to follow the lead of their more productive neighbors. Thus a process was set in motion that led to the private appropriation of virtually all available land. In time, hunting-and-gathering was no longer a viable way of life. Productivity increased and absolute scarcity diminished. But relative scarcity intensified inexorably.

In the original state of nature, the size of the human population and the capacity of the land to support it were in equilibrium. It is not clear why Rousseau thought that population pressures develop as productivity increases. Perhaps he believed that agricultural production runs up against inexorable physical limits – a reasonable expectation, especially in a preindustrial age. In any case, it is plain that Rousseau did not believe that the primordial harmony of the original state of nature could be maintained with rising productivity. The more there was to distribute, the larger the number of individuals demanding a share. Scarcity therefore became increasingly important. Indeed, it came to shape individuals' interests and to transform their wills.

With settled agriculture came the family, patriarchically structured and based on blood ties. In Rousseau's account, the family is an institution for organizing the labor process and reproducing labor power. It is also an institution for transmitting land and other productive assets from one generation to another. With rising populations, family plots were divided among surviving sons, each of whom established his own family in turn. Thus, with land resources remaining constant and population rising, the amount of land per family – and per person – diminished from generation to generation. This situation motivated the intensification of labor and the introduction of new technologies, increasing overall productivity and diminishing absolute scarcity. But these palliatives were insufficient to offset population growth. Though vastly more productive than the hunting and gathering technology that preceded it, settled agriculture brought relative scarcity into being; additional "progress" then intensified relative scarcity, turning it into the aspect of the human condition that, more than any other, makes a social contract necessary.

But relative scarcity also plays a role in the emergence of the conditions that make a social contract possible. In order to survive with scarcity intensifying, individuals were obliged to develop capacities dormant in the original state of nature. Thus they became the full-fledged (instrumentally) rational agents they potentially always were – setting long-range goals, deliberating prudently, and acting strategically. Their behaviors were increasingly governed by a determination to anticipate future wants, a momentous development with far-reaching implications for individuals' interests and dispositions. The fleeting impulses that directed the behaviors of the first men and women gave way to sustained projects organized around the relentless accumulation of resources.[11] In a sense, acquisitiveness is only a continuation of self-love after private property has transformed the human condition and human beings' capacities to adapt to it. But the disposition to accumulate eventually took on a life of its own. "Human nature" became acquisitive, just as Hobbes thought it always was.

Before economists appropriated and developed this idea, it was tacitly if unreflectively supposed that individuals always want more of everything. But, of course, no one does. People become satiated, and their desires for particular things usually diminish as these things are consumed or acquired. For greater verisimilitude, therefore, it has become standard to hold that leisure is a universally desired good that agents trade off against other goods that they can only acquire through effort. Thus, for most goods, individuals' utility functions will be such that, beyond a certain point, additional units will be desired in diminishing degrees – and leisure desired more.

11 For adherents of the view of rational agency assumed by those who consider private volition ubiquitous, accumulation per se is neither rational nor irrational. But, given the human condition and individuals' "natures," rational *human* agents will, as a matter of fact, want (virtually) unlimited quantities of resources.

47

It will be useful to represent Rousseau's position not in the vague way that he advanced it but with this clarification in mind. Then, if we introduce a universal measure of exchange, money, we can say that more money will always be desired. Leisure too is always desired. What will vary is the degree of intensity of these desires. The shape of an individual's utility function is, strictly speaking, indeterminate, even for full-fledged private willers. But, typically, when additional amounts of money can only be acquired by sacrificing leisure, individuals' utility functions will at some point exhibit diminishing marginal utility for money increments. In other words, the utility of yet more money will never be negative.

In any case, it was only after the introduction of private property that individuals became rational economic agents.[12] For this outcome to result, it was not necessary that everyone be burdened with acquisitive natures at the inception of civil society. It suffices if only some individuals are. A process analogous to natural selection can do the rest. We have seen how the presence of even a few accumulators among persons moved by self-love worsens the situation of the majority. As selection proceeds, this process fuels itself. The more rational economic agents there are, the more rapidly the processes that engender rational economic agency work their effects. Accumulation becomes the order of the day, propelled by ever-increasing (relative) scarcity but also by an ever more acquisitive "human nature."

12 It is worth remarking, again, that this destination of the protracted process Rousseau depicts was, for Hobbes, a universal feature of human psychology. Hobbes's picture of relentless accumulation effectively secularized an aspect of St. Augustine's account of human psychology after the Fall, according to which an inexorable passion to accumulate is one of the afflictions visited upon humankind in consequence of Original Sin. See Herbert A. Deane, *The Political and Social Ideas of St. Augustine* (New York: Columbia University Press, 1963), Chapter 2. Thus what Hobbes considered normal and even desirable Augustine thought a sign of human degradation. In effect, *The Second Discourse* revives the older Augustinian understanding. In Rousseau's account, the mentality that emerges in consequence of private property *is* an affliction and a result of a fall from an earlier condition of felicity. However, for Rousseau, the Original Sin of the first men and women was not Pride or Disobedience but the introduction of private property in alienable means of production. Although Rousseau had no specifically economic alternative to private property in mind, he did think that rational economic agents could – and would – rectify the antagonisms it engenders at the political level by means of a social contract. Thus, in his view, in contrast to Augustine's, "salvation" is possible through human efforts – thanks, ironically, to the very circumstance, the predominance of private volition, that makes it necessary.

Had "the true founder of civil society" not succeeded in privately appropriating a piece of land, *amour de soi* might have survived indefinitely. But with the end of the original state of nature and the ensuing transformation of human beings' interests and dispositions, the demise of self-love became inevitable. Rousseau called its successor *amour propre*, rational egoism. Individuals moved by amour propre are essentially the idealized agents of nineteenth- and twentieth-century economic theories, the rational calculators emblematic of "the spirit of capitalism." Strictly speaking, one need not be a rational egoist in order to count as a rational agent. But the rational agents who enter into the social contract are moved by amour propre. In fact, Rousseau's usage effectively conflates amour propre with (Hobbesian) rational agency. We can, of course, disaggregate these claims conceptually. But it remains true that the paradigm case of private volition is precisely the rational egoist whose origins *The Second Discourse* describes.

It should be noted, finally, that Hobbes's conception of individuals' interests is not quite the same as Rousseau's. In Hobbes's view, individuals have interests in accumulating resources. But they also have interests in dominating others and in diminishing the unrelenting fear that results from recognizing their vulnerability to mortal assault. People are not just "competitive" but also "vainglorious" and "diffident." Thus scarcity is less important in Hobbes's account of the war of all against all than in Rousseau's. Its role in the state of nature is to exacerbate antagonisms and to direct them into struggles over things. But Hobbes's individuals would find themselves at war even in a world of abundance. For what mainly sets them at odds is the fear of violent death. In a state of nature, relatively equal and instrumentally rational agents driven by this fear have an incentive to attack each other preemptively whenever an appropriate occasion arises. Thus any collection of human beings without a sovereign to keep their natures in bounds would evince a generalized disposition to combat which, Hobbes tells us, is precisely what a state of war is.[13]

---

13 "Hereby it is manifest, that during the time men live without a common Power to keep them all in awe, they are in that condition which is called Warre; and such a warre, as is of every man, against every man. For Warre, consisteth not in Battell onely, or the act of fighting; but in a tract of time, wherein the Will to contend by Battell is sufficiently known; and therefore the notion of Time, is to be considered in the nature of Warre; as it is in the nature of Weather. For as the nature of Foule weather, lyeth not in a showre or two of rain; but in an

49

However, for Rousseau, human beings are not, by nature, diffident or vainglorious or even acquisitive. When they act *as if* they are it is because they live in the grip of a civil society based on the private ownership of alienable productive assets. Inexorably, individuals in these conditions lock themselves into a condition of generalized conflict. As it was for Hobbes, this situation is dire. "The human race would perish," Rousseau insists, "unless it changed its mode of existence."[14]

DE FACTO STATES

Rousseau's warning is susceptible to at least two readings. Both are warranted and perhaps even intended. In *The Second Discourse*, what I shall call the neo-Hobbesian reading predominates.

The use of Hobbes's name in this context requires qualification. In recent years, a number of writers have deployed game-theoretic concepts to reconstruct and assess Hobbesian positions.[15] Doing so is, of course, anachronistic. But as a way of productively joining Hobbes's concerns with current issues in political philosophy, the fruitfulness of this approach is plain. It is in this spirit, even at the risk of distorting Hobbes's views, that I shall describe a Hobbesian state of nature as a game.

But what game? There is no uncontroversial answer. However, for our purposes, a deeper understanding of Hobbes matters less than a clearer grasp of Rousseau's purchase on the emergence of the mentality Hobbes described. Therefore, without any pretense of getting Hobbes right or even of siding with the stronger case, I will stipulate that a Hobbesian state of nature is a generalized Prisoner's Dilemma in which individually rational (maximizing) choices lead to outcomes that are worse, in terms of each individual's own interests, than outcomes that might otherwise be

inclination thereto of many dayes together; So the nature of War, consisteth not in actuall fighting; but in the known disposition thereto, during all the time there is no assurance to the contrary." *Leviathan*, Book I, Chapter 13.

14 *The Social Contract*, Book I, Chapter 6.

15 Cf., among others, David Gauthier, *The Logic of "Leviathan"* (Oxford: Clarendon Press, 1969); Gregory S. Kavka, *Hobbesian Moral and Political Theory* (Princeton: Princeton University Press, 1986); and Jean Hampton, *Hobbes and the Social Contract Tradition* (Cambridge: Cambridge University Press, 1986). This genre of philosophical reconstruction epitomizes "the standard philosophical interpretation" of Hobbes referred to in the Introduction, note 11.

		B	
		cooperate	*defect*
	cooperate	2nd, 2nd	4th, 1st
A			
	defect	1st, 4th	3rd, 3rd

Figure 1

achieved.[16] The situation can be represented as a game with two (or more) players and two moves – "cooperation" and "defection." To cooperate is to refrain from choosing what is individually best in order to produce outcomes that are better, given each player's private interests, than the outcomes that would result from straightforward maximizing choices. Cooperation is self-regulated coordination; it entails that some players sometimes not do what is individually best. To defect is to fail to cooperate – to act, move by move, with a view toward realizing one's own private interests. For players with private wills competing for scarce resources, it is desirable that there be cooperation – if only because the continuation of the war of all against all necessitates defensive measures that deflect efforts away from accumulation. For Hobbes, cooperation would also mitigate the pursuit of vainglory and diminish the anxiety that weighs on each individual in a state of war. But, for each player, it is better if only the *other* players cooperate. Thus, if there are two players A and B, A is better off if B cooperates and A defects than if both A and B cooperate; and similarly for B. Both A and B are better off, however, if both cooperate than if both defect. Finally, A is worst off if A cooperates and B defects; and similarly for B. Schematically, representing A's choices in order of preference on the left, and B's on the right, the payoff matrix shown in Figure 1 obtains. The payoff to A depends on what B does and vice versa. But whatever B does, A is better off defecting. Since the payoffs are symmetrical, whatever A does, B is better off defecting too. Therefore, if A and B are rational players, both will defect, and each will do less well than they might have done had they cooperated. But they cannot cooperate. Insofar as they are rational, when they confront Prisoner's Dilemma payoffs, they can only act in ways that produce suboptimal outcomes.

If Hobbes was right, the rational pursuit of private interests in the absence of political arrangements leads to the virtual certainty of outright annihilation in a war of all against all, a supremely

16 For a different and probably sounder view, see Hampton, *Hobbes and the Social Contract Tradition*, passim, but esp. pp. 58–63, 132–138.

suboptimal outcome. In this plain sense, "the human race would perish unless it changed its mode of existence." Thus a neo-Hobbesian reading would construe Rousseau's warning literally. I think there are good reasons to resist this construal, but it is instructive to see where it leads.

For Hobbes, there is a qualitative gap in individuals' orderings of outcomes in the Prisoner's Dilemma they confront. Third choices rank somewhat higher than fourth choices, inasmuch as individuals can at least hope to emerge as victors in a generalized state of war but face certain annihilation if they cooperate alone. To a much greater degree, each player's most preferred outcome, lone defection, dominates universal cooperation. Lone defectors enjoy the benefits of cooperation without having to pay the costs. But the intensity of these preferences pales before each player's preference for universal cooperation over universal defection. Since players cannot expect to be lone defectors but will instead remain in the war of all against all if they attempt to bring about what they deem individually best, it is overwhelmingly in the interest of each of them to implement mutual cooperation, their second-best choice. But how can they do so? Individuals who choose to cooperate, so long as they play against rational agents, will find their least preferred outcome realized. Their dilemma is plain: To advance their own (private) interests, they cannot allow defection to continue, but neither can they act rationally and avoid this result.

To "solve" this otherwise intractable problem, Hobbes would have individuals change the game they play by instituting sovereignty, supreme authority, through a covenant concocted to be advantageous to each contracting party. The sovereign would then organize his subjects into a "police" for enforcing his commands. With enforceable sanctions in place, defection or, as we then should say, disobedience becomes irrational, given individuals' interests. In virtue of being able to issue enforceable commands, the sovereign coordinates individuals' behaviors – and individuals attain the peace that they cannot achieve directly through cooperation.

Although *The Second Discourse* describes the emergence of an essentially Hobbesian state of nature, there is an important difference between Hobbes's story and Rousseau's account of the origin of de facto states. Because Hobbes's state of nature is ahistorical, and because he viewed relative equality (not just in physical and mental endowments but also in possessions) as given, Hobbes imagined that the individuals who establish "a common power to hold [themselves] in awe" do so from roughly the same starting point. Rousseau, on the other hand, depicted the onset of the war and all against all as a consequence of processes that result in considerable inequalities of condition. For Rousseau, therefore, the establishment of de facto sovereignty is not a solution contrived by equals. It is a response to a problem confronted by individuals of unequal wealth, where the burdens of war weigh most heavily on those who have the most to lose. States are formed whenever the rich are able to convince the poor that it is in their interest to end the war of all against all by political means. In Rousseau's view, it is the guile of the well-off and the gullibility of the rest that gives us de facto sovereignty.

In *The Second Discourse*, this trick, foisted on the vast majority, is promoted by Hobbesian arguments tempered by professions of concern for those who are destined to become the principal victims of the new order. Thus Rousseau imagines an individual "enriched by industry," invoking "the horror of a situation which armed them all against each other and made their possessions as burdensome as their needs," entreating his propertyless neighbors in these words:

Let us unite . . . in order to protect the weak from oppression, restrain the ambitious, and assure everyone of possessing what belongs to him. Let us institute rules of justice and peace to which all will be obliged to conform, which will make special exceptions for no one, and which will in some way compensate for the caprices of fortune by subjecting the strong and the weak to mutual obligations. In short, instead of turning our forces against ourselves, let us gather them into one supreme power that governs us according to wise laws, that protects and defends all the members of the association, repulses common enemies, and maintains us in eternal concord.[17]

In short, let us establish "a common power to hold us in awe," a Hobbesian sovereign, for our mutual advantage.

Rousseau suggests, as Marx would half a century later, that the citizenship the rich offer the poor masks and reinforces the underlying inequalities of civil society, and that the institutions that transform possessions (*biens*) into property (*propriété*) institutionalize the poverty of the asset-poor. But the argument the rich advance, though disingenuous and disadvantageous to "crude and easily seduced men," is nevertheless sound. The untrammeled reign of private interest in a world of scarcity does threaten even

17 SD, p. 177.

those who have nothing more to lose than their lives, and the establishment of de facto states does remove this mortal danger. If Rousseau's warning that "the human race would perish unless it changed its mode of existence" is understood in the neo-Hobbesian way, as a prediction of universal physical annihilation, the people of *The Second Discourse* have indeed contrived a solution.

FREEDOM

The de facto state arises in consequence of a process set in motion by the introduction of private property in alienable productive assets. As private property increasingly determines social life, the state of nature turns into a Hobbesian war of all against all, a condition that everyone has an incentive to transform. By authorizing a sovereign to act in their behalf – agreeing to obey his commands and to enforce his will against disobedients – individuals constitute a force sufficiently powerful to ensure the order that they all desire.

But what order? For Hobbes, the function of the state is to keep human nature from destroying humankind. Thus he would have the state suppress anything that threatens to disrupt the fragile peace it establishes. Revolutionary challenges to existing regimes are particularly dangerous, but any destabilizing political intervention can unleash a course of events likely to devolve into a war of all against all. The order that states exist to protect is therefore the existing order, whatever it may be. Hobbes did value freedom in the sense of "negative" liberty, "the absence of external Impediments."[18] But, in his view, order takes precedence over freedom and everything else. For Rousseau, on the other hand, disorder is not so odious in itself, nor is it inscribed in the "natural" course of events. Political arrangements serve a different purpose.

In Rousseau's view, there exists a fundamental interest that Hobbes failed to acknowledge and that legitimate political institutions must protect. This interest is intimately bound to

18 *Leviathan*, Chapter 13. This is, roughly, the understanding of freedom that liberals would later make their own. I discuss aspects of post-Hobbesian freedom in *Liberal Democracy: A Critique of Its Theory* (New York: Columbia University Press, 1981), Chapter 2, and *Arguing for Socialism*, 2nd ed. (London: Verso, 1988), Chapter 1.

"one's dignity as a man, the rights of humanity and even its duties."[19] If we focus on this interest and reflect on its implications, a nonliteral – Rousseauean – reading of Rousseau's warning of the impending demise of the human race suggests itself. On this understanding, what is put in jeopardy by a Hobbesian war of all against all is not human life as such but essential humanity.[20]

What Hobbes ignored and what individuals moved by amour propre fail to see is what Rousseau proclaims in the first words of *The Social Contract:* that "man is born free."[21] Of course, no one is "born free" from "external Impediments." But negative liberty is not what Rousseau had in mind. What he intended by "freedom" was *autonomy*, self-determination, "obedience to a law of one's own making." What is essential to being human, according to Rousseau, is the possibility of becoming the master of one's own projects and undertakings. For reasons Kant would later explore, it is reasonable to value autonomy absolutely because it is the condition for the possibility of moral agency, which alone makes human beings "ends in themselves."[22] Autonomy therefore takes precedence over other interests – including the universal human interest in order and the more particular but still pervasive interest in rational accumulation that has developed after the introduction of private property.

Even if the human race could physically survive a war of all against all, Rousseau's concern is that essential humanity, autonomy, cannot survive this condition. "Man is born free, but is everywhere in chains." The humanity of the human race will perish if these chains – made more burdensome by the establishment of de facto states – extinguish the very hope of genuine self-determination. But this is just where the process set in motion by the introduction of private property tends. *The Second Discourse* recounts the transformation of the human race into a collection of unfree, heteronomously determined individuals – in Rousseau's terms, into "slaves." When Rousseau insists that the preservation of life is not a sufficient reason for an individual to enter into the

19 *The Social Contract*, Book I, Chapter 4.
20 See Levine, *The Politics of Autonomy*, Chapter 1.
21 *The Social Contract*, Book I, Chapter 1.
22 Cf. Immanuel Kant, *The Foundations of the Metaphysics of Morals*, passim, but esp. Part 2. What follows draws on Levine, *The Politics of Autonomy*, pp. 20–29. Autonomy is discussed in Chapters 6 and 7 herein.

social contract, he is simply drawing out an implication of this view.[23] If autonomy is the source of all value, life itself is of no value, except as a condition for exercising autonomous choice. Thus in a war of all against all, where autonomy is at risk of becoming irretrievably lost, the physical continuation of the human species is not the issue. The issue is humanity itself.

This is why Rousseau insists that autonomy can never be advantageously exchanged:

Renouncing one's liberty is renouncing one's dignity as a man, the rights of humanity and even its duties. There is no possible compensation for anyone who renounces everything. Such a renunciation is incompatible with the nature of man. . . . [I]t is a vain and contradictory convention.[24]

Autonomy is *priceless*; its value knows no bounds. There is nothing, including peace or wealth, that can compensate for its loss. Any social contract that grounds legitimate political institutions must therefore respect autonomy. Thus the de jure state is an assembly of autonomous agents. In contrast, the de facto states *The Second Discourse* describes, the states whose origins Hobbes explained, are associations of slaves. "The fundamental problem of political life" is therefore not quite the problem Hobbes engaged: the institution of a regime capable of rendering impossible the war of all against all. It is Hobbes's problem with a very non-Hobbesian proviso added on. Individuals must somehow contrive a way to avoid a war of all against all while retaining or, more precisely, realizing essential autonomy; they must, in short, reconcile autonomy with authority.

So, far from solving this problem, Hobbesian sovereignty exacerbates it. This is not the place to assess Rousseau's attempt at a solution: his insistence that each individual "place himself and his powers under the supreme direction of the general will."[25] What matters for now is just that "the exercise of the general will" is introduced to address a problem private willing generates and inten-

23 See, especially, *The Social Contract*, Book I, Chapter 4, where Rousseau argues that pacts of involuntary slavery, in which individuals conquered in wars agree to become the slaves of their conquerors in return for their lives, do not establish legitimacy. Arguably, Rousseau's claims for the worthlessness of life in the absence of freedom are exaggerated for rhetorical effect. But this conclusion literally does follow from his view of autonomy as a necessary condition for the value of everything else. See Levine, *The Politics of Autonomy*, pp. 9–19.

24 *The Social Contract*, Book I, Chapter 4.

25 Ibid., Chapter 6. For an extended discussion of the merits of Rousseau's case, see Levine, *The Politics of Autonomy*, passim.

sifies. According to Rousseau's story, general will coordination becomes possible, desirable, and eventually indispensable only *after* the private will has transformed the human condition.

EPHEMERAL HOBBESIANISM

The individuals we encounter by the end of *The Second Discourse* are Hobbesian in the sense that, without a sovereign to constrain them, they would find themselves in a war of all against all. But their Hobbesianism is triggered by particular social conditions and is destined to pass from the scene. Hobbes thought mutual antagonism an inevitable consequence of human nature. For Rousseau, human nature can support this state of affairs, but it hardly necessitates it. In fact, essential humanity points in a different direction. As *The Social Contract* completes the story begun in *The Second Discourse*, the essence Rousseau imputes to human beings finally works its effects. Then what had previously been only a notional possibility becomes increasingly feasible and even necessary. Thus the Hobbesianism that is the destination of *The Second Discourse* is ephemeral. It is a "dialectical" moment in the history of the human race, "overcome" when its immanent development undoes the conditions for its possibility.

It is tempting to conclude that Rousseau's solution to "the fundamental problem of political life," the subordination of private to general interests, is a "self-effacing" Hobbesian solution, according to which Hobbesian individuals undertake to end the Prisoner's Dilemma they confront by ceasing to advance the private interests they acknowledge.[26] But this characterization is misleading because Rousseau's political philosophy is non-Hobbesian at its core. Its fundamental commitment to human autonomy is foreign to Hobbes's conception of political life. True Hobbesians would deny that "man is born free." For Rousseau, however, autonomy is the condition sine qua non of humanity itself.

From a Rousseauean point of view, Hobbes concocted a general theory of political life by focusing on only one phase of human "history." This phase, the age of private interests, is a Dark Age for humankind. It is a time in which the passion to accumulate forges chains of unfreedom. So pervasive are its effects that human nature itself stands increasingly at odds with essential humanity. But

26 On self-effacing theories, see Parfit, *Reasons and Persons*, pp. 23–24, 43–45. See also Joshua Cohen, "Reflections on Rousseau: Autonomy and Democracy," *Philosophy and Public Affairs*, vol. 15, no. 1 (1986), pp. 281–284.

as the reign of private property unfolds, a realization of unfreedom dawns. Individuals become aware that the social order they have constructed is a mortal threat to their most fundamental interest, to their own autonomy and therefore to essential humanity itself. In *The Social Contract*, this *prise de conscience* leads Hobbesian individuals to end the unchallenged reign of private volition and to put the Hobbesian "moment," whose origins and ascendance *The Second Discourse* recounts, definitively to rest.

Since these reflections on *The Second Discourse* have stayed close to Rousseau's own meandering thoughts, it will be helpful, by way of conclusion, to draw together some of the principal claims that can be teased out of the tale Rousseau concocted in that text and its continuations in *The Social Contract*. Thus we can say that Rousseau holds:

(1) that what it is to be a human being is to be free (autonomous); and therefore that autonomy takes precedence over all other ends that human beings might will. Essential autonomy is asserted as a metaphysical claim about the nature of human beings. Autonomy is therefore a condition that all legitimate institutional arrangements must accommodate.

(2) that human beings' essential freedom has no direct implications for human psychology. Thus, in humanity's "natural state," neither private nor general wills govern individuals' lives. Individuals are instead moved by *amour de soi*, "self-love," in just the way that higher animals are. This "natural state" is a happy condition and also a stable one.

(3) that this condition is alterable. Unlike higher animals, human beings are capable of developing (instrumentally) rational capacities; and, as a matter of fact, these capacities did develop. Among other things, people discovered ways to augment the productivity of land through agriculture. But the first men and women were unable to deploy agricultural technologies in the social conditions of the original state of nature.

(4) that, thanks to a change in "social relations" that might well not have occurred, the successful introduction of private property in land, it became socially possible to shift from hunting and gathering to settled agriculture. The implementation of this advance in productive technology had momentous consequences: augmenting population and diminishing the stock of land available per person. But scarcity – in a relative, not absolute, sense – intensified as productivity increased. This change in the human

condition had profound ramifications for human nature. Self-love gave way to amour propre, and instrumentally rational individuals developed properly *private* wills. Thus human beings became indomitable accumulators, and the happy and peaceful state of nature turned increasingly into a Hobbesian war of all against all.

(5) that this process is replete with dire consequences for humankind. Among other things, it explains "the development of inequality among men." More important for a philosophical theory of the state, the war of all against all puts essential autonomy in peril.

(6) that the story *The Second Discourse* tells therefore culminates in a condition that makes the establishment of de jure political communities, resting on a supremacy of the general will, both necessary and possible, if the human race is not to forfeit essential humanity irretrievably. "The human race would perish if it did not alter its mode of existence" – that is, if it did not become what it always essentially was, a union of autonomous beings.

Thus, after the process begun with the introduction of private property has run its course, each individual has in principle two wills: a private will and a general will. Each is compatible with transhistorical constraints on human psychology, and each can be actualized under different social and historical conditions. Paradoxically, the prolonged supremacy of the private will eventually makes the supremacy of the general will possible; and the essential nature of humanity makes it desirable. What is morally imperative converges on what is historically feasible. The emblematic expression of this idea is the social contract itself: the earthly instantiation of the notional possibility of genuine self-determination.

The general will plays no role in *The Second Discourse*, and its cogency is assumed in *The Social Contract*. Thus neither text adequately addresses the hesitations of those who find the idea incoherent or obscure. But *The Social Contract* does help clarify what is intended by the contrast between an individual's general and private will; and *The Second Discourse* helps even more. By telling a story about the "origins" of the private will, an account that emphasizes the historicity of private volition, it works to diminish the influence of this idea over contemporary thinking. General will coordination is certainly problematic. But if *The Second Discourse* story is at all plausible, its ostensible rival is as well.

Chapter 3

Solidarity

To gain a better purchase on what general will coordination is, it will be helpful to contrast it with a form of social interaction it appears to resemble: acting in solidarity. In our political culture, "solidarity" is often used imprecisely and in a variety of vaguely related senses. However, what follows focuses on only a very few legitimate uses of the term. An investigation of solidarity is useful especially for the insight it provides into the central political problem Rousseauean political philosophy confronts: the problem of transforming a world where private interests hold exclusive sway into a social order in which "the exercise of the general will" plays an important role.

A POINT OF DEPARTURE

It is seldom enlightening to investigate political phenomena by reflecting on obscure and oracular dicta. But, in this case, there is a venerable and celebrated saying that, though virtually featureless, suggests what is essential. According to the portion of the Mishnah called the Pirke Aboth, "The Sayings of the Fathers," Rabbi Hillel is supposed to have said: "If I am not for myself, then who will be for me? And when I am for myself only, what am I?"[1] These often quoted words are sufficiently vague to support a variety of plausible interpretations. They might be held, for instance, to assert the moral importance of self-respect. But in the popular sermonizing directed to those who seek wisdom in this saying, a

[1] Hillel's dictum then continues, irrelevantly for our purpose, "if not now, when?"

consensus interpretation has emerged according to which Hillel's words are taken to recommend what is nowadays understood by "solidarity." This is a defensible and fruitful interpretation, even if it is not an incontestable rendering of Hillel's intent. It is this understanding that I shall assume in utilizing these ancient words as a point of departure for investigating solidarity.

The question "when I am for myself only, what am I?" seems easy for readers of Hobbes and Rousseau. I am the sort of individual who populates a Hobbesian state of nature, a being moved by amour propre. If Rousseau was right, such individuals exist only in determinate social conditions. Perhaps, however, amour propre is even more historically particular than *The Second Discourse* suggests, enough so to make this answer an anachronistic response to Hillel's question. But even if individuals did not always think of themselves (and others) as bearers of private wills in quite the way Rousseau intended, the behavior the term has come to designate (or some very close approximation) surely has existed since time immemorial. "Being for oneself only" – what the moralists call selfishness – has long been considered a moral flaw. Hillel's words suggest that it is something else besides: that being for oneself only is often unwise or, as in a Prisoner's Dilemma, self-defeating. Individuals for whom this description fits do less well for themselves (in just the sense that they intend by being for themselves only) than they otherwise might.

The question "If I am not for myself, then who will be for me?" is more problematic. Construed as a rhetorical question, the answer is surely "no one." And the presumed implication is that this is not a happy state of affairs; that it is better – in general but also for me – that others be for me too. Since the "me" in question is plainly intended generically, to designate everyone, the claim evidently is that it is good – or, more precisely, beneficial – for people to be for one another, to help one another, and that it is beneficial also (apparently not just for independent reasons) that the people who help others also help themselves.

If it is fair to read this much into a question asked at a remote time for an obscure purpose, it is only fair to note an ambiguity in the inferences we are led to draw. The position Hillel asserts admits of two distinct understandings:

(1) that a world in which people generally help one another is preferable to a world in which they do not; and that a condition for

bringing such a world into being is that all people be to some degree (but not exclusively) for themselves; or

(2) that a world in which people generally help one another is preferable to a world in which they do not; and that some degree of being for oneself *is an essential part of that state of affairs.*

At issue is whether "being for oneself," but not for oneself only, is a means to a desirable end or whether it is also an end in itself, irrespective of its efficacy for promoting the practice of helping others. I would venture that, in our political culture, both readings properly attach to "solidarity" but that the instrumentalist conception is more fundamental.

Since private volition today seems "normal," it is natural to suppose that what Hillel's dictum endorses is "enlightened" self-interest – egoism, being for oneself, in conjunction with *altruism*, being for others. In a world in which it is generally advantageous to everyone that people help one another, it is well, Hillel might be taken to have asserted, that egoism and altruism be joined.

However, "altruism" is an ambiguous term. Sometimes whatever is not egoistic is deemed altruistic. I suspect that this usage attests more to the prevalence of the mentality whose origin *The Second Discourse* recounts than to any analytical exigency. In effect, it categorizes motives as ordinary (egoistic) or extraordinary (non-egoistic) and then groups all the extraordinary motives together under the same designation. This construal of altruism evidently obliterates important distinctions. In particular, it obscures the distinction I want to draw between general will coordination and acting in solidarity.

An egoist seeks to advance his own welfare position. An altruist, then, will be an individual who seeks to enhance the welfare position of at least one *other* individual. Anyone who acts for a non-welfarist motive would therefore be neither an egoist nor an altruist. The egoism–altruism distinction is not even exhaustive within a strictly welfarist frame of reference. What utilitarians call "benevolence," a commitment to enhance the welfare positions of all relevant others (including one's own), would elude both categorizations.

This understanding of altruism lends precision to Hillel's aphoristic advice. Of course there is no reason to think that Hillel intended either "being for oneself" or "being for others" in a welfarist way or even that the intuitions behind contemporary welfarism were available to him. But Hillel's dictum is sufficiently indeterminate to accommodate this reading and, in so doing, to serve as a point of departure for contrasting solidarity with general will coordination.

WHAT IS SOLIDARITY?

Like most terms of political discourse, "solidarity" is used with enough imprecision to encompass a wide range of meanings. Any account is therefore likely to exclude some legitimate uses of the term. With this warning in mind, I shall characterize solidarity as a kind of conditional altruism. To be sure, Hillel's words appear to endorse *unconditional* altruism; he advises us to enhance the welfare position of others irrespective of whether or not they seek to advance our own. However, for beings moved by *amour de soi*, unconditional altruism would be difficult to sustain if unrequited. To be unconditionally for others when others are for themselves only, to give without receiving back, is likely to cause even the most dedicated altruist to falter. Therefore *lone* altruists will likely not persist in being for others very long. Instead, they will become like their neighbors. But then, as Hillel might have asked, "What would they be?" Thus, if only to assure that altruism survives, it is reasonable to infer, according to the spirit if not the letter of Hillel's rhetorical questions, that the disposition he recommends is *conditional* altruism: where individuals are for others if and only if others are altruists too.

However, solidarity is only one form of conditional altruism. Conditional cooperation is another. A conditional cooperator is for others if and only if others directly reciprocate. People cooperate when, for the sake of some common objective, they forbear from doing what they would do were they not cooperating. In a world in which private volition predominates, the overwhelmingly most important reason to cooperate is, of course, to advance one's own welfare. This reason pertains almost universally in the context of interdependent actions – where an agent's payoff depends, in part, on what other agents do. Of particular importance in this respect are social interactions that have the structure of Prisoners' Dilemmas. In these circumstances, as we have seen, individuals would do better by cooperating than by not cooperating. But we know that rational agents may find themselves unable to cooperate. Then their only recourse is to alter the conditions under which they interact – as individuals in a Hobbesian state of nature do when they successfully institute "a common power to hold them in awe." It is now understood that, when Prisoner's Dilemma games are iterated indefinitely, individuals can successfully adopt cooperative strategies.[2] Being more successful in (iterated) Prisoner's Dilemma games, if they occur at all, they will eventually predominate. In consequence, in Prisoner's Dilemma situations in which players interact indefinitely many times, conditional cooperators will come to find the conditions under which they are disposed to cooperate fulfilled.

Conditional cooperators are conditional altruists in the sense that they sometimes act to enhance the welfare positions of others – specifically, those individuals with whom they cooperate. But their altruism redounds directly to their own advantage; they (reasonably) expect those whom they help to help them in return. Genuine solidarity, however, is conditional altruism without regard to reciprocal aid. Thus North Americans or Europeans who act in solidarity with workers in Central America or Africa have little reason to think that the individuals whose welfare they seek to enhance will ever be in a position to reciprocate their help. Solidarity therefore designates a more selfless form of other-regarding welfare-enhancing activity than conditional cooperation.

But this form of conditional altruism is not entirely selfless. Those who act in solidarity are indeed "for others" but also "for themselves." It is not reciprocity but the general practice of helpfulness that these conditional altruists seek to promote; and they benefit because they, like everyone else, are better off in a world in which people help each other than in a world in which they do not.

I argued in Chapter 1 that general interests and private interests sometimes do conflict and that the moral esteem often accorded those who promote (putative) general interests at the expense of private interests cannot be construed as a (morally praiseworthy) refusal to free-ride. However, the esteem accorded solidarity can be depicted in these terms. Helping is relevantly like a public good (as opposed to a general interest). A true public good spills over to everyone regardless of contribution. If unconstrained, pure egoists would therefore be inclined to free-ride; that is, to ob-

---

2 See Robert Axelrod, *The Evolution of Cooperation* (New York: Basic Books, 1984). See also Michael Taylor, *The Possibility of Cooperation: Studies in Rationality and Social Change* (Cambridge: Cambridge University Press, 1987), and Jon Elster, *Ulysses and the Sirens* (Cambridge: Cambridge University Press, 1979), pp. 141– 146.

tain the benefits without incurring the costs of contributing to the good's production. Helping is not a pure public good because, in principle, help can be withdrawn from nonhelpers. But it is hard to imagine, in practice, how information about an individual's contribution might be disseminated and how the selective withdrawal of help might be organized. We can therefore regard helping as if it were a public good in the strict sense, and acting in solidarity as a contribution toward producing it. Whatever moral praise attaches to promoting this beneficial practice – or to forbearing from free-riding on it – then accounts, in part, for the esteem accorded helpers. However, I will suggest presently that this explanation, though apt, by no means exhausts the insights to be gained by reflecting on the moral phenomenology of solidaristic actions.

Conditional altruism can also appear among individuals whose dispositions are better described as charitable than as solidary, individuals who help (particular) others by improving their welfare positions, conditional on others doing so too but without regard to beneficial welfare consequences, direct or indirect, that might accrue to themselves. Charity can, of course, be given unconditionally. But if, in addition to wanting to help particular others, individuals also care about the *efficacy* of the help they provide, their altruism is more likely to be conditional. For, in many cases, charity will be futile or insignificant if it is not coordinated with the charity of others, and few people will want to waste their efforts. Therefore even selfless givers are likely to be conditional altruists most of the time. They are not genuinely solidary agents, however, because their generosity is not intended to promote a practice of mutual aid from which they themselves can expect to derive benefits. There are a variety of motives that can lead people to perform charitable acts – from the morally base (opportunism, social pressure) to the lofty (outrage at outrageous conditions, a wish to identify with "the wretched of the earth," a desire to save one's soul). There are, correspondingly, a host of reasons for being altruistic if and only if others are altruistic too. However, to explore these situations is to investigate the psychology of charity, not solidarity.

Solidarity and conditional cooperation are strategies for advancing one's own welfare interests. Of course, in practice much of what passes for charity is undertaken for self-interested reasons too. But in principle the charitable strive to realize a different ideal. Charity is by its nature *disinterested*. Self-interested generosities that purport to be charity are, as it were, inauthentic – products of self-deception, disingenuity, or outright hypocrisy. Solidary agents, on the other hand, are not disinterested. They are authentic creatures of the world *The Second Discourse* describes. If they are not simple egoists it is because of an enlightened perception of where their private interests lead, not because they aspire to the saintliness of the truly charitable.

Nor do they aspire to Rousseauean citizenship. Thus solidary agents do not abandon private interests in the way that the individuals of *The Social Contract* do. To act in solidarity is to seek to advance the well-being of atomic individuals generally – in order, ultimately, to help oneself. Acting for the sake of a "moral and collective body" is, we have seen, a different matter altogether. In circumstances where no one will be for anyone if people are not also for themselves, and where being "for oneself only" is generally detrimental, it is rational even for Hobbesian individuals to be solidary agents. If the Hobbesian men and women of *The Second Discourse* are not themselves solidary agents, it is because solidarity is difficult to implement in practice, not because it is unreasonable for self-interested rational agents to exemplify it.

THE PRACTICE OF SOLIDARITY

Real-world experience attests that solidarity is best promoted through its own practice. Curiously, this idea too can be teased out of a venerable and familiar teaching, originally advanced in a religious context but nevertheless relevant to real-world concerns. I have in mind Blaise Pascal's celebrated Wager on the existence of God.[3]

Pascal thought belief in God reasonable, so long as there is any probability at all that the belief might be true. If I believe in God and God exists, my "payoff," eternal salvation, is infinitely high; if I do not believe in God and God exists, my payoff, eternal damnation, is infinitely low. On the other hand, if God does not exist, then whether I believe or not, my payoffs will be finite and roughly similar. In these circumstances, given the risks attendant on non-

3 Blaise Pascal, *Pensées*, trans. A. J. Krailsheimer (London: Penguin, 1966), pp. 149–155.

belief and the possible gains, a reasonable person will believe.[4] But since the *subjective probability* that God exists is sure to be low for anyone aware of the challenge posed to religious beliefs by the discoveries of the new sciences of nature, belief in God is difficult to instill and sustain. Moreover, it is psychologically impossible to establish this belief directly, simply by deciding to believe. Thus, for those who would believe but find themselves unable to do so, Pascal advised the adoption of an *indirect* strategy. He suggested that they act as *if* faith were already established. *Pratiquez d'abord:* Practice first. Then faith will follow; a faith that is unwarranted by criteria of rational or evidential support but that is nevertheless reasonable in light of the expected utilities of belief and nonbelief, respectively.

For fostering solidaristic dispositions, *pratiquez d'abord* is good advice too. Become more solidary by acting in solidarity. Successful solidaristic interventions will enhance trust and also transform preferences. By helping others and being helped by others in turn, individuals become more helpful.

It is worth remarking that, despite his apparent conviction that human nature cannot be changed, Hobbes effectively anticipated Pascal's observation. To end the war of all against all, Hobbes would have individuals change the payoff structures they confront by authorizing a sovereign to make and enforce rules that impose sanctions on rule violators. But since individuals in a state of nature can only invest sovereignty in one of their own, and since individuals are relatively equal in their natural endowments, the individual chosen to be sovereign cannot have significantly more physical power than anyone else. By himself, therefore, he is as unable as anyone else to issue commands that others will obey. But a Hobbesian sovereign is not just one individual among many. He is the authorized "representative" of each of his subjects. In authorizing the sovereign to act in their behalf, individuals in a state of nature agree, conditionally on others agreeing too, to become the sovereign's police: to enforce his commands against others as others would against them. In this way, the sovereign acquires the power to issue enforceable commands. Since this agreement is a covenant, a promise to be executed in perpetuity,

4 Taken at its word, this argument is sound only if, contrary to what nonbelievers believe, the alternatives are partitioned in the way Pascal suggests; and if, contrary even to what many believers think, salvation can be achieved by wagering on God's existence. It is therefore unlikely that many people will be persuaded by Pascal's argument.

individuals, upon entering into the pact, provide themselves the opportunity to form expectations about each other's behaviors. They come to see that the condition upon which they each transfer all their rights to a common representative is in fact fulfilled. In this way, even Hobbes's social contract depends on a prior aptitude for cooperation. To be sure, individuals cooperate only enough to constitute a credible threat. It is because they cannot co-operate more extensively that sovereignty takes on the character Hobbes ascribes to it and even that sovereignty is necessary at all. Nevertheless, even for Hobbes, *trust* is indispensable for political life. Hobbesian commonwealths are possible only insofar as indi-viduals have more reason to fear the sovereign than they have to fear each other, and their fear of the sovereign is reasonable only to the extent that they trust each other to execute his commands. The covenant Hobbes contrived builds on this trust and extends it.

To launch Hobbes's social contract, conditional cooperation, not solidarity, is required. But Hobbes's account of the self-fulfilling consequences of acting *as if* the conditional altruist's conditions were fulfilled, even before they are, applies to conditional altruism generally and therefore to solidarity as well. So long as some in-dividuals are prepared to "practice first," to act as if it is already reasonable for rational agents, directed by private wills, to be gen-erally helpful, then, other things being equal, it will in fact become increasingly reasonable to be generally helpful. Barring (unlikely) countervailing factors peculiar to particular circumstances, soli-daristic struggles transform people and their preferences, making them more inclined to act to enhance each other's well-being. In short, the more solidarity there is, the more solidarity there will be. The larger solidaristic movements are, the faster they grow.

BEYOND SOLIDARITY

Between solidarity and general will coordination there exists the difference Kant identified between (enlightened) prudential delib-eration and moral agency. The "moral point of view," evident in Kant's categorical imperative but emblematic too of non-Kantian moral philosophy, is the standpoint of agent neutrality or impar-tiality. From this vantage point, individuals decide what to do on the basis of interests moral personalities share, in disregard of fac-tors that distinguish particular agents from one another. Thus the moral point of view resembles the attitude Rousseau would have citizens adopt in the assemblies of the people, the perspective of generality. The difference is that Rousseau envisioned general will deliberations occurring within particular communities, whereas the moral order that Kant conceived encompasses all rational agents.[5] However, since *The Social Contract* nowhere addresses criteria for membership in particular communities and since it effectively regards the just state as a universe unto itself, citizenship, as Rousseau conceived it, is tantamount to membership in a (Kantian) "republic" (*Reich*) of ends. What Kant called a "harmony of rational wills" describes the self-regulated inner workings of a Rousseauean state in just the way that it describes the moral order.[6]

For Kant, following Rousseau, moral deliberations differ qualitatively from prudential considerations, including those that motivate solidaristic politics. Thus Rousseau assimilated group interests (and coalitions of group interests) to the interests of egoists in a state of nature, depicting them all as "private." In this sense, Rousseau would oppose solidarity as much as straightforward egoism. But in *The Social Contract*, where the affinity with Kant's disparagement of prudential calculation is most pronounced, Rousseau's aim was to demonstrate the coherence of the idea of a just state and its possible applicability. He sought to defend a timeless, Platonic ideal. But actual politics, as Rousseau knew better than anyone, is inextricably historical and something less than ideal.[7] In the real world of politics, solidarity and morality do not stand quite so far apart as they do in the Platonic realm of *The Social Contract*.

In reflecting on the *connection* between solidarity and the general will, it will be useful to take the role the term plays in our political culture seriously. In contemporary political discourse, "solidarity" has an oppositional flavor. Historically, the term entered political discussion through the labor movement – in the course of an "industrial revolution" that brought large numbers of people, from diverse backgrounds, into a common class position. Solidarity continues to bear the mark of its origin. In rhetorical contexts and

5 Kant's view of practical reason and therefore of rational agency is not, like Hobbes's, strictly instrumental. For Kant, reason does not prescribe particular ends, but it does *proscribe* those that fail to meet the test of universalizability or, equivalently in Kant's view, that fail to respect persons as ends-in-themselves. On differences between Kantian and Hobbesian views of rational agency, see Levine, *Liberal Democracy*, Chapter 4.
6 This claim is defended expressly in Levine, *The End of the State*, Chapter 1.
7 Cf. Levine, *The End of the State*, Chapter 2, and *The Politics of Autonomy*, Part 2.

as a term of art, it is much more frequently invoked by militants in collective struggles of a progressive character than by the Right or by politicians executing normal administrative operations.[8] Virtually everywhere in the world today, there is more cooperation among elites than among dominated peoples. But solidarity remains largely the province of subordinate groups. At least it is this sort of solidarity that inspires such ideals as "solidarity forever" and that elicits something close to the sentiment Kant, in reflecting on "the good will," called "reverence" (*Achtung*).[9]

I have already suggested that the (moral) esteem accorded solidarity derives, in part, from the realization that solidary agents contribute toward the promotion of a public good, the practice of helping others. But there is also, I think, another dimension to the esteem accorded solidarity.

It is instructive to follow Kant's lead by reflecting on the fact that solidarity, especially when practiced by subordinated individuals or groups, typically does elicit a sentiment akin to what "reverence" seems to denote, even among "impartial observers" uncommitted to the particular objectives of the individuals or groups acting in solidarity. In investigating the conditions for the possibility of the good will, Kant used the phenomenology of moral experience as a basis for reflection.[10] This methodology is seldom deployed today by moral philosophers, and it is surely moot whether anything reliable about morality can be learned from the subjective experiences of (potentially) moral agents. But the fact that the sentiments morality and solidarity induce are similar is at least suggestive. So too is the realization that general will coordination at the level of "the whole community" often seems unattractive even when it may be feasible. These pieces of phenomenological "data" suggest a hypothesis that bears further con-

8 Of course, class-conscious elites can and do frequently act in solidarity with other elite individuals and class fractions. When they do, it is not inconceivable that they would declare themselves to be acting in solidarity. However, this usage is unlikely, especially in times and places where the labor movement has not already brought the expression into wide currency.

9 See Kant, *The Foundations of the Metaphysics of Morals*, Part 1.

10 For example, in Part 1 of *The Foundations of the Metaphysics of Morals*, Kant suggested that the feeling of reverence that the moral law inspires is the source of its imperatival force – rendering the moral law something to *do* rather than merely to contemplate. Thus the conclusion that morality is a system of categorical imperatives, to the extent that it depends upon the "regressive analysis" of moral experience Kant provides in the *Foundations*, rests on an account of the feeling the moral law elicits in human beings.

sideration: that in the actual world genuine impartiality is not always desirable and that, paradoxically, in existing or imaginable political contexts respect for moral personality may actually be better promoted by solidarity than by "the exercise of the general will." Insofar as our sensibilities are informative, we recognize that, in a world of moral recalcitrants, replete with obstacles in the way of the vision Rousseau and Kant elaborated, solidarity may sometimes be preferable even to morality itself. Thus it may sometimes be well for solidarity to "stand in" for universal morality in those less than ideal circumstances where, if worthwhile political aims are to be realized, real generality cannot stand in for itself.[11]

That there is a problem in reconciling political exigencies with private morality has been acknowledged at least since Machiavelli. Perhaps the best known modern formulation of the dilemma is Max Weber's observation that whoever would choose "politics as a vocation" must frequently confront a sometimes irreconcilable tension between an "ethic of responsibility" and an "ethic of ultimate ends."[12] In Weber's view, this conflict is inevitable if only because responsible political action sometimes requires using persons as means, in violation of the demands of the (Kantian) "ethic of ultimate ends" that he endorsed. The tension between these ethics takes on a qualitatively greater dimension for political actors intent not just on muddling through in the manner of politicians in our political culture but on implementing a definite end in view – the Jacobins' republic of virtue, for instance, or Marxian communism.[13] In addition, since revolutionary politics inevitably involves extraordinary political interventions at odds with the demands of a universal morality, the tension is even more acute for political visionaries who are also revolutionaries. This moral dilemma carries over to historical assessments. Since there is seldom agreement about the desirability of the visions motivating political

11 The idea behind this contention is not peculiar to Kantian understandings of what morality is. The same idea can be expressed, for example, in utilitarian terms. Thus it might be held that the way to advance well-being overall is not, as utilitarianism maintains for ideal cases, to seek to advance individuals' well-beings, counting all individuals' utilities equally, but instead to seek to advance the well-being of individuals in some groups, if need be at the expense of individuals in other social categories.

12 See Max Weber, "Politics as a Vocation," in H. H. Gerth and C. Wright Mills (eds.), *From Max Weber: Essays in Sociology* (New York: Oxford University Press, 1958).

13 Cf. Steven Lukes, *Marxism and Morality* (Oxford: Oxford University Press, 1985), Chapter 6.

actors, even in retrospect, sympathy for their aims will not always mitigate judgments of their means. And, of course, condemnations of revolutionaries' ends abound as well. Nevertheless, displays of solidarity, insofar as they can be distinguished from contentious aims and dubious means, remain remarkably immune from reproachful judgment. The otherwise unavoidable tension Weber identified, even intensified to the extreme in revolutionary contexts, seems to pale in the face of unequivocal manifestations of genuine solidarity.

In this respect, solidaristic politics differs instructively from other means to (putatively) desirable ends that can also diverge from the requirements of an ideal morality. Imagine a consensus favoring peace in a world where relations between states (or individuals) fall short of this ideal. Pacifists would have persons act as if the desired end were already established, the better to bring it about. Nonpacifists, though they may acknowledge a presumption in favor of pacifist means, nevertheless maintain that violence may sometimes be necessary for advancing the ideal they and the pacifists share. They might argue, as Sartre did, that, in some circumstances, a person who acts as if peace were already attained is unwittingly complicitous in the violence pacifism is intended to redress.[14] Or imagine individuals who value the emancipatory effects of liberal tolerance in a genuine "marketplace of ideas" but find themselves in a world in which formal tolerance functions "repressively," as Herbert Marcuse famously maintained – by marginalizing opinions genuinely oppositional to a status quo very much in need of transformation.[15] Civil libertarians, by analogy with pacifists, might hold that the best way to bring about a genuine marketplace of ideas in these circumstances would be to

14 Cf. Jean-Paul Sartre's Preface to Frantz Fannon, *Les damnées de la terre* (Paris: Maspero, 1961); English translation by Constance Farrington, *The Wretched of the Earth* (New York: Grove Press, 1963).
15 Herbert Marcuse, "Repressive Tolerance," in R. P. Wolff, H. Marcuse, and B. Moore, *A Critique of Pure Tolerance* (Boston: Beacon Press, 1965). Marcuse did not literally mean that tolerance was repressive but that, in societies relevantly like mid- and late-twentieth-century America, it functioned in the way genuine repression does – to enforce conformity to an oppressive social order. It is not entirely clear why Marcuse thought liberal tolerance had, as he put it, "turned into its opposite." Its practice in a world rife with economic inequalities is part of the story, but Marcuse also seems to have believed that the nature of communications technology in a television age also plays a role – by diminishing peoples' moral and intellectual capacities for functioning as competent consumers in a marketplace of ideas.

act as if the ideal were already achieved. Marcuse disagreed. Like Sartre on violence, he acknowledged a presumption against interfering with speech but insisted that intolerance – toward positions that undergird the system that makes formal tolerance a sham – may sometimes advance the ideals tolerance ostensibly promotes. In each case, there is a consensus on ends and a disagreement over means. To adjudicate these disputes, it is necessary to assess the relevant evidence and to speculate about the likely outcomes of different social practices. Those who are persuaded by Sartre or Marcuse plainly face the dilemma of reconciling what they think right with what they think they ought to do. Pacifists and civil libertarians also face a potential difficulty insofar as they concede that their positions depend on empirical considerations that might support conclusions different from the ones they draw.[16] However, in anticipating the ends they and their opponents share, pacifists and civil libertarians do sometimes evoke emotions similar to those elicited by displays of solidarity. They too anticipate a genuinely moral order – with appropriate consequences at the level of moral phenomenology. But because their political strategies are so eminently contestable, the sentiments they evoke are frequently mitigated and sometimes take on a meretricious aspect. In contrast, for most people most of the time, the solidarity of the oppressed seems unequivocally worthy of esteem. Conceived as a means for ending domination, it is also an anticipation of a world without domination.

SOLIDARITY FOREVER?

Solidarity and general will coordination are distinct phenomena. But phenomenologically, the solidarity of "the wretched of the earth" foreshadows a time when the actual world approximates the ideal, when the real impartiality of general will deliberation, the antithesis of a generalized "war of all against all," can take its rightful place in human affairs. I have used these phenomenological data, in conjunction with the feeling of apprehension that general will coordination sometimes evokes, to suggest that, in a world still recalcitrant to the moral point of view, the ends of morality may be better served by solidaristic politics than by the adoption of a more "general" perspective. This contention is consistent

16 They could avoid this problem by maintaining that violence or intolerance is categorically proscribed regardless of its consequences. But then they would confront the far greater problem of justifying these prohibitions.

73

with the widely acknowledged idea that political exigencies can sometimes force responsible political actors to diverge from the strict requirements of private morality. It is, in effect, a partial elaboration of that idea.

Will this conclusion always pertain, or will solidarity eventually undo the conditions that now make it both necessary and estimable? Traditional procommunists inclined toward the latter view. But the conviction that solidarity can "wither away" entirely is eminently contestable.[17] We will find that even under communism the conditions that make solidarity indispensable cannot be altogether "superseded." Hillel's words therefore apply to communist men and women, just as they do to us. But we will also find that the generalized practice of helpfulness that Hillel recommends and the attention to individual well-being that I have imputed to him will pale in importance in comparison with their current urgency. In other words, solidarity will wither away *somewhat*. Thus the traditional view, despite its evident exaggeration, contains more than a kernel of truth.

17 See Chapter 8 herein.

Chapter 4

Democracy in the Age of States

I have suggested that the "state" envisioned in *The Social Contract* is not a state at all but an internally coordinated "republic of ends." However, in this respect as in so many others, Rousseau is revealingly equivocal. "The moral and collective body" founded by the social contract does sometimes coordinate individuals' behaviors through force and does concentrate the means of coercion into a single institutional nexus. If the state is conceived in the standard way as an institutionalized monopoly of the means of violence, the social contract therefore does establish a state or, at least, a social order superintended by institutions with statelike properties.

However, the ambiguity that surrounds the state of *The Social Contract* is submerged during what I shall call the Age of States, the time when states that accord no place for "the exercise of the general will" reign everywhere on earth. These are the states Hobbes had individuals establish in order to end the war of all against all, the states whose "origins" Rousseau recounted in *The Second Discourse*. For both Hobbes and Rousseau, the opposition of private wills makes states necessary. But states that only coordinate private wills will not solve the "fundamental problem of political life." They will not "defend and protect with all common forces the person and goods of each associate" while assuring that each individual "obeys only himself and remains as free as before."[1] Hence, for Rousseau, unlike Hobbes, the state of *The Second Discourse* must give way to the state of *The Social Contract*.

There is, in addition, a related complaint against existing political forms that is implicit in some of Rousseau's descriptions of legitimate authority relations. This line of criticism is more

---

1 *The Social Contract*, Book I, Chapter 6.

pronounced, however, in Marx's writings on politics, especially those composed after the defeat of the Paris Commune. In this strain of Marxist political theory, the focus is not on autonomy per se but on democracy. States and the word system of nation-states are faulted for failing to implement democratic values. This shortcoming is not a contingent feature of particular de facto states. On this view, obstacles to the fullest possible realization of democracy are inherent in the very idea of the state as a form of political organization. To be sure, lack of democracy can be ameliorated without abandoning the state altogether. Indeed, what Marxists consider the "last state," the state that superintends the transition to communist statelessness, is distinguished from other states precisely by its radically democratic character.[2] But if this position is sustained, democracy cannot be realized fully until the Age of States has finally passed from the scene.

DEMOCRACY

The autonomy Rousseau faulted de facto states for thwarting is a property of individuals. If we resume the atomic individualist picture and conceive individuals as independent centers of volition, then an individual atom is autonomous if it determines its own velocity and direction. It is not enough that the atom's inertial motion be unblocked. The freedom that matters for Rousseau is self-mastery, the setting of ends before oneself. We are autonomous or free to the degree that we are self-directing. The idea of self-direction links autonomy with democracy. It is even fair to say that autonomy and democracy represent the same idea – from the standpoint of the individual and of the whole community, respectively. Since this affinity is obscured by contemporary and historical uses of the term, it will be well to reflect briefly on what "democracy" has meant to its defenders and detractors. In doing so, the connection with autonomy will become evident. More importantly, we will gain a better purchase on the intuition that motivates these values.

From the time of the ancient Greeks until roughly two hundred years ago, "democracy" was universally despised. Nowadays, it is endorsed by nearly everyone – from celebrants of the systems of governance in place in advanced capitalist countries to defenders

2 See Chapter 5 herein.

of popular democracy in the Third World and in the countries that used to form the "socialist bloc." In short, the term has become "essentially contested," adopted by all sides, even as disagreements abound about its meaning. Support for the term, if not the idea, is so widespread that the core principle genuine democrats have always promoted, despite their differences, is now at some risk of being lost in the morass. This situation is evidence for an important transformation in human history. The universal support now accorded "democracy" attests to the entry of the *demos*, the (ordinary) people, into the political arena. It represents a general recognition that the claim of "we the people" to rule ourselves is legitimate and incontrovertible.

In earlier times, "democracy" meant rule by the demos. This was the democracy that political philosophers, if not the people themselves, almost universally despised. Today it is more apt to consider a political community democratic if its institutions implement "peoples' power" in some *procedural* sense.

It has become commonplace for mainstream democratic theorists in the West and, more recently, throughout the entire world to identify "democracy" with the governmental forms in place in the so-called Western democracies.[3] For reasons that will become evident shortly, this understanding is both tendentious and inappropriate if "democracy" is to retain even a tenuous connection with its traditional meaning. A more plausible and historically grounded view of democracy is implicit in the theory of collective choice, in welfare economics, and in some contemporary political philosophy. A political community is democratic, on this view, if its collective choices are functions of the choices of its citizens, where citizens' choices, expressed in voting, count equally and where rights of citizenship are enjoyed regardless of such irrelevancies as class, gender, ethnicity, or race. In other words, democracy is conceived as a mechanism for making social choices – for legislating – that can be modeled by a "device" that combines individuals' votes in an appropriate way. Thus we can depict the votes of individuals 1, 2, . . ., n as inputs and the social choice as an output, and then construct a collective choice rule for aggregating the votes as pictured in Figure 2. If voting rights are distributed in such a way that no one is excluded for irrelevant reasons,

3 See Joseph Schumpeter's *Capitalism, Socialism, Democracy* (New York: Harper and Row, 1942), the *locus classicus* of this definitional move.

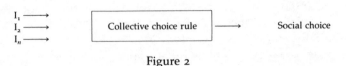

Figure 2

and if the collective choice rule is properly responsive to individuals' choices,[4] we have a genuine democracy. This definition is roughly coextensive with the older idea of democracy, given the size and composition of the demos in existing political communities. To the extent that the two definitions overlap extensionally, the more modern understanding, in suggesting a picture of universal political equality, obscures what the older idea takes for granted: the existence of real social divisions in political communities, and the intrinsic conflict in all socially divided societies between popular masses and social elites. It will be important to my argument eventually to bring the class content of democracy back in. However, for now, if only to accord with how the word is nowadays used, it will suffice to think of "democracy" as rule by the people tout court.

|What democrats value is collective self-mastery – rule by the people, not by elites. Rule by elites is a form of collective heteronomous determination. In the spirit of Rousseau's definition, it is "slavery," a form of governance in which the *other* rules. Similarly, democracy is autonomy at the level of political communities. It is autonomy for "the moral and collective body" established by the social contract.|Democracy is rule of the people by the people – and, presumably also, for want of a sufficient reason otherwise, for the people.|

Where freedom is understood as the absence of (coercive) restraint, unfreedom may admit of degrees in the sense that one can be more or less constrained from doing what one wants. But one can be absolutely free. If freedom is held, in addition, to involve an agent's ability to do what he or she wants, then freedom

4 Collective choice theorists represent responsiveness to individuals' choices by stipulating conditions on collective choice rules that articulate "democratic" intuitions. It has been known since Kenneth Arrow's pathbreaking investigations in the early 1950s that impossibility results can be generated even from very weak sets of conditions. See Kenneth Arrow, *Social Choice and Individual Values* (New York: Wiley, 1951; 2nd ed., 1964). Recent, comprehensive accounts of collective choice theory include Thomas Schwartz, *The Logic of Collective Choice* (New York: Columbia University Press, 1986), and Norman J. Schofield, *Social Choice and Democracy* (Berlin: Springer-Verlag, 1985).

too admits of degrees. Finally, autonomy, the ability to set ends before oneself, also admits of degrees. Autonomy is always conditioned by circumstances. We can make our own way, as it were, but not, to paraphrase an expression of Marx's, in circumstances of our own choosing. Among other things, institutional arrangements affect the level of autonomy individuals are able to realize.[5]

It is plain too that democracy, autonomy writ large, admits of degrees. It is not just that individuals collectively are unable to set their own course apart from the circumstances they confront. Conditions internal to political communities affect the extent to which the people are able genuinely to rule themselves. The contention here is that the state itself affects self-rule detrimentally; that so long as states coexist with *material* conditions compatible with statelessness, economic, social, and political arrangements can be more or less democratic, but always less democratic than they could otherwise be. States are obstacles in the way of realizing democratic values. In the Age of States, the people in power is, at best, a regulative ideal that cannot be very well approximated. To make democracy as real as humanly possible, it will be necessary, finally, to end the state.

I will go on to advance a number of considerations in support of this claim. But it will become plain that the view of democracy it supposes – democracy as *peoples' power* – is misleading, not only because it obscures the class nature of human societies in the Age of States but also for its ahistoricity. In Chapter 5 I will argue, on broadly Marxist grounds, that static representations of democracy are always, in some measure, deceptive. In the real world of politics, in contrast to the Platonic realm of *The Social Contract*, a commitment to democracy is a commitment to the process of its enhancement: to *democratization*. Rousseau is equivocal on this point; the strain of Marxist theory that envisions the end of the state under communism is more straightforward. From that vantage point, in any conceivable political formation this side of communism, democracy, by its nature, is always in movement, and its trajectory is what is especially of concern. Properly understood, what democrats favor – now and well into even the most distant future – is not quite *the people in power,* a static condition, but the process of enhancing power to the people.

5 These claims are defended expressly in Levine, *Arguing for Socialism*, Chapter 1.

MODELING DEMOCRACY

Contemporary democratic theorists typically ignore democracy's dynamic aspect, just as they ignore the fact that, historically, democracy meant rule by the demos. Collective choice models therefore serve them well. If "democracy" is construed synchronically and understood to mean rule by an (undifferentiated) citizenry, it is fair to model it, as in Figure 2, by a flow diagram – with individuals' choices as inputs and the social choice as the output – provided citizenship rights are properly distributed and fairly represented, and provided the aggregating device is positively responsive to individuals' choices and to nothing else.

All models abstract from features of the phenomena they represent. However, the collective choice model favored by many contemporary democratic theorists is excessively abstract. To its detriment, it incorporates a number of assumptions, endemic in many strains of political theory and throughout the dominant political culture, that more careful scrutiny cannot support. It therefore blocks insight into the nature of democracy, even allowing that democracy is properly construed synchronically and from a perspective that excludes class divisions. More importantly for our purposes, it impedes understanding the roles the state can play in facilitating or impeding the implementation of democratic values.

The most misleading of the assumptions that this model supports is the idea that voting – in particular, majority rule voting – unproblematically implements collective self-rule. Majority rule voting plainly does what its proponents intend in a wide range of circumstances. But the issue is more complicated than may at first appear.

The temptation to identify majority rule with democracy is easy to explain. When the majority rules, social choices reflect individuals' choices in the sense that the outcome selected is preferred by more voters than any other alternative in contention. Of course, the most preferred alternative would also win in any voting system in which a majority greater than 50 percent plus 1 is decisive, up to and including unanimity. But, in cases where more than simple numerical majorities are required, the method of voting is biased against new enactments; a minority can block any measure. Where unanimity is required, a single individual can stop any proposed enactment! In contrast, the method of majority rule introduces no bias for or against the status quo. Of all conceivable voting schemes, it therefore seems best able to implement the idea that the people should rule themselves. However, this conclusion holds only if it is assumed that an individual's vote represents a genuine choice that warrants recognition as a proper input to a collective choice rule, and if it is assumed that majority rule voting aggregates these choices in such a way that the outcome actually is determined exclusively by the choices individuals make. Neither assumption can be sustained.

The case for majority rule voting is particularly compelling if it is also assumed that interests are private. Individuals' votes then register *preferences* for alternative, feasible outcomes. On this assumption, majority rule voting can be defended on grounds of both fairness and welfare. The procedure is fair in the sense that individuals' preferences are equally represented in the output. And it is welfare-promoting because each individual does as well as possible, given the constraint that other individuals too are seeking to do as well for themselves as they can – in a world where wills are radically independent of each other and where collective choices must be made.

Rousseau too advocated the method of majority rule,[6] but *not* as a mechanism for aggregating private wills. A state where the majority rules but where votes represent private interests would be, for him, at best a benevolent form of slavery. Arguably such a state is preferable to the regimes in place in existing states. It would at least exhibit greater sensitivity to the (private) interests of its subjects. But it is still a creature of the Age of States.

Implicitly, Rousseauean political philosophy therefore does fault the identification of democracy with democratic collective choice. For Rousseau, the method of majority rule is necessary but not sufficient for collective self-mastery – still conceived statically and *as if* no fundamental social divisions obstructed equal membership in "the whole community." For the people to rule themselves, it is also necessary that the choices aggregated be of the right kind: specifically, that they represent judgments about what is best for "the moral and collective body" of which individual voters in de jure states are indivisible parts. For Rousseau, therefore, individuals do not ipso facto rule themselves whenever they arrive at social choices by paradigmatically democratic procedures.

However, it is not necessary to invoke Rousseauean views about the general will to arrive at this result. A similar conclusion can be

6 See *The Social Contract*, Book IV, Chapter 2.

reached from a perspective more consonant with mainstream thinking about political legitimacy.

We can define imprudence as a failure to recognize or act upon true (private) interests. There are, we know, many reasons why an agent in a particular choice situation might act imprudently. Individuals can fail to reflect adequately on the alternatives in contention or can reflect on the basis of false or inadequate information or, for any number of other reasons, can hold false beliefs that impede rational choice. When choices represent imprudent preferences, the social choice that results from combining them is not unproblematically an expression of individuals' interests. In these circumstances, the rationale for according moral weight to the aggregation of individuals' preferences fails to obtain, and the intuition that joins majority rule voting with democracy is impugned.

Even conceding that there is reason to combine preferences, does it follow that the best way – or even a good way – to do so is to count votes?[7] Following the long-standing practice of welfare economists, collective choice theorists typically construe the objects of individual and social choice as *social states*, exhaustive and mutually exclusive sets of (already individuated) items that constitute the context of choice. When collective choice models represent voting, alternatives in elections are conceived as social states. But, as such, they are not well partitioned for realizing democratic values. Welfare economists work with indifference curves that represent individuals' preferences as sets of trade-offs between constituents of commodity bundles. Preferences are expressed by the relative prices individuals will pay for particular goods. But this picture does not carry over well to interpretations of collective choice rules as voting systems. When individuals vote, they do not choose among social states that can be decomposed and reassembled at will. In elections, alternatives are, so to speak, prepackaged, and trade-offs are generally impossible. Voters are therefore not able to choose among social states generally but are forced to select from among only a few – having exercised little, if any, control over their constitution.

This situation impugns the democratic character of many voting systems. Let *a* and *b* be social states that voters will decide between – say, by the method of majority rule. Even allowing that each voter will have a clear preference, say, for *a* over *b*, the voter

7   Cf. John Burnheim, *Is Democracy Possible?* (Berkeley and Los Angeles: University of California Press, 1985), pp. 82–96.

will often prefer aspects of the less preferred social state *b* and may also be indifferent to much that *a* and *b* contain. The voter's preference for *a* over *b* will then represent a preference *all things considered* – for social states that are antecedently partitioned and presented for social choice. The individual will prefer *a* to *b* on balance and because a choice must be made, but that choice is not an unequivocal expression of the preferences that motivate it. In idealized economic interactions, on the other hand, agents partition alternatives as they please. They set ends before themselves. In this sense, they enjoy a degree of autonomy that is elusive even in theory in electoral contexts.

There is yet another, more subtle, disanalogy. Indifference curves model individual-level cost–benefit analyses. Taking their beliefs and desires as given, individuals compute their own ideal commodity bundles by calculating how much of a particular good they would be willing to sacrifice for others. In contrast, voting is typically costless or very nearly so. Indeed, a motive for voting for one alternative over another is sometimes to help shift costs onto others. Therefore the information a vote conveys is different from the information conveyed by an agent's idealized economic behavior. Through voting, we can discover which, among antecedently given social states, an individual prefers, taking all relevant considerations into account. In the cases economists regard as paradigmatic, we learn what, given only their budget constraints, individuals actually prefer.

There is an additional difficulty, finally, for anyone who would assume that votes generally represent preferences. In actual voting situations, individuals often have incentives not to vote for the (prepartitioned) social state that they prefer on balance but instead to misrepresent their preferences for strategic reasons. Suppose that *a*, *b*, and *c* are candidates in an election, and that individual *i* prefers *a* to *b* and *b* to *c*. Suppose too that *i* believes that *a*'s chances of winning are slight, whereas the contest between *b* and *c* is likely to be so close that a single vote could be decisive. Suppose, finally, that *i* strongly prefers *b* to *c*. In these circumstances, *i* will have good reason to vote for *b* over *a*, despite the fact the *i* prefers *a* to *b*. If *i* votes for *a*, the probability that *c*, the least preferred alternative, will win increases. If *i* votes for *b*, however, it is more likely that *b* will win. In this case, one serves one's preferences best by not voting for the alternative one most prefers. Incentives for strategically misrepresenting preferences increase as voting communities develop relatively stable populations. Thus *i* may prefer *a* to *b* and even believe that *a* can win over *b* but will nevertheless vote for *b* over *a* in order to induce someone else, *j*, who strongly prefers *b* to *a*, to vote with *i* at some future time for *y* over *z*, a matter about which *i* cares more. As we move from highly idealized representations of voting situations to real-world voting behavior, mechanisms inducing strategic misrepresentations of preferences are likely to become increasingly important. But even in the most idealized cases, strategic interactions among voters are likely to cause electoral systems to fail to represent individuals' preferences in the way that market transactions represent consumers' choices in the models welfare economists propose.

Markets and electoral systems, conceived abstractly, are each interpretations of the "device" pictured in Figure 2. The difference is that in markets individuals do as they please, subject to budget constraints and the exigency of interacting with others through market relations, whereas in voting the majority determines the minority. But at a slightly less abstract level, the analogy between markets and voting breaks down. In economic models of market arrangements, individuals order all the items in a particular choice context according to the prices they are willing to pay. Willingness to pay is therefore a reasonable proxy for preference or, more precisely, for preference subject to budget constraints. In voting, however, because items are typically bundled into social states in ways that lie outside a voter's control, because choices generally do not come with "prices" attached, and because there are so many incentives to misrepresent preferences strategically, voters' choices are much less adequate proxies. There is therefore good reason to question the idea that majority rule voting combines individuals' preferences fairly and in a welfare-enhancing way even if, *pace* Rousseau, we consider these objectives desiderata in their own right.

Collective choice theorists have raised doubts mainly about collective choice rules, supposing in effect that the inputs collective choice rules combine are unproblematic. They have focused on the rationality of devices for combining individuals' choices, understanding rationality as a weak (or "thin") normative standard – amounting to consistency. In general, the problem collective choice theorists since Arrow have identified is that collective choice rules that satisfy minimal and ostensibly unexceptionable conditions can take consistent orderings of alternative social states as inputs and still generate inconsistent outputs. Inconsistencies are manifest as cyclical or intransitive orderings. Given the intuitions that drive democratic theory, inconsistencies are clearly undesirable. If *i* prefers *a* to *b* and *b* to *c* but *c* to *a*, in violation of the transitivity requirement, *i* is literally unable either to choose or to act exclusively in accord with his preferences when confronted with a choice between *a*, *b*, and *c*. A similar problem confronts public officials presented with inconsistent social orderings generated from sets of consistent individual orderings. Inconsistency, then, is a severe, albeit a minimalist, reproach to both individuals and societies.

The objections raised here, however, assume a "thicker" standard of rationality. I have faulted voting systems for admitting and even encouraging imprudent choices and for failing to ensure that voters' choices, their "revealed preferences," coincide with the preferences, prudent or not, that they actually hold.

The problems collective choice theorists have identified with aggregating mechanisms are relevant to political arguments that depend on the thin rationality of voting systems. They ought therefore to be of grave concern to anyone intent on providing liberal democracy – or relevantly similar forms of the state – with justifying theories.[8] But the problems collective choice theorists raise, serious as they are, arise only as a theoretical limit on aggregating choices. In real-world voting situations, paradoxical effects seldom, if ever, emerge. The problems with voting in our political culture therefore have less to do with the difficulties collective choice theorists focus upon than with what collective choice theory – with its penchant for abstraction – tends to obscure.

DEMOCRACY IN A WORLD OF STATES

States, again, exercise supreme authority over particular territories or populations. In a world divided into de facto states, political authority is centralized intranationally and divided into distinct (though possibly interdependent) units internationally. Within each unit, authority is supreme. Between units, no authority relations exist at all – though there may be (largely) unenforceable rules that regulate the interactions of sovereign entities. For democrats, the division of the world into nation-states is, on balance, a misfortune because, at the international level too, states are obsta-

---

8 Cf. Levine, *Liberal Democracy*, Chapter 3.

cles to collective self-rule. This problem was not salient at the time of the formation of the modern state system. But today it has become unavoidable.

As Marx and Engels insisted in *The Communist Manifesto*, the nation-state was instrumental for the development of national economies. In the period of its inception, as feudal solidarities gave way to market arrangements, decentralized feudal arrangements became "fetters" on economic development. Thus, as national economies formed, human populations sorted themselves out into discrete and unitary communities, a fact registered at the political level by the development of a unitary nexus of state institutions. Nation-states would, from time to time, interact – in disputes over territory or over commercial or security interests. There was diplomacy and war. But these "affairs of state" were marginal to political life. Politics was, in the main, an affair of individuals, not political communities. Intercommunal wars and their continuations by diplomatic means were, at most, impositions upon self-sufficient political systems. In monopolizing authority relations within a territory or over a population, states were supreme and complete unto themselves.

However, with capitalist development on a world scale and especially with technological innovations in communications and transportation, national economies have become increasingly superseded. In consequence, nation-states, as superintendents of national economies, have become inappropriate units of the world political order. With production and distribution organized on global lines, and with environmental problems from resource management to pollution controls crossing state boundaries, the state has become an obstacle in the way of addressing many fundamental human concerns.

The problem is not just that the state system divides the world into units that are too small to address the challenges the world's peoples confront. The greater problem is that the dispersal of political authority into nation-states, the existence of competing centers of supreme authority, produces antagonisms that exacerbate these problems. What may once have been a natural division has become an anachronism and a source of potentially devastating animosities.

The obvious remedy, it seems, would be to expand the boundaries of the nation-state to include the entire world. On this view, the early defenders of the state were essentially right; their error, from a contemporary vantage point, though not from their own, was only in their conception of the state's proper boundaries. Needless to say, the world system of nation-states generates political facts that are self-perpetuating. Therefore a different political organization of the planet may not be feasible in practice. It may not even be desirable in any remotely foreseeable future, given the enormous social and cultural divisions the state system has generated or exacerbated. But there is no hope for change without first articulating a different, more unitary vision of political order. It would therefore seem to follow that democrats and perhaps others as well should promote the idea of One Big State. In doing so, it would be necessary to rethink much of what has long been maintained about political institutions. Among other things, one would have to contrive, if only in the imagination, an administrative apparatus appropriate for a state of global dimensions. But the core ideas, articulated in the years since the nation-state first appeared, would remain robust under these transformations in political institutions. If it was right in earlier times to construct *nation*-states, it is right today to devise a state to rule over the entire world.

However, democrats cannot be happy with this conclusion. Expanding the size of the state, ultimately to include the entire planet, probably would render many problems more tractable administratively than they now are. But in some respects a world state would actually intensify conflicts between the state form of political organization and democracy. The problem is not just that each citizen's control over the state would tend to decrease as the size of the state expands. The more telling problem is that, no matter what their size, states enjoin the partitioning of alternatives according to the exigencies of centralization, not the interests – not even the *private* interests – of individuals. The larger the administrative unit, the more acute the divergence would tend to become. A world state, because it is the largest possible administrative entity, is the limiting case. If the voting behavior of citizens in relatively small nation-states differs significantly from the idealized market behavior welfare economists model, the behavior of voters in a world state would differ even more markedly – rendering the insult to democracy more severe.

The problem, then, is not just that the nation-state is too small. It is also too large and, worse, too all-encompassing. It draws into itself more authority than is required for realizing democratic intuitions, with detrimental consequences for the implementation of democratic values. Just as some problems are too global to be addressed at the level of the nation-state, many questions of social choice are too parochial, too much an affair of those who are immediately involved, to warrant relegating authority over them to centralized concentrations of power. Much more appropriate would be a system that vested authority in functional entities of varying sizes positioned at the real interstices of social and economic life. Then social choices could be made by all and only those directly affected. In doing so, the quality of these choices would surely improve, as would the level of public deliberation and debate. More in point, decentralizing political authority would promote the formation of collective choice problems that more nearly resemble those that democratic theorists assume when they represent voting systems in the manner of idealized market arrangements. But, of course, were authority relations decentralized and diffused, we would no longer have supreme authority concentrated in a unitary entity. In a word, we would no longer have a state.

The end of the state system at the international level, like the end of the state itself, is, at best, a *distant* goal. The problem is not just the difficulty of getting from here to there. More important, from a normative point of view, is the nature of the goal itself. Among the consequences of humanity's long tenure in the Age of States is the unavoidable fact that national and other group identifications have become intertwined with the existence of the state system. To be sure, the communal values that states now foster are not unequivocally estimable. Even Rousseau, the ardent defender of patriotism, would likely not endorse its many deleterious consequences: militarism, xenophobia, international animosities. But the values Rousseau sought to instill through a common civil religion, public spectacles, and a patriotic education are not without merit. In any case, the purchase on community that the state system currently provides cannot be legislated away. Therefore, in order not to unsettle needlessly the group identifications people actually make, it is wise to proceed with caution.

LIMITS TO DECENTRALIZATION

It is unlikely, in any event, that the state form of political organization could be replaced completely. For in even the most radically democratized system of governance, centralized authority – at the level of the nation-state or perhaps a world state – will remain necessary indefinitely to settle disputes authoritatively when they arise between the larger or smaller administrative units to which other state functions devolve, and to address fundamental resource allocation problems.

Even today, some "judicial" functions are performed by institutions tied to both nonstate corporatist associations and to the formal court system of nation-states. Many professions, for example, police themselves through their own institutional mechanisms, and many intragroup conflicts are resolved by these means. To the extent that enforcement powers too devolve onto decentralized institutions, the decentralization of "the administration of justice" could be expanded considerably. But then as now there would remain a need for "courts of last resort" – to resolve issues that remain intractable by other means or that have consequences that spill over from one jurisdiction to another. It is likely, then, that a thoroughgoing decentralization of the judicial system, even were it desirable for the sake of democratization, would be impossible. Unless we were to assume, contrary to what can reasonably be expected, that interindividual conflicts will someday disappear completely, there will always remain a need for something like a "supreme" court and its associated institutional arrangements.

On the other hand, economic affairs can certainly be organized without a central funding agency to allocate resources and direct investments. Thus, throughout the world today, capitalist markets allocate resources and individual capitalists make investment decisions. But these matters affect everyone in varying degrees. Insofar as democrats are committed to the vague but compelling idea that individuals ought to make the decisions that affect their lives, democrats therefore have at least a prima facie reason for keeping these matters in the hands of "the whole community."[9] But in order to allow basic questions about the allocation and use of productive resources to be made democratically, it would seem that there would have to be, as it were, a single site where at least the most fundamental budgetary decisions are made. In the former socialist countries, economic affairs generally were centrally planned. In light of the economic performance of these regimes, it now seems clear that efficiency considerations alone suffice to discredit this degree of control from the center. However, microlevel

---

9 Thus there is also a prima facie reason why democrats ought to oppose property rights that confer the power to make investment choices on particular individuals. In this way, democratic values weigh in against capitalism. Cf. Levine, *Arguing for Socialism*, pp. 127–134.

economic planning is not necessary for control to be exercised collectively over economic life. It should suffice if only the most fundamental budgetary decisions are centrally planned. Even so, the extent to which it is desirable that institutions of a decentralized kind replace centralized, state institutions would be, to some degree, constrained.

What can vary, however, is the impact of these constraints. Even under existing conditions, it may sometimes be feasible and desirable, from a democratic point of view, to devolve social investment decisions to decentralized funding agencies with varying jurisdictions. Prototypes for this kind of institutional arrangement are state and (sometimes) international institutions that supply capital for research projects or development schemes. Proposals are submitted, evaluated by peers, and allocations are made. Of course, the funds to be allocated are ultimately set by state or international authorities. But it is fair to speculate that, with the growth in productive capacities prerequisite for moving toward the end of the state under communism, these budgetary constraints will diminish in significance and with them the impact of centralized allocating mechanisms. Increasingly, ventures will be undertaken because peers acknowledge their promise; not because, as in existing capitalisms, individuals have special access to capital or because, as in previously existing socialist societies, state or party bureaucrats decide to pursue them. In short, centralized economic institutions may be unavoidable even into the remotest future, but their importance can diminish progressively.

In any case, this side of communism, the crucial question, for democrats, is how best to democratize the political regime. To this end, a number of dogmas of our ostensibly democratic political culture must be rethought.

REPRESENTATION

Representative governments, Rousseau (sometimes) maintained, are not second-best approximations of impracticable direct democratic institutions but insidious alternatives to genuine democracy.[10] When the people elect representatives to rule in their behalf, they forfeit essential autonomy – turning themselves into

10 See *The Social Contract*, Book II, Chapter 1, and Book III, Chapter 15, for Rousseau's most celebrated strictures against representative government. When Rousseau was engaged not in ideal theory but in speculation on feasible political arrangements in a world he thought already irreversibly corrupted, his

slaves of the masters they have elected. However, in this regard too, there is no need to accept Rousseau's stringent and idiosyncratic conditions on political legitimacy to accord credibility to his dismissive assessment of representative institutions. A similar conclusion follows from the observation that the best arguments in favor of representative government are non- or even antidemocratic in character.

In general, these arguments are of two kinds.[11] There are, first of all, those which assume the characteristic liberal distinction between civil society and the state and then support liberalism's celebration of civil society at the state's expense. On this view, politics is, at best, a necessary evil, wisely relegated to "public servants," while the vast majority pursue their interests free from its deleterious effects. It is of course desirable that political affairs be conducted well, that public servants be competent and perform according to expectations. Politics should therefore be structured as a career like others, with appropriate penalties and incentives, the better to attract able personnel and to reward merit. In addition, there should be measures in place to assure that governance will accord with established institutional norms. It is therefore useful, if only to facilitate accountability, that the people vote in periodic elections and otherwise participate minimally in political processes. Elections also enhance de facto legitimacy, particularly in political cultures where democratic values have become established. But in no case should politics be, as it was for Rousseau and the entire "classical" tradition in political theory, an inseparable and essential feature of human life. However necessary states may be in the face of an otherwise devastating war of all against all, what makes life worth living transpires outside the political arena – in civil society. Representative government is justified, on this view, because it makes the best of this bad situation. Though only a pale facsimile of real democratic control, it is instrumental for implementing a feasible approximation of an apolitical and therefore nondemocratic ideal in which individuals pursue their interests and express their natures in a civil society free from political intrusions.

views on political representation were far more favorable. For a comprehensive account, see Richard Fralin, *Rousseau and Representation: A Study of the Development of His Concept of Political Institutions* (New York: Columbia University Press, 1978).

11 For elaboration of some of the points that follow, see Levine, *Arguing for Socialism*, pp. 134–141.

Arguments that appeal to considerations like these are not strictly antidemocratic. They do not fault democracy so much as exclude it from their conception of what is normatively desirable. In contrast, the other kind of argument adduced in support of representative government does challenge democratic values. Thus it is sometimes claimed that the peoples' representatives are likely to rule better than the people themselves because the people are ill informed, mercurial, susceptible to demagogic manipulation – in short, unfit for the tasks of governance. Representatives are better qualified, if only because, with governance their principal occupation, they are able to cultivate the capacities required for directing political institutions. In opposition to the claims of participatory democrats, direct democratic institutions, for antidemocrats of this stripe, undermine political competence, educating citizens away from civility and sound judgment. Representative government is then defended as an alternative. The case for representative institutions can itself be less or more antidemocratic. According to the less antidemocratic version of the argument, representative institutions are defensible because they foster capacities for governance better than the feasible alternatives. According to the more antidemocratic version, political representation is no better – and is perhaps worse – than other nondemocratic forms of governance but is preferable to its rivals for fostering a sense of legitimacy in a world where "democracy" is everywhere endorsed and where representative government and democracy are commonly confounded. In either case, the class bias that formerly motivated hostility toward rule by the demos also motivates the case for representative government. At root is the conviction that the ordinary people are not to be trusted; that government "of the people, by the people, and for the people" – the reality rather than the slogan – is a peril to be avoided.

Of course, it is precisely faith in the demos that motivates genuine democrats. But even the staunchest democrat must concede that the arguments invoked in behalf of political representation contain a grain of truth. Oscar Wilde is supposed to have said that socialism would take too many evenings.[12] Obviously, it was *democratic* socialism he had in mind. Wilde was right; there is a danger that, in a genuinely democratic order, projects that might other-

---

12 Cf. Michael Walzer, "A Day in the Life of a Socialist Citizen," in *Obligations: Essays on Disobedience, War, and Citizenship* (Cambridge, Mass.: Harvard University Press, 1970), pp. 229–238.

wise be pursued constructively would be dissipated in endless deliberations and public assemblies. Therefore there is reason to relegate public tasks to public servants. It is also beyond dispute that governance requires special competences that, very likely, cannot be universally attained or equally distributed. Certainly these competences are not now generally evident in the vast majority of the population. Proponents of participatory democracy may be right when they insist that democratic participation is itself an educator; that, in the right conditions, public deliberation and democratic collective choice transform individuals into democratic citizens. But even if democracy is an effective means toward its own enhancement, there is still less reason to invest faith in the citizenry at large than in subsections of it selected for political skills.

These arguments must be weighed against the value democrats accord collective self-determination. It is unlikely that anyone would be persuaded to abandon democratic convictions on their account, but democrats would nevertheless be wise to incorporate the insights these arguments convey into their reflections on democratic institutions. To this end, it is well to note that plausible hesitations about democracy seem less compelling if we imagine political authority situated not as it now is in de facto states but in larger and smaller institutions corresponding to the natural administrative divisions of particular social orders. It has already been suggested that democratic values are better implemented under such arrangements than within states. It also seems plain that non- and antidemocratic hesitations about peoples' power are less worrisome under these arrangements too. If individuals exercise power mainly in institutions that involve them directly, fewer evenings would be taken up with meetings, freeing time for extrapolitical projects and interests. And people immediately involved with particular institutions are likely already to have a level of expertise sufficient for governing these institutions soundly. In any case, they are prime candidates for transformation through political participation. Even those who are otherwise disinterested in public affairs are likely to have their attentions focused and to deploy their energies constructively on administrative matters of immediate concern to themselves, when the impact of the decisions they make is likely to be directly experienced. Lenin's celebrated polemical (or genuine) declaration notwithstanding, cooks may not generally be suited for running the state but, in the right conditions, they surely can run their own kitchens well. Admittedly, in the Age of States, faith in the demos has a utopian flavor in light of what is everywhere observed. But if *The Second Discourse* story makes a sound point, the Age of States is only a moment in human history, and what is humanly possible in any particular period depends, to a considerable degree, on what its institutional arrangements allow and on the effects of political forms upon human beings' mentalities and characters.

REPRESENTATION VERSUS DELEGATION

Political representation is commonly promoted, incorrectly, as a second-best approximation of direct democracy. But if the point were really to approximate this ostensibly impractical ideal, it would be better to restrict the independence of legislators, requiring them to operate as delegates rather than independent representatives. Revolutionary institutions have typically gravitated toward systems of delegation – the Paris Commune and the 1905 and 1917 revolutions in Russia are conspicuous examples – and Marxist political theory, or rather the strain of it epitomized by *The State and Revolution*, endorses it emphatically. The practical difficulty of communicating the choices of large numbers of people is a mark against delegation and a reason for supporting the independence of representatives. However, modern communications technologies substantially undermine this rationale. Systems of delegation, approximating direct democracy, are probably now feasible. With existing (or feasible) communications technologies, direct democracy itself may even be possible. Therefore representation by independent legislators no longer wins out over its rivals on grounds of practicality alone. If a case is to be made for representation, delegation, or direct democracy, it must be on the respective merits of these political forms.

As remarked, justifications for representative government typically appeal to non- or antidemocratic considerations. But there is an argument favoring representative institutions that accords well with democratic intuitions and that, paradoxically, has a vaguely Rousseauean flavor. It is instructive to draw this argument out in order to clarify, by way of contrast, what a genuinely Rousseauean position would be.

The argument turns on the observation that political representatives are freer than delegates to assess alternatives according to their respective judgments about what is best for everyone, not just their own constituents. Insofar as representatives are able to rise above their constituents' desires, they approximate, it seems, the *dis*interestedness or impartiality that Rousseau imputes to citizens generally in a de jure state. Thus, if generalized impartiality is desirable but unfeasible, an approximation of this desideratum is provided by political representation.

It should be noted, first, that, despite its appeal to the interests of the whole community, this argument is only superficially like Rousseau's. The will, Rousseau insists, must be general both in its object *and in its source*.[13] It is therefore as crucial that the people themselves decide as it is that the decision they make be in the interest of "the whole community." This is not an arbitrary stipulation. Rousseau would have "the whole people decide" for just the reason that he would have individuals subordinate their private to their general wills – in order to enhance their autonomy. In *The Social Contract*, Rousseau twice claimed that political representation is tantamount to the alienation of liberty.[14] We need not follow Rousseau to this dire extreme to see that a system of legislation based on relinquishing decision-making power through the election of representatives who rule on the peoples' behalf is, on the face of it, autonomy-diminishing. In any case, it is plain that the affinity of the argument in question with Rousseauean views is largely illusory.

More importantly, the argument is ambiguous. It might seem to warrant the conclusion that independent representatives, because they are able to adopt a global perspective, are better equipped than delegates (or, for that matter, the people at large) for ascertaining what the general will is. But a more natural – and very different – reading of its conclusion would be that impartial representatives improve the probity of private will aggregation because they are less bound than delegates to the parochial interests of their constituencies.

Imagine that the assembly of the people must decide some question of social allocation: say, whether or not to invest in highway construction and, if so, how much to invest and where and how the money should be spent. Were the point to aggregate private wills, the task would be to assure that all (private) interests are represented and combined fairly. According to the argument in question, independent representatives have a signal advantage over more rigidly controlled delegates in this regard. In addition to

13 *The Social Contract*, Book II, Chapter 6.   14 See note 10.

representing their constituents' immediate interests, they are able to attend to broader concerns and ultimately to the common interests of everyone. So long as these common interests are not also the particular interests of some constituency, they might not otherwise register in the political process at all. Let us suppose that certain concerns about the environmental consequences of highway construction fall within this description.[15] The claim, then, is that independent legislators would have a better purchase on these interests than delegates would – for all the private interests that bear on the collective choice, not just some subset of them, could be represented in their deliberations. Then, assuming that votes are combined according to fair procedures, the outcomes they generate would be fairer than under a system of strict delegation.

But we know that "the whole community" can have general interests that are not reducible to the interests of its constituent parts – even when all pertinent private interests are accorded their fair weight. As remarked in Chapter 1, the nature of the interests different entities have will vary with the entities in question. For purposes of normative theory, welfare interests are of obvious importance for human beings – now and in any imaginable future. But they are not the only kinds of interests that matter. We will see that for "whole communities" under communist conditions an interest in autonomy enhancement has a supremely important role to play alongside welfare interests. General interests are tantamount to interests of this sort.[16]

Independent representatives can, of course, assess alternatives according to any standard whatsoever. Therefore they can seek to enhance autonomy, if they wish, even at the expense of welfare. It is also conceivable that autonomy is best served by an institutional structure that prevents individuals from making collective choices directly. The considerations adduced to this point make these outcomes unlikely but not impossible. It is not necessary, however, to rely on speculations about probabilities to discount these possibilities. We will find in subsequent chapters that Rousseau's insistence that the will be general in its source as well as in its object is a theoretically well-motivated and defensible claim.

---

15 These interests are political analogues of externalities in (idealized) free markets. Externalities are costs or benefits that are not represented in an item's efficiency price.

16 See Chapter 8 herein.

In any case, it is plain that an interest in enhancing autonomy, a general interest, might not coincide with even the most fairly aggregated set of private interests, "the will of all." Thus it is conceivable that decisions about whether, where, and how to build highways, say, will differ according to which standard is used. It is also conceivable that there will be a genuine general interest with respect to none or only some of these questions. Thus it may be in the general interest that a highway be built and that it be built in one of several ways but indeterminate with respect to which of these ways. In those circumstances, on that question, even a well-ordered communist society might rightfully accede to "the will of all."

Whatever standards are appropriate for assessing the respective merits of representation and delegation, it is clear that insofar as the point is to approximate direct democracy delegation, not representation, is the better choice. Why not have the ideal directly? There are some obvious reasons: Whole communities cannot be gathered together for deliberation and debate, and it would be burdensome, if not impossible, to aggregate the choices of every citizen on all matters upon which decisions must be made. But suppose, as suggested, that these difficulties can be mitigated technologically. Other hesitations about direct democracy would remain – in particular, those that motivate the non- and anti-democratic arguments that support representative institutions. The case for representation revolved around two claims: that direct democracy and, to a lesser degree, its close approximations are *too demanding*, and that they fail to draw on and cultivate *special competences* required for governance. In both respects, delegation may actually be superior to the direct democracy that it approximates. A hierarchically structured network of delegatory institutions could relieve individuals from the burden of too many meetings; and delegates are as well situated as independent representatives for cultivating capabilities for governance. A system of administrative units composed of delegates could therefore address hesitations about democracy at least as well as the representative institutions characteristic of existing liberal democracies. The difference is that liberal democracy addresses these qualms at democracy's expense,[17] whereas the alternative can better accord with democratic aspirations.

17 See Levine, *Liberal Democracy*, Chapter 8.

97

The general will

ELECTIONS

It would be foolish to speculate on the nature of the institutions that could implement democratic values once the obstacles placed in the way of democracy by the concentration of authority into a single administrative nexus are past. Rousseau thought that political institutions could not be specified, except in a very general way, apart from contingencies of time and place. Marx voiced similar hesitations about communism. In this respect, as in so many others, it is wise to follow their lead. Thus it is hardly possible here and now to decide where the interstices of social and economic life in societies of the future will lie, or to advise administrative units situated at these points how to conduct their affairs. However, if the preceding discussion has been on track, there is at least one very general suggestion that does seem apt for as long as any system of delegation or independent representation remains in place. This suggestion may appear paradoxical inasmuch as its objective is to advance democracy. The suggestion is that legislators, whatever their degree of independence, not be elected but selected by chance.[18]

The ostensible reason to elect legislators is to assure that constituencies are well represented. The rationale is the same as for majority rule voting generally: The winning candidate is the individual most voters want to represent them from among the individuals who present themselves for candidacy. But we have seen that candidates, because they are individuals, are, so to speak, prepackaged social states. Thus there is even less reason than in the general case to expect that the trade-offs voters make in selecting from among candidates accurately reflect their choices. Moreover, in elections for candidates, more than in the general case, opportunities for strategic misrepresentations of preferences abound. In addition, experience has shown that political representatives, despite their differences, tend to constitute themselves into a political class with what Rousseau would designate "private interests" of their own. On the other hand, were members of legislative and administrative units selected periodically and for short intervals – say, by lot from among appropriate constituencies as in the ancient Greek democracies or as juries are selected today – the

18 In *The Social Contract*, Book IV, Chapter 3, Rousseau cites with approval Montesquieu's contention that "voting by lot is the essence of democracy."

benefits of elections could be achieved without the obvious short-comings and without the unhappy consequence of fostering a political class distinct from the general population.[19]

It might be objected that legislators chosen at random would be even less preferred than those chosen by elections. Perhaps so. But what matters, for a democrat, is that the measures enacted in legislation represent the peoples' will, not that the individuals who make these enactments be preferred to their electoral rivals. Here, again, there is a plain advantage for delegation over representation. To be sure, since individuals have different skills and different knowledge, one individual could not quite substitute for another without consequence even in a delegatory system. But, whoever they are, delegates are required by their mandates to do as their constituents desire. For this reason, who the incumbent is matters far less than in a representative system.

DEMOCRATIZATION

Throughout most of this chapter, democracy has been conceived statically, as a collection of institutional arrangements that implement a certain (synchronic) understanding of collective self-rule. Also, as is appropriate in the Age of States, political forms have been assessed on the assumption that politics is exclusively or mainly an affair of private interests. Eventually it will be necessary to abandon both assumptions. But my aim in this chapter has only been to fault the state system from the standpoint of democracy. For that purpose, assumptions that are standard in our political culture suffice.

However, I have also contrasted the positions under consideration with Rousseauean views, and I have very tentatively proposed general strategies for democratization. Since the chapters that follow address these topics from a perspective closer to Marx's than Rousseau's, it is well to point out here that the strategies proposed in this chapter do not depend on the transformation of capitalism into socialism, communism's "lowest phase" in the historical materialist scheme. These measures merit consideration as means for moving toward communism. But they can also be assessed and implemented in their own right. In the present historical conjuncture, this is at least a significant practical advantage.

19 See Burnheim, *Is Democracy Possible?*, pp. 9–12 and passim.

We will find, however, that there is an important sense in which Marxists were right in joining socialism with democracy, even as they failed to acknowledge the (relative) independence of the socialist and democratic projects. We will find too that there was a sense in which Marxists were right in distancing themselves from liberalism – both in theory and in practice. But, again, they erred tragically in failing to acknowledge the evident merits of liberal institutions. Democratization and liberal concerns will be at issue throughout the chapters that follow – independently and from the perspective of Marxist theory. Both themes come together perspicuously in the Marxists' conception of the "last state," the state that superintends the transition to communism.

Chapter 5

The last state

Even those who are convinced of the feasibility and desirability of moving beyond the Age of States to an earthly "republic of ends" might wonder if statelessness is, in fact, a viable political ideal. Rousseau's despair of the possibility of establishing a just state in real history provides a cautionary note. If Rousseau was right, the damage already done to the mentality of human beings and therefore to their wills is irreversible. By instituting de facto states, the inhabitants of the state of nature concocted a seeming remedy for the affliction diagnosed in *The Second Discourse*. But this palliative has altered the condition of humankind beyond the possibility of a genuine cure. Rousseau's deeply pessimistic reading of the world *as it is* deserves serious attention, as do the convergent judgments of conservative and liberal philosophers. Nevertheless, there is reason to think that humanity can move beyond the Age of States; that the road from here to there, however difficult to traverse, is not insurmountably blocked.

It would be foolhardy to aim for a definitive theoretical defense of this contention. Institutional arrangements, by their nature, are too closely linked to peculiarities of time and place for general considerations to be decisive. What follows, therefore, are only reflections on one sustained attempt, the most important to date, to broach this problem in theory and practice: the project for revolutionizing the state pursued by Marxists committed expressly to the end of the state under communism. To reflect on "the dictatorship of the proletariat," as these Marxists called the "transitional" state they envisioned, is to continue the discussion of institutional means for implementing democratic values broached at the end of Chapter 4. If only for this reason, the designation Marxists use to describe this form of the state is needlessly misleading. But since the expression "dictatorship of the proletariat" has standing in the

Marxist tradition and since it suggests claims worth defending, despite its unfortunate connotations, the expression will be retained here. What follows is not an attempt at a general account of the institutions appropriate for a state committed to its own withering away. An account of that kind is impossible, given the essentially conjunctural nature of political practice. The most that we can expect is to appropriate lessons learned in ventures undertaken in circumstances quite different from our own, and bound to differ even more markedly from the conditions future partisans of statelessness will encounter.

There is however a plainly philosophical problem, appropriately broached at this level of abstraction from actual politics, suggested by the idea of a state concocted to implement its own demise. Such a state, whatever its institutional forms, wields power in order to implement a vision of ideal social arrangements. It does, in short, what virtually all political philosophers thought eminently proper before the advent of the modern era but what hardly anyone today thinks right – it uses state power to implement a particular and controversial conception of the good. Neutrality with respect at least to controversial conceptions of the good is a tenet – some would say a defining feature – of modern liberalism. The state communists envision to lead the transition to statelessness therefore seems at odds with what had become the consensus view. It is a theme of this chapter and the next that this observation is itself misleading. But before examining the dictatorship of the proletariat in light of its differences from the state liberals advocate, and before reflecting on neutrality as an ideal, it will be well to say as much as possible, albeit not very much, about the nature of the ostensibly offending polity. The burden of this chapter will therefore be to reflect on the dictatorship of the proletariat as Marxists have traditionally conceived it.

DEMOCRACY AND DICTATORSHIP

Throughout our political culture, democracy and dictatorship are opposed. In democracies the people rule; in dictatorships the people are ruled – by a dictator. But on even a cursory scrutiny of the most paradigmatic instances of real-world "dictatorships" – or on common-sense reflection on the nature of governance – it is evident that dictatorship in this sense is impossible in a state of any size or complexity. An individual can hardly rule alone. A "dictator" can predominate among those who rule – prevailing, typically, in setting agendas and making decisions. But a dictator cannot literally "dictate," and we saw in Chapter 4 that the people hardly rule at all in so-called democracies. Thus neither "democracy" nor "dictatorship," as these terms are widely used, designates anything like what it suggests.

It might be thought that democracies are based on the rule of law, whereas dictatorships, like ancient tyrannies, are based on the wills of those who govern. This suggestion has merit. But the idea of the rule of law is itself problematic. No putative dictatorship has ever dispensed with at least the appearance of legality – with "legalism" as a means for legitimating existing power relations.[1] What is called "the rule of law" plainly involves more than legalism. But it is far from clear that the difference will serve to distinguish democracies from dictatorships.

In any case, current usage matters very little for the Marxist understanding of "the dictatorship of the proletariat."[2] The "dictatorship" Marx discussed in his writings on the Paris Commune and that Lenin resumed in *The State and Revolution* was not the "dictatorship" of contemporary political culture and is not intended to contrast with "democracy." Representative governments, the paradigm case of democracy in the current view, are bourgeois class dictatorships, according to Lenin's use of the term; and the dictatorship of the proletariat, as Lenin conceived it, is radically democratic. "Dictatorship," according to a celebrated formulation of Lenin's, is "rule based directly upon force and unrestricted by laws."[3] But, in this sense, for anyone persuaded by a generally Hobbesian view of the state, all states are dictatorships. Marxists are Hobbesians in this respect. Indeed, they have a reason Hobbes never imagined for supporting the Hobbesian view. For Marxists, laws are not sufficiently independent of state institutions to operate *substantively*, not just formally, as constraints on the sovereign's power. Indeed, in the Marxist view, both the state and the law depend substantially on a third, genuinely independent, factor – the economy. In traditional Marxist terminology, the state and the law are superstructural. Both *rest upon* an "economic base." How then can the one also rest upon the other?

1 Cf. Judith N. Shklar, *Legalism: An Essay on Law, Morals, and Politics* (Cambridge, Mass.: Harvard University Press, 1964).
2 What follows resumes claims defended in my *Arguing for Socialism*, Chapter 6, and *The End of the State*, Chapters 7 and 8.
3 V. I. Lenin, "Proletarian Revolution and the Renegade Kautsky," in *Collected Works* (Moscow: Progress Publishers, 1972), vol. 28, p. 236.

This question is unanswerable as long as these notoriously obscure metaphors remain unexplicated. This is not the place to pursue this issue very far, but this much is clear: For Marxists, superstructural phenomena are constrained by the economy in a way that – and to a degree that – the economy is not constrained by them.[4] Moreover, superstructural phenomena are constrained in this way and to this extent only by the economy, not by each other. It is therefore plain that, unless the Marxist metaphors are denuded of their intended sense, it is inconceivable, from a historical materialist vantage point, that the state could rest upon the law. From this perspective, democracies are just as much "tyrannies" in the classical sense as the "dictatorships" of mainstream political discourse.

We might conclude, then, that in the sense that Lenin intended the term, there is in fact nothing controversial in the contention that all states are dictatorships. This claim, it seems, asserts no more than the widely held idea that states are, according to the consensus view, institutionalized monopolies of the means of (de facto) legitimate violence, a definition meant to apply as well to states with "autonomous" legal systems as to those without them.

---

4 Despite what Marxists, following Marx, have believed, the claim that the state and the law are "superstructural" need not imply that all aspects of these institutional arrangements and practices belong to the superstructure. The base–superstructure distinction is best construed as a claim about *explanation*. Very generally, then, the idea is that the base explains the superstructure more than the superstructure explains the base. As remarked, Marxists have tended toward the view that the economic base explains *everything* about legal and political superstructures – and also forms of consciousness. But it is plain that no Marxist, no matter how doctrinaire, could plausibly have maintained that literally *everything* having to do with the state, law, and consciousness has an economic explanation. Judges in Britain wear wigs; in the United States they do not. Must Marxists be committed to the idea that this fact can be explained economically? Evidently not. The standard view, then, was that important or fundamental political and legal phenomena and forms of consciousness belong to the superstructure. But what counts as "important" or "fundamental"? It has lately become clear that there is no theoretically well-motivated way to answer this question in general; and also that, strictly speaking, it is only necessary to hold that those aspects of the state, the legal system, and "forms of consciousness" *that bear on economic structures* need be explained economically to accord with historical materialist precepts. Thus the superstructure may encompass much less than Marxists have traditionally supposed. These claims are advanced and defended in G. A. Cohen, "Restricted and Inclusive Historical Materialism," in *History, Labour, and Freedom: Themes from Marx* (Oxford: Clarendon Press, 1988). See also Wright, Levine, and Sober, *Reconstructing Marxism*, Chapter 5.

What is nonstandard and even distinctively Marxist in this strain of theorizing is the idea that states are *class* dictatorships, that state power ensures and reproduces class domination.

However, this conclusion is easily misunderstood. As remarked, for political philosophers after Hobbes, the most fundamental concern has been to justify the coordination of *individuals'* behaviors. But from the perspective of historical materialism, social classes, defined by the social relations of production in which individuals are implicated, are the proper starting point for theorizing human societies and their political arrangements. With this crucial emendation, the core problem of modern political philosophy takes on a different cast. The interindividual coordination problem political philosophers since Hobbes have addressed becomes an *intraclass* coordination problem. This new problem is then "solved" in just the way the old one was: by creating an apparatus that allows for the preeminence of a single will and for its enforcement. This will cannot be a general will in Rousseau's sense, for in a class-divided society there can be no general interest. Nor is it a sovereign's will in Hobbes's sense, since there is no individual or collection of individuals who can genuinely represent the whole community. In the Marxist view, the will that directs the state is the will of the economically dominant class. The state allows the members of this class to act in concert – for the purpose of maintaining their domination of subordinate classes.

There therefore is a sense in which Marxists go beyond the claims of standard political theory in calling states dictatorships. Arguably, there is even a sense in which, in their view, democracy and dictatorship conflict. The contrast, however, is not with democracy per se but with democracy purged of its class-centered connotations. When democracy is understood to designate rule by the (undifferentiated) people, it is a form of what Hegel called a *Rechtstaat*, a state grounded in the (supposed) universality of Right (*Recht*). However, a dictatorship, according to contemporary understandings, is not a Rechtstaat. Like ancient tyrannies, these polities are based on the will of the dictator, a will that is arbitrary with respect to Right. In calling states dictatorships, Marxists effectively maintain that the Rechstaat is an illusion, that so long as class divisions remain, the universality of Right is an impossible and even harmful ideal.

In this respect, the characterization of states as dictatorships is part of a broader challenge to any notion of morality or law that stands beyond class divisions. For Marx, so long as class divisions persist, class interests remain fundamental. They cannot be assimilated to private wills, as Rousseau proposed in *The Social Contract*, nor can they be dissolved into a putative general will. The standpoint of universality, emblematic of the moral point of view, is therefore flawed and deeply ideological. It works to impede the emancipation of subordinate classes by representing ruling class interests as universal interests. The idea of a Rechtstaat, a universal state, is correspondingly flawed and similarly ideological so long as class domination, organized by the state, persists. To depict states as dictatorships, then, is to continue a distinctively Marxist assault on a widely accepted conception of morality. It is, from the perspective of political theory, to fault the idea of Right. The insistence that states are *class* dictatorships is additionally informative. It helps explain why the idea of a Rechtstaat cannot be sustained. More importantly, this insistence joins the theory of the state with the idea that history is a history of class struggles. The term "dictatorship" in Marxist political theory is therefore neither so contentious as may at first appear nor so standard as further investigation suggests.

But the fundamental Marxist claim is indeed that states are *class* dictatorships and therefore that they figure in a broader process of class struggle that shapes the nature and trajectory of human history. In this process, there is no conflict between dictatorship and democracy. Quite the contrary. The dictatorship of the proletariat is that form of the state that superintends the process through which the Age of States is finally superseded. To this end, democracy – in the fullest sense of the term – is essential to its nature.

RELATIVE AUTONOMY

In *The State and Revolution*, Lenin is emphatic in insisting that the old regime be "smashed," not "seized," and replaced by a new type of state. Following Marx's own reflections on the Paris Commune and its tragic aftermath, Lenin maintained that institutions of the old form, by their very nature, promote bourgeois class rule and that a proletarian class dictatorship, correspondingly, requires institutional arrangements of a different kind. It is fair to generalize this claim. If we accept the thesis, fundamental to the Marxist view of politics, that state power is always a class dictatorship, then, if Lenin was right, there exist relations of compatibility and incompatibility between types of state power or different class dictatorships, on the one hand, and the institutions through which state power is achieved and maintained, on the other.[5]

Writing in the summer of 1917, between two great revolutionary "moments" and in the flush of rapidly changing and suddenly momentous events, Lenin was disinclined to draw out many of the implications of this claim, particularly those that focus on how revolutionary victories can become deflected. But although he does not quite acknowledge the point, it is a plain implication of his view that a working class that seizes but does not smash the offending institutions of the class dictatorship it overthrows would not, in fact, control a proletarian state. In time, if the old institutions remain in place, they would reestablish compatibility by reconstituting a *bourgeois* class dictatorship, perhaps administered by erstwhile revolutionaries or their successors.

Real history seems to have vindicated this unhappy inference. But in the Soviet Union and elsewhere where the "Soviet model" was imitated or installed, the failure to advance toward genuine communism was, at most, only partly explained by the survival of old institutional forms. The indefinite prolongation and eventual entrenchment of repressive and ideological arrangements inappropriate for the permanent revolutionizing of the state were at least as much to blame. Nevertheless, Lenin's implicit recognition of a likely and profoundly debilitating danger facing revolutionary Russia seems remarkably prescient.

It is unclear in general to what extent forms of state power limit institutional arrangements and vice versa. It is one thing to hold that not all institutional forms are compatible with all class dictatorships and something else to assert particular incompatibilities. Nowhere in the Marxist corpus is any general guidance offered on this more vexing question. This is just what we should expect if it is true that no general theory of institutional arrangements is possible. However, *The State and Revolution* makes much of one sort of incompatibility – that alleged to hold between a "relatively autonomous" repressive state apparatus, proclaimed the hallmark of bourgeois class rule, and the dictatorship of the proletariat. It is now plain that this claim is dangerously flawed.

What motivates the suggestion that an independent judiciary be replaced by popular tribunals or that a specialized police and army

---

5 To say that a type of class dictatorship and a set of institutional arrangements are *incompatible* is to say that their coexistence is structurally unstable to an extent that the configuration cannot be maintained indefinitely. One or the other must give way.

be superseded by peoples' militias is the same principle that underlies the injunction to smash parliamentary forms of governance and establish workers' councils in their stead. It is a commitment to enhance direct popular control over state institutions – in a word, to democratize them. But historical experience belies this conclusion. It is plain that the "relative autonomy" of institutions for "the administration of justice" in existing liberal democracies is a signal advantage of these regimes that very much enhances individual and collective well-being. It is equally plain that the comparative lack of independence of the judiciaries and police of the formerly "socialist" countries worked to the detriment of the citizens of those states.

It could be argued that the superiority of liberal democracies in this respect follows only from the failure of states constructed on the Soviet model to democratize their repressive institutions. The regimes that controlled those countries did "smash" the institutional forms of liberal democracy. But, virtually without exception, they did so preemptively, inasmuch as liberal institutions were never actually established in the social orders they replaced. In any case, they did not institute democratic arrangements in their place. Instead, the repressive apparatus of the former socialist polities was directed by a party and bureaucracy even more remote from popular control than the relatively independent judiciaries and police of liberal democracies. The repressive apparatus of a bureaucratized state socialism in a political community bereft of liberal traditions and with very limited democratic experience could hardly have been expected to realize the vision advanced in *The State and Revolution*. Sadly, experience has vindicated this prediction.

Nevertheless, it would be hard to deny that the history of the Soviet model from its inception to its demise tends to corroborate that pessimism about human nature that pervades liberal political culture and that motivates its support for institutional safeguards designed to save human beings from themselves and from each other. It is important for democrats to address this wariness and to reflect on its implications.

Pessimism – some might say "realism" – about human nature is the principal source of the zeal with which liberal democrats defend the relative autonomy of state institutions. Characteristically, radical democrats counter liberal doubts by ascribing transformative effects to democratic participation itself. For radical democrats, liberal democrats err not so much in their view of the psychology of present-day human beings but in thinking that the human nature one observes must remain forever impervious to a genuinely democratic "education." The citizens of liberal democracies and of other non- or only minimally democratic states do have reason to fear their own natures and should therefore prefer relatively independent judiciaries and police to more democratic alternatives. For them, the tyranny of the majority is at least as much a menace as more conventional tyrannies. But, in the view of radical democrats, the very real shortcomings of the human nature we observe can be altered profoundly. In this respect, Rousseau was a pioneer participatory democrat. In his view, when "the whole people rule concerning the whole people,"[6] human beings become citizens who, by the very nature of their wants, effectively realize liberal values without recourse to non- or antidemocratic liberal constraints.[7]

However, the belief that democratic participation has these effects is more an article of faith than a corroborated hypothesis. Participatory democracy has seldom been attempted even in small-scale organizations, and never broached at the level of the nation-state. Therefore evidence that would compel assent to or rejection of participatory democratic claims is unavailable. But enough is known about human nature to speculate with some confidence, and there is anecdotal evidence too. On these bases, it is fair to conclude, albeit tentatively and awaiting empirical confirmation, that faith in the positive transformative effects of democratic participation is eminently reasonable.

The tyranny of the majority is a plausible threat insofar as the majority of individuals are ill informed, mercurial, susceptible to demagogic manipulation, and generally lacking in the virtues of civility. For such a citizenry, it is appropriate – and even crucial – to limit the scope of democratic collective choice as liberals propose and to move from direct democratic to representative institutions as liberal democrats do. However, even the most irresponsible individuals, invested with real power over particular decisions, can become responsible decision makers – especially if there are mechanisms in place that hold them accountable for the decisions they make. The reason why is clear enough: Genuine control encourages interest, and interest, in turn, encourages knowledge, competence, and responsibility. In cases where individuals' choices and activities are palpably effective, self-interest

6 *The Social Contract*, Book II, Chapter 6.
7 See Levine, *The Politics of Autonomy*, pp. 72–80.

alone should suffice to focus individuals' interests in the workings of the institutions they control. Thus we observe that the most politically ill-informed citizens are often knowledgeable about matters like music or sports that, for one reason or another, engage their interest. We can therefore infer that, for most people, genuine control over institutions is likely to concentrate the mind and spark sufficient concern to address liberals' fears. Of course it remains unclear how much confidence to invest in these speculations. But it is plain that the deficiencies one observes in the citizenry of existing states does not inevitably carry over to other aspects of social experience and should not be assumed unalterable under different institutional arrangements.

In contrast to many contemporary defenders of participatory democracy, Marxists who support radical democratic positions focus less on individuals' activities in non- or quasi-political contexts than on their behavior in revolutionary undertakings – the Paris Commune of 1871, the 1905 revolution in Russia, the events of the spring and summer of 1917, the October Revolution, the (failed) revolutionary eruptions in Central and Eastern Europe in the aftermath of the October Revolution, and the host of Third World revolutionary ventures of the past several decades. They infer that the masses are indeed able to govern well from the fact that hosts of downtrodden and oppressed individuals have assumed control of their destinies and participated competently in insurgent organizations and revolutionary institutions in the course of these momentous upheavals.

However, these "data" are unlikely to assuage liberals' fears. There is first of all the problem of maintaining competence and civility as revolutionary events subside and give way to other, more "normal" concerns. It is far from clear that what is normal in extraordinary circumstances can be indefinitely sustained. In addition, in revolutionary situations, revolutionaries commonly take severely illiberal measures against real or imagined enemies, and this fact has weighed heavily on the liberal imagination. Indeed, from the last days of the French Revolution until the dread of nuclear weaponry impinged on human consciousness, revolutionary Terror was, according to Hegel's celebrated portrayal, the very emblem of unthinkable horror.[8] Arguably, *excess* is endemic to revolutionary politics; it has certainly been characteristic of it. In any

---

8 See Hegel, *The Phenomenology of Mind*, section BB, VI, B, III, "Absolute Freedom and Terror."

case, the history of revolutions and of popular rule within revolutionary situations can reinforce the fears that lead liberals to distance political institutions from direct popular control as much as it can reinforce the hopes of radical democrats for bringing them closer together.

There is little hope, at present, of intervening in this debate decisively or of changing settled convictions. No available evidence is likely to persuade those who believe human nature incapable of respecting liberal values "spontaneously" from thinking that limitations on self-rule can be safely relaxed for democratic reasons; and those who think otherwise are not likely to be dissuaded by the host of contrary observations that can be adduced in support of the need for keeping democracy within bounds. It is not just that partisans of one or another view are obstinate; the bearing and even the relevance of the data that exist are too unclear. The experimental introduction of increasingly democratizing institutional forms along the lines suggested at the end of Chapter 4 would probably generate evidence of a less equivocal sort. But it is unfair to prejudge the outcome of experimental ventures not yet undertaken – indeed, not yet on any actual political agenda.

Even if new or existing data were approached without prejudice, an unlikely assumption on so charged an issue, threshold effects or significant discontinuities in the consequences of democratization are likely to make the interpretation of the evidence controversial. Not even the most ardent proponents of participatory democracy have offered principled reasons for thinking that the (alleged) beneficial effects of democratic participation rise or fall continuously with increasing or decreasing levels of participation. For participatory democrats, it would seem to be enough if some (presumably, far-reaching and radical) levels of participation enhance democratic citizenship. Therefore it need not embarrass participatory democrats if, at some levels, enhancing or diminishing participation has no significant effects on individuals' capacities for democratic citizenship and, at other levels, increasing participation is actually detrimental.

In any case, the accumulation of relevant evidence ought to be a high priority for democrats, even if there is little prospect of settling debates about participatory democracy definitively. Democratic commitments rest ultimately on faith in the demos and in democracy's beneficial consequences. If this faith is not to degenerate into a dogma, with potentially dire consequences for humankind, it is well to construe it, by analogy with experimental hypotheses, as a plausible but inconclusive conviction awaiting the test of experience. Unlike those with otherworldly convictions, democrats can test their faith. Wise democrats will be eager to do so.

BEYOND LIBERAL DEMOCRACY?

The crucial test is to see if it is indeed possible to realize liberal values without recourse to liberal institutions – by relying on individuals' *characters* or, as Rousseau would prefer, on the nature of their wills. Through popular self-rule – and in other ways too – individuals are to be educated to respect the moral equality of persons and all that it implies. No less a liberal than John Stuart Mill also emphasized the importance of character for implementing liberal and democratic values.[9] But he foresaw no possibility of dispensing with liberal institutional safeguards. Historically, Marxists have disagreed. I will argue that, ultimately, they may be right, but only if their disagreements with liberals are based on principled democratic convictions and only if the nonliberal institutional forms they envision are deferred to the very long run. Historically, Marxism has been deficient in both respects.

A conservative sensibility, attuned to the dangers inherent in tampering with established political forms, would tend to support Mill against Marx. In general, it is wise to act in accord with this sensibility. However, conservatism, so conceived, need not entail immobility, nor need it even proscribe revolutionary undertakings.[10] It only militates against the impatience that seems always to afflict revolutionaries – advising caution in anticipating the *pace* of change – and warning against the idea that mentalities developed over centuries and shaped, in part, by psychological and cultural factors remote from any "economic base" or political "superstructure" can be rapidly and profoundly transformed.[11]

---

9   The effects of institutional arrangements on individuals' characters is a central theme of both *On Liberty* and *Considerations on Representative Government*. See also Dennis F. Thompson, *John Stuart Mill and Representative Government* (Princeton: Princeton University Press, 1976).
10 See Levine, *The End of the State*, Chapter 4.
11 Questions about the pace of change are distinct from questions about the appropriateness of attempting revolutionary transformations (of real property relations) at particular historical moments. It is one thing, for example, to fault the Bolsheviks for attempting too much too quickly and something else to claim that the Bolshevik Revolution itself was premature, given prevailing con-

Respect for what some liberals would call the "rights" of others is eminently achievable for most people most of the time even now. In uneasy coexistence with the opposite inclination, the character traits from which such respect flows can flourish to an extraordinary degree in the exceptional, revolutionary conditions Marxists invoke as support for democracy's beneficial effects. But sufficient confidence in individuals' capacities to respect "rights" in "normal" circumstances and without institutional constraints would require, at the very least, a protracted period of character formation – possibly lasting generations. Marx and Lenin and their cothinkers went wrong in imagining that this process could be cut short, that the old institutional forms could be changed quickly and extensively without conjuring up the perils they protected against. One need not quarrel, then, with their view of the nature of the changes needed for realizing democracy fully, or even with the means they proposed for bringing the requisite changes about. They erred only in their estimates of the rate at which these changes can safely proceed. Marx, it seems, was clear-sighted to a fault about what human beings could achieve but willfully blind to the all-too-human obstacles standing in the way of his vision.

If, as Plato said, a *virtue* of a thing is that which makes it perform its function well, and a *vice* is that which has a contrary effect, then impatience is a serious vice in a revolutionary. Perhaps more than any other factor, impatience makes otherwise sound revolutionary ventures turn out badly. Marxists, including Marx, can be faulted for this vice – in their practice and in its theory. Lenin's injunction to smash rather than seize the old repressive state apparatus was, in context, a clear expression of impatience that has had dreadful consequences. It *is* true that the old repressive state institutions, relatively insulated from each other and from the main governing bodies of the state, are obstacles in the way of democratization and its (potentially) beneficial effects. It is also true, therefore, that the dictatorship of the proletariat, in order to fulfill its historical mission, must eventually replace these institutions with more directly democratic forms. But it is wrong to undertake to democratize prematurely and without liberal protections. To do so is to foster the tyranny of the majority (or of those who purport to rule in their

ditions in Russia in 1917. Historical materialism, Marx's theory of history, bears on the latter question; the kind of conservatism that revolutionaries would do well to incorporate is concerned, on the other hand, with the pace of change.

behalf) and to put individuals' "rights" – and the dignity they express – in jeopardy. On even the most optimistic assessment of democracy's transformative potentialities, it will be a long time indeed before liberal values are sufficiently instilled that liberal "constitutional" protections can be significantly relaxed, as they must eventually be to pave the way for the unprecedented and unfettered democratization communism entails.

Those who acknowledge the possibilities historical materialism identifies and who are eager to wager on democracy's transformative effects should therefore forbear from calling for the last state, the state in transition to statelessness, to "smash" relatively autonomous institutions for the administration of justice and the maintenance of civil order. To issue such a demand is to neglect the central problem a state in transition must confront: the recalcitrance of deeply entrenched undemocratic and illiberal inclinations, and the difficulties these habits of mind pose in the process of transition. In well-functioning liberal democracies, programs with illiberal implications are unlikely to gain many adherents. Not so, however, in illiberal regimes where few have much to lose by relinquishing nonexistent liberal protections. Thus the call to "smash" liberalism preemptively – in conditions where liberal institutions have not produced their own (limited) transformative effects – is particularly reckless. Liberal democracy is a preschool for real democracy. It is evaded at great peril. As history attests, the likely outcome of attempts to pass over liberal democracy is tyranny – at first, perhaps in the guise of democratic forms, eventually without any disguise at all.

Even with liberal democracy as an established point of departure, the way ahead for the last state remains problematic and uncharted. It is therefore pointless to speculate on time frames for the protracted transformative process of building securely liberal character types, liberals without liberalism, even conceding the feasibility of the project. All that can be concluded with confidence is that the process will be facilitated greatly if the institutional safeguards liberal democracy has evolved to protect against the tyranny of the majority remain in force – now and for the foreseeable future, though not for an indefinite future. The dictatorship of the proletariat must find a place, as it were, for relatively autonomous repressive state institutions. For a long time to come, perhaps a very long time, it must remain liberal, however incompatible liberalism may ultimately be with its general democratizing tendency.

But then how can the last state advance toward statelessness? How can it be a state of a new type? To begin to answer these questions, it is well to follow the lead of some Marxists after Lenin – Gramsci, for example, and Althusser – and to look back, again, to indications provided by political philosophers before Marx. Thus partisans of the last state should take to heart Hume's celebrated declaration that "opinion is the true foundation of the state."[12] This view is entirely in accord with Rousseau's thought too, insofar as Rousseau conceived politics as a contest between the private and the general will – a struggle for the "opinion" of each citizen. In short, it is insufficient for defenders of the last state to look only at repressive state institutions, as Lenin did. The real battle in and over the dictatorship of the proletariat is ultimately waged at the level of opinion.

THE IDEOLOGICAL STATE APPARATUS

It was perhaps with this idea in mind that Althusser identified what he called "the ideological state apparatus," a formulation plainly intended to parallel "the repressive state apparatus" of orthodox Leninist theory.[13] The expression is Althusser's, but the idea is Gramsci's. Among Marxists, it was Gramsci who first privileged the role of ideology in the struggle for socialism and, by implication, in the process of moving socialist societies toward communism. And it was Gramsci who first conceived ideological institutions as state institutions, even when they are not juridically "public."[14]

Gramsci's aim was to provide a theory of socialist transformation suitable to Western European conditions. Without quite saying so, he effectively acknowledged that the Russian Revolution was not an appropriate model. Because it took place in a society that was underdeveloped economically and politically, it could be waged, like the French Revolution more than a century before, as a frontal assault on the principal institutions of the old regime.

12 David Hume, *A Treatise of Human Nature*, ed. L. A. Selby-Bigge (Oxford: Clarendon Press, 1888 and subsequently), Book III, Part 2, Chapter 8, pp. 539–549.
13 Louis Althusser, "Ideology and the Ideological State Apparatus," in *Lenin and Philosophy and Other Essays* (London: New Left Books, 1971).
14 See Antonio Gramsci, *Letters from Prison*, ed. and trans. L. Lawner (New York: Harper, 1973), and *Selections from Political Writings*, vol. 1 (1910–1920), ed. and trans. Q. Hoare and J. Mathews (New York: International Publishers, 1977), vol. 2 (1921–1926), ed. and trans. Q. Hoare (New York: International Publishers, 1978).

The repressive apparatus of the czarist autocracy and then the Kerensky government, weakened by war and mired in a feudal past, proved incapable of withstanding the pressures of a popular insurrection directed by a "professional" leadership organized on quasimilitary lines. However, states that superintend more developed societies are likely to have considerably greater means for maintaining themselves in power. A frontal assault on such a state is therefore unlikely to succeed. What is required, instead, is a protracted struggle – metaphorically, a "war of attrition." At stake in this war is what Gramsci called "hegemony" – moral, cultural, and intellectual leadership. If the working class and its allies could gain hegemony, the old order would lose the battle for "opinion," the basis for its (de facto) legitimacy and hence for its very existence. The conquest of the old state apparatus therefore ratifies an earlier, more fundamental victory won on the ideological front. Socialist revolution, on Gramsci's view, is not essentially a matter of storming a Bastille or seizing a Winter Palace. In developed countries, revolutionary events like these can be of only symbolic or expressive importance. The real task is to combat the old regime ideologically, to assault its legitimacy, precipitating a crisis that is finally resolved by the ascension to power of a new hegemonic class.

In his account of ideological struggle, Gramsci was an innovator. But his depiction of revolutionary politics as a struggle for hegemony recalls familiar Marxist accounts of the "bourgeois" revolutions through which capitalism decisively and irreversibly defeated feudalism. In the traditional view, a new mode of production "matured" in the "womb" of the old. In other words, the great bourgeois revolutions cemented economic transformations that had already largely transpired within the old regime. A strictly parallel development is inconceivable under capitalism. Capitalist economies can accommodate prototypes of socialist economic organizations – workers' cooperatives, for instance, or publicly controlled enterprises – but, so long as the economy remains capitalist, these organizations must deal with one another and with the larger economy in capitalist ways. Whatever their internal structure or juridical status, they are therefore capitalist firms. For this reason, pockets of socialism cannot arise within capitalist economies.[15] But it is possible for socialist "opinion" to form and

15 This formulation presupposes that capitalism and socialism are indeed historical alternatives in the way that Marx's theory of history claims and that the broader intellectual culture largely assumes. Eventually, this presupposition

gain hegemony. In this sense, a new form of civilization can indeed grow to (near) maturity in the womb of the old – not in consequence of inexorable economic processes but as a matter of conscious design. The venerable metaphor therefore remains apt even if the phenomenon it describes is not quite the same. Bourgeois revolutions became possible and even necessary because the political superstructure of feudal societies grew increasingly incompatible with emerging capitalist production relations. In Gramsci's view, in order to prevail in developed capitalist economies with "normal" states, socialist revolutionaries must create a parallel incompatibility – between the economy and the state, on the one hand, and opinion or hegemonic ideology, on the other.

The signal achievement of state building in the modern period has been to consolidate all (de facto legitimate) means of violence into a single institutional nexus. No parallel consolidation has occurred for the institutions that shape opinion. Indeed, a much remarked characteristic of capitalist societies – especially those with liberal democratic states – is the separation of the state from many spheres of individuals' lives and concerns and the consequent placement of many of the institutions Gramsci's analysis implicates outside the state – in "civil society." To be sure, this exclusion is seldom, if ever, complete. Some of the institutions involved in the struggle for hegemony – schools, for instance – are typically established, administered, and funded by the state. The press and other mass media are rarely public in this sense, particularly in liberal democracies. Religious organizations, which still play a role in shaping the mentalities of many citizens, are, at most, only tenuously affiliated with official state institutions and may even be "separated" from the state by law – as required, for

---

may prove untenable. Then, despite what Marxists and also non-Marxists have long believed, the capitalism–socialism distinction would have to be redrawn. It would be necessary, in other words, to disaggregate "capitalism" and "socialism" as these terms are traditionally understood. It is unclear what would follow from so fundamental a revision of received ways of thinking about the economy and society, but one possibility might be, paradoxically, that the traditional Marxist view of economic transitions – according to which modes of production mature within the modes of production they are destined to supersede – would be vindicated. At this point in the reconstruction of historical materialist themes, these reflections are too speculative to warrant dwelling on them. I do, however, venture some very tentative suggestions supporting a qualified version of the idea that it may be well to disaggregate traditional understandings of "capitalism" and "socialism" in Chapter 9 herein; see also Wright, Levine, and Sober, *Reconstructing Marxism*, Chapter 5.

example, by the United States Constitution. Despite these differences, Althusser, elaborating Gramsci's idea, subsumed all of them or rather aspects of them under the concept "ideological state apparatus," to which he added opinion-shaping organs emblematic of civil society – like the family.[16] It is true, of course, that the state, through the legal system, impinges upon family life and other ostensibly "private" matters, sometimes to the detriment of liberal values, sometimes unexceptionably. Ideally, the state superintends and supports the private sphere. In this sense, it is a condition for its possibility. But this fact hardly warrants collapsing the distinction liberals draw between civil society and the state. The ideological state apparatus of Althusser's formulation straddles this difference and, by implication, discounts it.

Nevertheless, there is some justification for Althusser's designation, and there is even a sense in which his formulation captures what is distinctive in Gramsci's political theory. For both Althusser and Gramsci, following Marx's depiction of the state as the set of institutions that reproduce existing class relations, the institutions state functionaries administer directly could not possibly exhaust the scope of the term. The "state," according to the assumed definition, would designate all the institutional arrangements that have the requisite effects. Civil society, as liberals understand it, should therefore be replete with state institutions. Insofar as even those institutions that paradigmatically distinguish civil society from the political realm work to reproduce existing relations of class domination, they are part of the state – effectively, though of course not juridically. As remarked, this usage can confuse and mislead. However, it also suggests an important challenge to mainstream political theory, motivated by Marxist views of the state's role in history. In its insistence that politics is not a realm apart but an inextricable aspect of all spheres of human life, Althusser's formulation points to a difference between Marxist and

16 For Althusser, the ideological state apparatus is, in effect, an ideal type, as is the repressive state apparatus. In his usage, these ideal types are defined functionally. Actual state institutions typically exhibit features of both of these ideal typical concepts. Thus the police are mainly part of the repressive state apparatus, but their existence also has ideological effects. On the other hand, schools are mainly part of the ideological state apparatus, but they also function repressively. It is unclear whether Althusser believed that these ideal typical concepts are exhaustive. In any case, there plainly are state functions – for instance, the regulation and coordination of productive activities and of finance – that are neither ideological nor repressive in his sense.

liberal political theory, and an affinity with Rousseauean thought and the broader "classical" tradition in political philosophy.

The Althusserian-Gramscian insight concerns the relation between civil society and the state. It can be appreciated if contrasted with the superficially similar distinction, fundamental to historical materialism, between a society's "economic base" and its "political superstructure." It is compatible with the historical materialist idea that a clearly differentiated "economy" is a relatively recent phenomenon in human history; that, as is often maintained, precapitalist societies conflated economic and political functions to such an extent that it was not until capitalism matured in the "womb" of European feudalism that the "economic" entered the conceptual scheme of individuals involved in production and exchange. Nevertheless, in the historical materialist view, a distinction between the economy and the state is of general explanatory importance throughout human history – even when it does not capture the lived experience of the people whose history it purports to explain. Similarly, liberals with a historical understanding of social and political ideas could concede the historical particularity of the distinctions they draw between civil society and the state. But it is tempting for them too to conclude that this distinction is of transhistorical normative significance, just as historical materialism claims transhistorical explanatory relevance for its own distinction between the economy and the state.

Historically, many liberals have succumbed to this temptation and for good reason. Without a transhistorically applicable private–public distinction, liberals would lack a critical tool for assessing nonliberal societies, and liberalism would be just one ideology among many. Marxists, of course, have long proclaimed the historical particularity of *all* normative views. But, strictly speaking, Marxists can be agnostics on the question of the universality of particular normative positions and even uphold the transhistorical standing of some normative standards.[17] In any case, nothing Gramsci or Althusser claims about "the ideological state apparatus" in any way impugns the transhistorical normative importance of the liberals' society – state distinction. This observation is hardly surprising inasmuch as neither Gramsci nor

17 It is even consistent with historical materialist claims to defend the opposing view, as do historical materialists who are also moral realists. See, for example, Alan Gilbert, *Democratic Individuality* (Cambridge: Cambridge University Press, 1990).

Althusser addresses the normative questions of interest to liberal political philosophers. But they do challenge the underlying, descriptive position that liberal moral philosophy suggests: the idea that there is a real difference between society and the state that is important for understanding the state transhistorically. Again, this claim is analogous to the historical materialist's distinction between the economy and the state. But there is no reason in general why a distinction drawn in the context of a moral philosophy, whatever its historical scope or metaphysical status, should be carried over into descriptive political theory. Nor is there any reason in this case to consider the general rule contravened. Thus it is the view of Althusser, insofar as a substantive thesis can be teased out of a provocative formulation, and implicitly also of Gramsci and perhaps of Marx as well, that the liberal's distinction, but not the historical materialist's, is of *only* historically transient importance; that, however natural it may be to treat these distinctions similarly, the two are not, in fact, on a par.

As remarked, this position is an implication of the idea that state institutions be defined as those which reinforce class domination. Is this view justified? In a word, it depends. For most explanatory purposes, the Marxist definition is too encompassing to be of much use. In class-divided societies, almost all institutional arrangements function, at least in part, to reproduce existing relations of class domination. In calling everything that has this effect a *state* institution, many differences of interest to political theorists are inevitably obscured. The juridical private–public distinction is likely to track political phenomena better. But, as Marxists instructed by the Eleventh *Thesis on Feuerbach*, Althusser and Gramsci were not so much interested in understanding the world in all its facets as in changing it. Their aim was to construct a "revolutionary theory," an understanding of the world capable of guiding revolutionaries in the task of transforming society toward communism. For this purpose, the more encompassing definition may indeed be apt, for it suggests a political agenda appropriate to the Marxist political project that is likely to elude adherents of a narrower view of the state.

CULTURAL REVOLUTION

To endorse a process of socialist revolution, from the defeat of capitalism to the establishment of communism, and to conceive this process as a struggle in and over *both* the repressive *and* ideological state apparatus is to imagine the state that overcomes the conditions that make states necessary, "the dictatorship of the proletariat," engaged in a protracted – Marx might have said "permanent" – ideological struggle. Marxist political movements in recent decades have produced a name for this phenomenon: cultural revolution. The team captures the spirit of the Gramscian-Althusserian idea. In Althusser's case, the connection was almost certainly intended. Althusser and his co-thinkers represented and defended a scarcely disguised Maoist politics,[18] where Maoism was held, according to Western perceptions at the time, to privilege ideological struggle as a means for overcoming the bureaucratic shortcomings and general immobility of Soviet Communism. It was Maoism, more than any other Marxist tendency, that promoted the idea of cultural revolution.

Today, even more than Marxism itself, the idea of cultural revolution has fallen into disrepute, thanks largely to the misuse to which the idea was put. Contrary to what was once widely believed on the left, it is now clear that the Great Proletarian Cultural Revolution, launched in China in 1966 and continuing for nearly a decade, was an unmitigated disaster. Its costs in human life and well-being, and its detrimental effects on economic development and political morality, are well known. Moreover, no one can plausibly claim that the Cultural Revolution moved China closer to communism. If anything, by its negative example and to compensate for the havoc it wrought, the Cultural Revolution encouraged a turn back toward markets and private enterprise that may not end before the full restoration of capitalism in China.

Of course, underdevelopment and the unrelenting hostility of world capitalism – and, in China's case, of the Soviet Union too – were mitigating circumstances. But it is impossible to explain away the Cultural Revolution or any of the other unhappy vicissitudes of Communist experience without blaming Communism itself. Needless to say, it is wrong to identify Communism with (small-*c*) communism or to see Communism as instrumental for communism's realization. Communism is not irrelevant to communism, but neither is it as great an embarrassment as is widely believed.[19]

18 See, especially, "Contradiction and Overdetermination" and "On the Materialist Dialectic," in Althusser, *For Marx*. Althusser's Maoism was always expressed in arcane theoretical terms – partly in consequence of the pervasive obscurantism of his intellectual style, partly to avoid direct conflict with the (pro-Soviet) French Communist party to which he belonged.
19 See Chapter 9 herein.

Nevertheless, in a period in which both Communism and communism are in disrepute, in part thanks to Communism's demise, there is an evident futility in defending the idea of cultural revolution – just as there is in defending the dictatorship of the proletariat. Short of awaiting a new historical moment, then, one can only argue for what is sound in these ideas in the hope of hastening the time when a political practice will emerge in which they assume their rightful place. One can hope too that the cultural revolutions of the future – and the class dictatorships in which they occur – will have little resemblance to the institutions and practices that bore these names in the past. So long as liberal constraints remain in place, and so long as the lessons of past misfortunes are taken into account, this hope is reasonable, no matter how improbable it may nowadays appear.

As it wages a political and cultural revolution, the last state transforms its own repressive and ideological "apparatuses" by radically democratizing them. But no matter how democratized they may be, the dictatorship of the proletariat uses public coercive force and ideological authority to promote a particular and contentious conception of the good. Thus, as noted, the last state appears to contravene the liberal desideratum of political neutrality. Inasmuch as political neutrality in its own right and in light of historical experience is a defensible ideal, it is crucial, in reflecting on Marxian communism, to confront this issue – and, more generally, the compatibility of core liberal commitments with the Marxist theory of the last state.

Chapter 6

The liberal state and/versus
the last state

For nearly two centuries, "liberalism" has designated a variety of ideas and institutional arrangements, sharing at least a family resemblance and perhaps also an essential core. In advanced capitalist countries, the dominant theory and practice of politics nowadays generally are liberal. In some capitalist societies, like the United States, liberalism has been a dominant ideology from the beginning.[1] Among political philosophers and moral theorists in the English-speaking world, liberalism has never been more ascendant than it now is. Part of the explanation for this phenomenon must lie with the enormous impression made by the work of some contemporary liberal philosophers. But their influence is itself explained, in part, by the undeniable appeal of liberal tolerance. Historically, liberals have sought to ensure tolerance by arguing for principled limitations on the state's – and also society's – power over individuals' lives and behaviors.[2] In contemporary accounts, liberal philosophers have propounded the idea of neutrality with respect to "conceptions of the good." On this understanding of the

---

1 In the political cultures of some Western states, particularly in nineteenth-century Europe, "liberalism" took on more particular connotations, based upon secularism (or anticlericalism) and tolerance, and a historical connection with laissez-faire capitalism. Ironically, in twentieth-century North America (and to some degree elsewhere), the term has come to designate (slightly) left-of-center political tendencies that endorse an affirmative use of state power to address social problems, sometimes to the detriment of laissez-faire arrangements. However, secularism in public life and, of course, social tolerance are persistent themes.

2 As remarked in Chapter 5, in contrast to Rousseauean thought and indeed to the entire "classical" tradition in political philosophy, all liberalisms acknowledge a distinction between the state – and, more generally, the political arena – and an essentially apolitical "civil society." The first liberals were concerned almost exclusively with limiting the power of states. John Stuart Mill was among

core liberal idea, the state – and, more generally, society through what Mill called "the moral coercion of public opinion" – should not seek to implement particular conceptions but should only guarantee that competing views, or at least those that are in any way controversial, be treated fairly. This contention is ostensibly at odds with Marxist accounts of the last state.

I will argue that the cogency and appeal of this position depend, in part, on how "conceptions of the good" are conceived. For now, in accord with prevailing understandings, the expression can be taken to designate overarching systems of value and belief that shape individuals' "plans of life" as well as some more limited projects. Not many centuries ago it was universally assumed that a legitimate function of political power was precisely to implement conceptions of the good in this sense. Even those who insisted on delineating the respective jurisdictions of sacred and secular authorities usually thought "defense of the faith" and the enforcement of moral restrictions legitimate political functions. Nowadays, as already remarked, the contrary idea has become hegemonic. Thus most "conservatives" in developed countries are today more liberal (in historically appropriate, if somewhat antiquated, senses) than genuinely conservative. In this respect, most radicals are liberals too. Not very long ago, it seemed clear that Marxists at least were not liberals. Now, even this verity seems problematic. It is increasingly plain that most of the normative concerns of declared Marxists fall squarely within the problematic of liberal social philosophy. Perhaps what has long been the case has only recently become evident. Nevertheless, it today seems fair to conclude what would have been difficult to imagine only a few years ago: that nearly everyone is a liberal.

To be sure, liberalism has many professed critics. Some philosophers fault liberalism for failing to take proper account of the value of community,[3] for its universalism,[4] and for a host of other shortcomings. But even declared critics of liberal theory and prac-

---

the first to articulate a broader conception of liberalism's claims. Mill's break from liberalisms that concerned only relations between the individual and the state is registered in *On Liberty*, perhaps the principal liberal document of the nineteenth century.

3 See, among others, Michael J. Sandel, *Liberalism and the Limits of Justice* (Cambridge: Cambridge University Press, 1982). For a critical survey of the literature, see Amy Gutman, "Communitarian Critics of Liberalism," *Philosophy and Public Affairs*, vol. 14, no. 3 (1985), pp. 308–322.

4 See, for example, Michael Walzer, *Spheres of Justice: A Defense of Pluralism and Equality* (New York: Basic Books, 1983).

tice generally uphold the fundamental ideals implicit in liberal tolerance – neutrality in the political arena and, in civil society, the active encouragement of diversity. For all practical purposes, liberalism's critics are liberals too.

It should be stressed, as some liberal philosophers recently have, that liberal tolerance is a political value and that support for it does not entail neutrality at the level of personal morality.[5] Tolerance is a virtue of states or societies, and of individuals only insofar as they are citizens of liberal states and members of liberal societies. Thus liberals need not be moral relativists, nor need they deny that there is a conception of the good to be discovered. Neither need they be agnostic on the question of knowing what the good is. Different views about the objectivity of moral discourse are as open to liberals as to anyone else. The liberal idea is just that *states* be neutral on questions of value and that "the moral coercion of public opinion" not obstruct "experiments in living" undertaken to advance knowledge about the good or, indeed, for any reason whatsoever – provided, of course, that others are not harmed.

There is plainly merit in construing liberal tolerance as a political value. Doing so frees liberalism from dependence on contentious metaphysical claims while dissipating otherwise troubling tensions in the thought of important liberal writers. Thus John Stuart Mill, as a dedicated utilitarian, plainly believed that there was a good to be discovered and pursued. At the same time, he eschewed deployments of state power or moral coercion in civil society aimed at realizing particular conceptions of the good. There is evidently no contradiction in these positions, so long as tolerance is deemed a virtue appropriately confined to the political sphere.

However, when liberal tolerance is cast as a political value only, there is some risk of obscuring an aspect of liberal theory that is central to Mill's moral philosophy and to the thought of many other prominent liberal philosophers too. Identifying this connection and reflecting on its implications are indispensable if we are to address the tension that exists between the last state in the Marxist scheme, a state that aims at undoing the conditions for its own necessity, and the core values liberal states aim to embody.

5 Cf. John Rawls, "Justice as Fairness: Political, Not Metaphysical," *Philosophy and Public Affairs*, vol. 14, no. 3 (1985), pp. 223–251; and Charles E. Larmore, *Patterns of Moral Complexity* (Cambridge: Cambridge University Press, 1987).

Rawls suggests that liberal tolerance came into prominence in consequence of a historical compromise reached implicitly in the aftermath of the Protestant Reformation and the religious wars to which it gave rise.[6] Individuals moved by the conceptions of the good represented by Catholic and Protestant ideologies were inclined to be intolerant of competing conceptions – in part thanks to the nature of their ideals, in part thanks to the psychology of religious conviction. But intolerance had, for generations, promoted devastating warfare – to the detriment of nearly everyone. Tolerance therefore emerged – as a more or less deliberate strategy for promoting civil peace. It was a necessary evil in the face of the havoc wrought by its absence. Then the necessary evil was transformed by liberal writers around the time of the Enlightenment into a positive ideal. What was originally only a modus vivendi, grudgingly adopted, became an indispensable feature of *just* political and social arrangements.

No doubt, in broad outline, this story does account for the emergence of tolerance in recent European history. Arguably, it also provides at least part of the explanation for the fact that tolerance is today most honored, if not always faithfully practiced, in those parts of the world whose history has been most directly touched by the Reformation and the Enlightenment. However, it does not account for what we most need to understand if we are to discover the deeper affinity joining the liberal tradition – or, more precisely, a certain strain of it – with Rousseauean and Marxist political theory. It does not explain why, for at least some liberals, tolerance became a positive ideal.

To put the question more sharply: all liberals, by definition, demand *as a matter of justice* that public coercive force not be used to enforce particular (contentious) conceptions of the good. Some liberals, however, have made tolerance in this sense an aspect of their vision of *good* social and political arrangements. Thus their view of the good coincides with their theory of the right.[7] We can only

---

6 See Rawls, "Justice as Fairness." See also Robert Paul Wolff Jr., "Beyond Tolerance," in Wolff, Marcuse, and Moore, *Critique of Pure Tolerance.*

7 Individuals whose conceptions of the good are illiberal – individuals, say, who not only oppose abortion but who want to live in a world in which abortions are legally proscribed – will, of course, be frustrated in genuinely liberal polities. More generally, liberal regimes will, as a matter of right, always favor tolerance (at the political level) over intolerance. There is therefore a sense in which liberalism cannot, except on pain of incoherence, be neutral with respect to neutrality itself. In this sense, liberalism effectively favors conceptions of the good

speculate about how this fortunate situation came about; perhaps much of the causal responsibility can be vested in the well-known human propensity to make a virtue of necessity. In any case, in order to understand the nature and importance of liberal tolerance for this strain of modern liberalism – and to discern its bearing on Marxist concerns – it will be necessary to look beyond strictly political motivations for neutrality and to bring more traditional moral philosophical concerns back in.

To this end, it will be helpful to reflect on aspects of the moral and political theory of John Stuart Mill. It need hardly be said that not all modern liberal theory is Millean in the sense I will identify; it could even be argued that Mill himself was not consistently or even preponderantly Millean in this sense either. But Mill's writings stand to this day as the preeminent liberal defense of tolerance, and his arguments are most convincing if considerations of the sort I shall adduce are allowed. Strictly speaking, my contention is just that there is, in fact, a strain of Mill's thought that advances the theoretical commitments I will, for the present purpose, impute to Mill tout court. I would hazard too that focusing on this dimension of Millean theory is useful for understanding his moral and political philosophy generally, and indeed for grasping the nature of liberalism generally – but these claims are at some remove from the issue at hand, and I will not pursue them here.

I will focus in this chapter on affinities between Millean and Marxist views of human nature. I must therefore repeat that what I shall have to say about Marx's philosophical anthropology is highly selective. It is plain that a good many of Marx's express reflections on human nature and essential humanity cannot be sustained. But there nevertheless is a "rational kernel" that is both sound and consonant with the aspect of Millean liberalism I will sketch. I will argue that, despite what is widely assumed, there is no deep incompatibility between the goals Mill sought to advance through liberal tolerance and the mission Marxist political philosophy imputes to the last state. Once what is misleading and unessential is set aside, it will become clear that similar commitments underlie both notions. Indeed, there is a sense in which Millean

that accord positive value to neutrality over conceptions of the good that are inimical to neutrality. More precisely, with respect to the advocacy even of illiberal views, liberalism is, by definition, neutral; what it cannot allow is their *coercive* implementation.

and Marxist political theory, from different vantage points and with different concerns, each articulate the same core idea.

At the heart of both theories is, of course, a commitment to autonomy but also, less conspicuously though no less centrally, to human flourishing – to a natural condition of excellence that human beings, properly cultivated and nurtured, can achieve. In this latter respect, Mill and Marx are "Aristotelian." But unlike Aristotle, Mill and Marx advance an essentially historical understanding of what human flourishing involves. For both writers, the natural condition of humankind is not temporally fixed but historically variable and generally progressive. They are each, as it were, historicized Aristotelians – assessing social and political arrangements according to how well they advance an ever-developing ideal of genuine humanity. Some of the more implausible and unappealing features of liberal and Marxist normative theory, as they are usually understood, can be explained in part by the failure – even of Mill and Marx themselves – to recognize the implications of this general orientation in moral philosophy.

ROMANTICISM/CAREERISM

In this category, pride of place must be accorded two unlikely notions that have come to be considered emblematic of Marxist and liberal theory, respectively: Marx's idea that a fulfilled human life is best not identified with any particular occupation or activity but is instead irreducibly multifaceted; and the ostensibly opposed liberal notion of a "plan of life," of a life conceived as a career. The latter idea has become so deeply entrenched in liberal thought in recent years that plans of life are commonly conflated with conceptions of the good – thereby entering into the definition of liberalism according to currently influential formulations.

It requires no particularly arcane psychological theory to fault the ideal of universal, polymorphous self-realization that Marx advanced in *The German Ideology* and that arguably continued to play some role throughout his later work.[8] To be sure, the idea does have critical force. The social inequalities capitalism generates exacerbate differences between individuals. Under communism or indeed in any regime more egalitarian than those that now exist, these differences would probably be less pronounced. But regardless of the economic structure in place, "the natural lottery" would

8 Cf. Jon Elster, *Making Sense of Marx* (Cambridge: Cambridge University Press, 1985), Chapter 2.

still distribute talents differentially. And even if, contrary to fact, anybody, potentially, could do anything well, so long as time remains scarce actually doing most things well would inevitably require developing only a few capacities at the expense of others. Perhaps we could hunt in the morning, fish in the afternoon, and criticize at night. But how many of us, even under the most beneficent communism, could fill teeth in the morning, repair jet engines in the afternoon, and work on differential equations after our evening meal?

Marx went wrong in *The German Ideology* in large part thanks to the residual influence of Feuerbach and other Young Hegelian philosophers and, more generally, because he was immersed in an intellectual environment beguiled by Romantic notions of a unitary human "essence." Following Hegel and his successors, Marx, in his early writings, was tempted to suppose that All is One. It was then not too great a "dialectical" leap to conclude that one is all, that human beings can realize themselves by actualizing undifferentiated capacities virtually without constraint – or, in more practical terms, that they can fulfill themselves by doing whatever they feel inclined to do, turning from one activity to another as they please, all the while performing well enough for the tasks they undertake.

It need hardly be pointed out that this view radically underestimates the time and effort required to cultivate the capacities human beings might want to develop, even supposing that people, supplied with full and equal access to the means for cultivating capacities, become vastly more able and multifaceted than the one-track individuals we observe in societies like our own. Plainly, Marx's proposal is psychologically unrealistic. It may also be logically flawed to the extent that some self-realizing projects necessarily involve doing some things better than others can do them or better than one can do other things oneself. Nevertheless, it cannot be denied that there is something attractive in the Marxist ideal, whatever its shortcomings, in the face of the rigoristic single-mindedness of liberal writers who, in advocating neutrality with respect to plans of life, assume totalizing conceptions of the good. If the former view can be designated Romantic, the latter conception can be called Careerist because it depicts a human life as a career, structured around overarching objectives and dedicated to the realization of specifiable goals.

Needless to say, many human projects require extensive and long-range planning; and some require lifetime commitments. But it is hardly intrinsic to human endeavors that lives be conceived as careers – that there be a single lifelong project with which individuals identify and against which their success or failure in life is assessed. Even single-minded dedication to a project requiring a lifetime to fulfill is not per se Careerist, so long as the project – at its inception and throughout its duration – is undertaken and pursued in a genuinely autonomous way. It is characteristic of capitalist societies that those who are more or less free to choose their roles in the economic system come to be identified with their occupational choices and to structure their lives, including their extraeconomic projects, around their "chosen" careers. As is observed reproachfully in *The German Ideology*, under capitalism people who hunt, fish, and criticize become transformed into hunters, fishermen, and critical critics. That autonomy should be diminished in this way, despite the existence of voluntary labor markets, is a deeply ironic offense to human freedom. Insofar as Marx, like Rousseau, conceived autonomous choice as a fundamental human interest that no social practice can legitimately infringe, this insult to freedom is a basis for indicting capitalist economic systems. Perhaps Marx's shamelessly utopian account of life under communism can be excused, to some extent, as a fervent expression of this indictment.

It is fair to suggest that Careerism will appear natural only to individuals leading forms of life that are already Careerist in broad outline. Before the advent of modern capitalism, then, Careerism probably would have seemed uncongenial and perhaps even unintelligible to most people. Even today, it is likely to seem appropriate only to those whose identities are effectively tied to careers.[9] Careerism is thus as historically particular as Romanticism is. And like Marx's Romanticism, it is an integument best peeled away from the "rational kernel" it partially obstructs.

What remains after this operation is performed is, in each case, an ideal of human life fused out of two complementary commitments: to freedom in the sense of autonomy and to self-realization; to the value Rousseau expressed in his insistence that "Man is born free" and to the Aristotelian ideal of human excellence. It is because, appearance to the contrary, careers are more imposed than chosen that they offend our interest in autonomy. And it is because polymorphous development is incompatible with the

9 Cf. Susan Moller Okin, "Justice and Gender," *Philosophy and Public Affairs*, vol. 16, no. 1 (1987), pp. 42–72.

cultivation of human excellences that we cannot be quite so multifaceted as *The German Ideology* would have us be. In the end, Careerism and Romanticism conflict with human flourishing – with the fullest possible satisfaction of our fundamental interests in autonomous choice and in freely developing our innate potentialities.

Strict Aristotelianism conceives human excellence in terms congenial only to the lives of privileged individuals in the Athenian *polis* or in close approximation of that condition. For Aristotle, the life of an Athenian gentleman, dedicated to contemplative pursuits, was ideal. This picture is static and undemocratic.[10] For Marx, in contrast, history is progressive in the sense that economic systems and corresponding superstructures rise and fall to adapt to ever-increasing levels of development of productive forces, and the resulting historical transformations expand the role of the demos in public life. Liberals have less theoretically elaborated accounts of what Mill called "the permanent interests of Man as a progressive being." Nevertheless, they too construe freedom and self-realization in roughly the same way. For Marx and Mill and the broader traditions they represent, the principal objective of political life is precisely to promote human flourishing by enhancing autonomy and self-realization. This commitment could, of course, be contested. But, at least in a modern and secular culture, it is hardly controversial in the way that particular conceptions of the good are.

Even were liberal–Marxist valuational commitments more controversial or less plausible than they are, it would still be the case that, from a liberal perspective, what justifies neutrality with respect to competing conceptions of the good would not enjoin that the state be neutral with respect to these core values. In philosophical discussions, the issue is seldom if ever posed in these terms. But it is worth remarking that not even the most ardent proponent of neutrality would maintain that the liberal state has no legitimate interest in protecting the autonomy of its citizens or the conditions under which they can become what they potentially are. In fact,

---

10 In other words, the Aristotelian picture of human excellence can be faulted not just for its historical limitations but also because its realization for some, in historically pertinent circumstances, depends upon its nonrealization by others – the vast majority of slaves and free men and women whose labor is necessary to sustain a gentlemanly existence for the few. Thus the Aristotelian ideal flaunts the core liberal – indeed, *modern* – sense of justice and the notion of moral equality that underlies it.

for Mill and the strain of liberal theory he epitomizes, it is precisely the idea that the state exists to advance these values that motivates liberal tolerance. For Mill, diversity and the development of individuality are not only effects of historical development; they are one of its most powerful motors. States are justified, in part, to the extent that, by encouraging diversity, they propel history along. Thus tolerance toward particular conceptions of the good is instrumental for bringing about the most fundamental objectives Mill and Marx endorse.

This instrumental connection provides a compelling reason for supporting liberal tolerance based on a notion of the good life for human beings. It is therefore distinct from, though consistent with, justifications for tolerance based on a notion of *equal respect* for persons in a world in which individuals have different and sometimes conflicting conceptions of the good. Appeals to equal respect are tantamount to appeals to justice in a distinctively modern sense; appeals to the good life, on the other hand, have a more traditional resonance, though conceptions of the good are historically variable and, as both Mill and Marx would insist, "progressive." The modern sense of justice may indeed be shaped, as Rawls and others maintain, by the need to accommodate to diversity in the face of the fundamental conflicts that divide modern societies. But whatever its genesis, it is plainly compelling to persons with modern, egalitarian sensibilities. However, it does not suffice to explain the positive valorization of heterogeneity and ideological diversity that liberals like Mill evince. To justify enthusiastic tolerance – the *active encouragement,* not just the grudging acceptance, of differences – it is necessary to appeal, as Mill did, to a certain view of "the permanent interests of man as a progressive being." In doing so, Mill and Marx are again of one mind. If their shared position is sound, it will become plain that, appearance to the contrary, the last state, the state that aims at overcoming the conditions that make states necessary, need offend neither the underlying values tolerance aims to promote nor even, in any significant way, liberal neutrality itself. Indeed, under certain conditions – precisely the conditions radical democracy aims to foster – liberal tolerance is instrumental and perhaps even indispensable for promoting the aims of the last state. Paradoxically, but in accord with the language traditionally deployed by Marxists to designate states that deliberately undo the conditions that make states necessary, liberal tolerance is a likely feature of any well-functioning proletarian class dictatorship.

ENHANCING AUTONOMY

Autonomy is only one sense of freedom, but support for it is implicit even in a commitment to the "negative freedom" with which it is sometimes thought to contrast.[11] Ostensibly, negative freedom is exemplified in Hobbes's definition of freedom as "the absence of Externall Impediments," the forerunner of the classical liberal view;[12] Rousseauean autonomy, on the other hand, epitomizes positive freedom. However, despite what is widely believed, these ideas are related. What reason could there be to value an absence of external impediments except to advance human beings' capacities to do what they want?[13] But doing what one wants is not yet acting freely, if wants are instilled by others. Thus the value

11 The idea that prevailing notions of freedom or liberty (using these words interchangeably) are distinct and even opposed was famously advanced by Isaiah Berlin in his essay "Two Concepts of Liberty"; see *Four Essays on Liberty* (Oxford: Oxford University Press, 1969). Berlin sets out to defend negative liberty against positive liberty, an idea that ostensibly includes autonomy in the sense of Rousseau and Marx. According to Berlin, negative liberty genuinely advances human well-being, whereas positive liberty contributes to oppressive state domination and ultimately to the demise of negative liberty itself. However, the distinction Berlin draws, whatever its pertinence for intellectual history, rests on a metaphor that is easily overdrawn. Proponents of negative liberty are said to be concerned with the *area* in which individuals are free, whereas proponents of positive liberty focus on the *source* of control. But the source of control is always a concern for partisans of the liberties Berlin extols, and the area of control is an issue for even the most ardent proponents of positive freedom. What Berlin has identified, at most, are strains of modern political and social theory that emphasize different aspects of the same general concept – a point argued incisively by Gerald MacCallum in his paper "Negative and Positive Freedom," *Philosophical Review*, vol. 76 (1967), pp. 312–334. If there is any merit to Berlin's hesitations about positive freedom, it is because the strain of political theory he opposes does tend, in some of its varieties, to conflate autonomy with rational self-determination in a way that arguably does suggest "totalitarian" usurpations of freedom in the name of control of the less by the more rational. But it is incorrect to impute these views to Rousseau or Marx, though perhaps not to some of their followers. More importantly, it is hardly necessary to construe autonomy in the way Berlin does. See, for example, C. B. Macpherson, "Berlin's Division of Liberty," in *Democratic Theory: Essays in Retrieval* (Oxford: Oxford University Press, 1973), and Levine, *Liberal Democracy*, Chapter 10.
12 It is commonplace, following Hobbes's example, to suppose that we are unfree in this sense only in consequence of what other human beings do – typically, in consequence of what they do *deliberately*. Bare nature does not render us unfree.
13 See Levine, *Arguing for Socialism*, Chapter 1, for an elaboration of some of the ideas sketched in this paragraph and the next.

attached to doing what one wants supposes that one's wants are one's own choice. In short, whoever values Hobbesian freedom ought also to value autonomy as well. For liberals as much as for Rousseau or Marx, individuals are free, in the final analysis, insofar as they are the authors of their own projects.[14]

Rousseau's use of "autonomy" suggests that autonomy is something individuals either have or lack. Whether or not this was his considered opinion, it is not a sustainable position. If freedom is conceived as the ability to exercise self-governing capacities like reasoning, imagining, or planning, it plainly admits of degrees. Autonomy is therefore something of which there is more or less; not all or none. It is even unclear what it would mean for agents to be the *sole* authors of the ends they set before themselves. But autonomy can be enhanced or impeded. The degree of autonomy agents attain will be, in part, a consequence of the social order in which they live. Institutions foster the capacity for autonomous determination or thwart it and also limit the degree of autonomy an individual can be expected to achieve. The real world of autonomy is socially relative and, since societies are irreducibly historical, historically relative too.

As remarked, Mill supposed that there exists a long-range secular tendency in human history for institutions to enhance individuals' autonomy.[15] In *On Liberty*, where this idea is most evident, it is more assumed than elaborated theoretically. But it is not difficult to supply a rationale consistent with the overall commitment of *On Liberty* to the Enlightenment idea of progress in human history. With expanding technological capacities, the material conditions for expanding human beings' abilities to do what they want are, in general, advanced. Of course, it is one thing to say that a

14 Most liberals, of course, do endorse autonomy, even if they also evince support for the distinction Berlin draws between negative and positive freedom. If, as I have proposed (see note 11), Berlin's distinction is understood descriptively, as a claim about how freedom has been traditionally construed, rather than, as Berlin would have it, a claim for the existence of two distinct concepts of freedom, then the commonplace liberal view is consistent with the position I am proposing. It is not clear, however, that my position is in fact what liberals generally intend: whether, in other words, they do not somehow conceive autonomy as a value distinct from freedom or even whether they do not sometimes conflate autonomy and negative liberty.

15 Cf. Thompson, *John Stuart Mill and Representative Government*, Chapter 4. Mill's commitment to progress is particularly evident in Chapter 2 of *On Liberty*, "The Freedom of Thought and Opinion," where the overall trajectory of human history is depicted as a story of technological and moral progress.

certain degree of autonomy is materially possible and something else to maintain that this potentiality is in fact achieved in real history. Mill believed that, in the long run, the ever-advancing material conditions for freedom prevail over impediments in the way of freedom's advance. Therefore, Mill thought that, as a matter of empirical fact, human beings become ever more free. Moreover, with the growth of individuals' abilities to do what they want comes an enhancement of their capacity to conceptualize possibilities and therefore to set ends before themselves. Thus the level of autonomy feasible at particular moments in human history rises too. This broadly technological account of history's driving force is, of course, essentially the idea Marx developed into a full-fledged theory of history, historical materialism. In its classical formulations, historical materialism's focus is on the rise and fall of economic structures, not on the enhancement of freedom per se. But autonomy is central to Marx's philosophical anthropology; and it is clear that, in Marx's view, the general human interest in advancing autonomy is implicated in real-world class struggles.[16] Like Mill, Marx thought that, in the long sweep of human history, despite setbacks and reversals, autonomy is, in fact, advanced. In Marx's Hegelian moments, especially in his early writings, the progress of freedom is not construed linearly, as *On Liberty* suggests, but "dialectically." Thus, in *On the Jewish Question*,[17] the

16 For an extensive listing of corroborative citations, see Rodney G. Peffer, *Marxism, Morality, and Social Justice* (Princeton: Princeton University Press, 1990), Chapter 1. Here follow two illustrative passages, the first from *The German Ideology*, reprinted in *The Marx–Engels Reader*, ed. Robert Tucker (New York: W. W. Norton, 1972), pp. 161–162; the second from *Capital*, vol. 3 (New York: International Publishers, 1967), p. 820

"With the community of revolutionary proletarians . . . who take their conditions of existence and those of all members of society under their control . . . it is as individuals that the individuals participate in it. It is just this combination of individuals (assuming the advanced stage of modern productive forces, of course) which puts the conditions of the free development and movement of individuals under their control – conditions which were previously abandoned to chance and had won an independent existence over against the separate individuals just because of their separation as individuals, and because of the necessity of their combination which had been determined by the division of labour, and through their separation had become a bond alien to them."

"The realm of freedom actually begins only when labour which is determined by necessity and mundane considerations ceases. . . . Beyond it [the realm of necessity] begins that development of human energy which is an end in itself, the true realm of freedom, which however, can blossom forth only with the realm of necessity as its basis."

17 Marx and Engels, *Collected Works*, vol. 3.

French Revolution and its aftermath are depicted as an advance for "political liberty" but also as a cause of an intensification of un-freedom ("alienation") in the sphere of production and throughout "civil society."[18] Ultimately, however, even this "negation" works toward freedom's further realization. It helps move human-kind toward communism, "the realm of freedom," where auton-omy is so far advanced in comparison to conditions in capitalist societies that it is fair to speak of a qualitative breakthrough.

Neither Mill nor Marx directly proposed a mechanism that would account for autonomy's progress in real history. But it is plain that an explanation consonant with the overall position of both thinkers – with Mill's historicized Aristotelianism and with Marx's declared philosophical anthropology – would advert, ulti-mately, to their shared conceptions of human nature. The idea that autonomy is advanced as history proceeds is not, for either thinker, only a general hypothesis about the trajectory of historical change. It is not a "fact" that could have failed to obtain, "taking men as they are and laws as they might be." For both Mill and Marx, this outcome is necessitated by a transhistorical disposition, inscribed in human beings' mentalities, that propels them to seek to become ever more free. This idea will be further elaborated in Chapter 7. For now, it will suffice to remark that, for Mill and Marx as for Rousseau, it is a salient fact of human existence, of tremen-dous pertinence to political philosophy, that "man is born free." Rousseau, who declared this inexorable fact, doubted that human beings could ever exercise their birthright in real history; Mill and Marx thought otherwise.

SELF-REALIZATION AND THE GOOD

In just the way that claims about the value of autonomy depend, ultimately, on claims about human nature and other matters of fact, views about the character and importance of self-realiza-tion are also empirical claims. As such, they are open to dispute in light of new evidence or reinterpretation of evidence already available. In principle, therefore, substantive assertions about self-realization are necessarily provisional and tentative. Never-theless, many conclusions can already be drawn with a high de-gree of confidence.

18 I argue in support of this claim in "Alienation as Heteronomy," *Philosophical Forum*, vol. 8, nos. 2–4 (1978), pp. 256–268.

To this end, it will be helpful to distinguish spontaneous conceptions of the good from the totalizing, Careerist conceptions widely invoked by liberal philosophers. A spontaneous conception arises "spontaneously" in the way Lenin thought "trade union consciousness" did – not without reflection but mainly in consequence of individuals' lived experiences. Careerist conceptions then integrate spontaneous theories into a single, overarching view – like class consciousness does, according to Lenin. Careerism, like class consciousness, is an imposition on what arises spontaneously. But unlike class consciousness in the Leninist scheme, Careerism is not a welcome integration of spontaneous conceptions. It can, in fact, be detrimental to human freedom.

Implicitly, the cardinal virtue of liberal societies, as Mill conceived them, is precisely tolerance for divergent spontaneous conceptions of the good. In practice, spontaneous conceptions differ enormously. No doubt, inequalities in the distribution of resources and in opportunities for cultivating innate capacities account for some of this divergence. But it seems plain, even so, that to some degree people's values and judgments are irreducibly diverse and that spontaneous conceptions of the good are therefore bound generally to differ. It would be rash to conclude that they are therefore unconstrained. But they are surely not so constrained that, other things being equal, they will invariably converge.

The idea that individuals' valuations and ultimately their spontaneous conceptions of the good are bound to be (somewhat) at odds raises the question of the extent and nature of the constraints that govern judgments of value. Mill's discussion of higher and lower pleasures in *Utilitarianism* is not quite focused on this issue, but what he says about higher and lower pleasures is germane to it. We know with considerable assurance that there are, as Mill believed, qualitative differences among the things we value.[19] In clarifying how this distinction can be made, drawing on Mill's account, some purchase can be gotten on the constraints that lead spontaneous conceptions of the good to converge, while

19 In fidelity to the principles of (Bentham's) hedonistic psychology, Mill called the objects of value "pleasures." However, in the account that follows, nothing hinges on these things actually being pleasures in Bentham's sense. Following Mill's practice, "pleasure" will here be used interchangeably with "value," but without any implication that the only thing valuable or the only thing people in fact value is pleasure.

remaining irreducibly heterogeneous. A deeper understanding of this situation will help, finally, to clarify the nature and historicity of self-realization.

HIGHER AND LOWER PLEASURES

To turn from spontaneous conceptions of the good to higher and lower pleasures in Mill's sense is, if nothing else, to focus on finer-grained judgments. In order to become clear about how these judgments are (psychologically) constrained, it will help to reflect on value judgments generally.

Judgments of taste provide an instructive example. Connoisseurs of, say, wine will usually agree about the ranking of wines with respect to quality – at least in general. But within broad limits, particular judgments may vary, the variations becoming more pronounced the finer the discriminations involved. There is, in other words, a tendency toward consensus about gross differences that becomes less pronounced when finer judgments are made. At the limit, there is no disputing taste. But people with taste are generally in accord – even if disputes about "fine points" cannot always be resolved to everyone's satisfaction.

One might explain this phenomenon simply by the internalization of norms. The connoisseur would then be no better equipped than anyone else to determine what is "really" better or worse. Perhaps there is nothing really better or worse to determine. Experts would only have learned better than others what experts are supposed to say. Then judgments of taste would ultimately be arbitrary even when there is a consensus of expert opinion. The fact of consensus would only establish the success of socialization. It would not address the reality of qualitative differences.

At the other extreme, it could be held that there are real differences in merit among wines that at least some human beings, connoisseurs, are equipped to discover. The acquisition of the requisite skills undoubtedly requires training of an appropriate sort. Connoisseurs are more made than born. But, properly trained, connoisseurs detect differences of quality. They do not prescribe them. Then disagreements about wines among connoisseurs would most likely arise in consequence of the uneven development of their evaluative skills. Unless there are real indeterminacies in the world of wine, equally developed connoisseurs should be in complete accord.

It will be helpful, at this point, once again to invoke an Aristotelian idea by proposing, as it were, a "golden mean" between these views of connoisseurship. For an Aristotelian, there are "objective" standards of judgment, but standards have to do both with how the world is and with the nature of human beings. In just the way that there is a natural standard for, say, an iris – that is, roughly, what an iris would become under ideal (or nearly ideal) conditions – there is, an Aristotelian would say, a standard of taste in wines that an ideally cultivated connoisseur would develop. Insofar as the faculty of taste (in wine) is roughly the same throughout the human population, judgments about wines among human beings, properly cultivated, should be roughly similar. Not all irises cultivated under ideal conditions will in fact look alike. Similarly, in all likelihood, not all judgments of taste will converge even in principle. Beings of the same natural kind in their natural conditions need not be similar in all important respects. The degree of variation will vary from kind to kind. But, among human evaluators, there will be enough similarity to undergird a recognizable and objective standard of taste. Therefore judgments of taste are not arbitrary on this view; they are determined both by the properties of the things judged and by human nature itself. How constraining human nature is must, of course, remain an open question. But it is fair to speculate at least with respect to wine connoisseurship that it will limit evaluations severely, and therefore that the area of convergence among individuals with full access to the means for cultivating their capacities will be considerable.

If, as seems likely, fine-grained value judgments would sometimes fail to converge completely even when people are provided with equal and sufficient access to the means for cultivating their evaluative capacities, this fact would not fully explain why people differ in what they choose to do. Differences in people's choices simply do not depend sufficiently on differences in judgments of value. Many of the difficulties philosophers encounter in thinking through the ramifications of the distinction between higher and lower pleasures arise because, following Mill, they assume an overly facile way of linking evaluative judgments with choices. The underdevelopment of an individual's intellectual and aesthetic capacities can explain a preference for pushpin over poetry, for one of Mill's lower over one of his higher pleasures; and so can weakness of will. But for a cultivated person, weakness of will is seldom the best explanation. In ways that remain largely unexplored in moral psychology, judgments of value do affect our desires and therefore our preferences and what we choose to do. But desire is not, and ought not to be, the slave of value judgments. Arguably, if objects of desire could be sorted out into natural kinds, then, when an individual desires something of a certain kind, it would be irrational to prefer what one judges to be worse. But there do not appear to be many natural-kind divisions among objects of desire, at least if they are specified in a fine-trained way. An individual may, at time *t*, judge wine A better than wine B but nevertheless prefer to drink B at *t*. Doing so would hardly warrant a charge of irrationality. It is unlikely that this assessment would change if A and B were grouped together under some finer category – whether or not the categorical determination somehow indicates a real division among wines. Perhaps the finer the categories are drawn, the less likely it becomes that a cultivated person would prefer something judged inferior. But this is an idle speculation awaiting a more careful investigation of the relation among judgment, desire, preference, and choice. For now, I would only suggest that there is no good reason in general to censure those who, knowing better, drink inferior wine or play pushpin when they could be reading poetry. Mill's writings sometimes reflect this high-minded attitude. Contemporary liberalism exemplifies it. But there is also the liberalism of *On Liberty*, which advocates tolerance and *laissez-vivre* not just because justice requires it but because the active encouragement of diversity is instrumental for each individual's learning what is required for his or her own flourishing.

It is fair to speculate that the range of variation for individuals' (freely chosen) projects and, more generally, for their judgments about the kinds of lives they want to lead will be greater than for judgments of taste. There is surely no "right way" for everyone to live, and probably no "right way" even for any particular individual to conduct his or her life. Any of a range of public or private pursuits and active or contemplative projects – and any of a variety of mixtures of these elements – will probably "satisfice" for self-realization. In the nature of the case, there is no point in looking for an optimal mix, even if some sense could be attached to the idea. In view of human differences and the contingencies of life, the only way to advance, as best one can and in the face of substantial indeterminacies, is through trial and error; in short, through practical experimentation.

EXPERIMENTALISM

The exploratory probes and tests of spontaneous conceptions of the good promoted by Mill in *On Liberty* and elsewhere are indispensable sources of insight for promoting human flourishing. What can now be concluded tentatively about higher and lower pleasures is based on such experiments and on extrapolations from the data acquired through them. Of course, judgments made today must also be based on informed speculation about what we would learn from experiments conducted under more favorable conditions, where the means for cultivating innate but historically developing human capacities are widely – and, in the ideal case, equally – distributed. It is pointless to try to say what experimentation in such conditions might reveal.

We can, however, speculate with some assurance that there will be considerable convergence of opinion on general matters, just as there is now convergence on gross judgments about wines among connoisseurs, and similarly significant variations of judgment on points of "detail." We will probably be able to make progress in distinguishing pleasures (and whatever else is of value) qualitatively, and we may be able to develop a sounder philosophical theory of the good and a better and more comprehensive moral psychology than we now have. Most in point, I would venture that the Careerism dear to contemporary liberals would eventually drop out of fashion. For whenever an entire life or a significant part of a life is viewed as a career, a long-range project that structures preferences and choices, practical experimentation is needlessly constrained. Of course, an overarching plan of life is not necessarily detrimental to the spirit of experimentation. A single career, if freely (autonomously) undertaken, can be as worthwhile, from an experimentalist standpoint, as projects of shorter duration. But when institutional structures themselves encourage single-mindedness, many of the constraints that liberals oppose when supported by the state or the moral coercions of public opinion are effectively reimposed internally. Career*ism* is a kind of intolerance in its own right, *intra*personal intolerance, resulting in the self-regulated discouragement of the diversity experimentation promotes.

It would be well therefore for liberals to resist the idea that there need be one thing that is necessarily and permanently one's own and to revert back to that side of Millean liberalism that actively promotes experimentation. Insofar as Mill's thought is representative, there is nothing essential to liberalism that under-writes an aversion to hunting in the morning, fishing in the after-noon, and criticizing at night – or, more plausibly, to the idea that one should try many things but not identify one's self with any of them in particular. This picture, in its Romantic elaborations, is transparently at odds with what we know of human psychology and the requirements of self-realization. Human flourishing will elude the dilettantes Marx depicts, just as it will elude individuals who unreflectively constrain themselves by pursuing plans of life. In a word, a dearth of high-mindedness is as wrong-headed as a surfeit. The point, in proper Aristotelian fashion, is to find the mean. If it is the right to hold that Careerism is not essential to liberal tolerance – indeed, that it is opposed to the spirit of liberal experimentation – then that is an indication of where the mean lies.

In any case, the objective, for both Mill and Marx and the os-tensibly opposing traditions they represent, is to promote human flourishing. What is to be done to this end is ultimately an empir-ical question that is better addressed experimentally than a priori. What can be concluded now is that it is well to cast impedances to experimentation aside, and that the Careerism that has become emblematic of liberalism today – like the Romanticism that afflicts Marx's speculations on communism – is an impedance of just this kind.

THE LIBERAL STATE AND THE LAST STATE

The standard view today is that equal respect for persons man-dates neutrality at the political level. I have just attributed to Mill a somewhat different justification for political neutrality that ap-peals to its role in promoting autonomy and self-realization and, more generally, to human flourishing in determinate historical conditions. Both rationales suffice to justify liberal tolerance. Both are compatible, ultimately, with Marxist views. But the rationale that appeals to equal respect, more than the appeal to autonomy and self-realization, is in evident tension with the Marxist idea of the last state. For that state is a "dictatorship" in which the work-ing class and its allies, the vast majority, deploy state power to suppress capitalism and its vestiges and therefore also those con-ceptions of the good for which capitalism and its vestiges are in-tegral. For Marxists, equal respect is a feature of ideal social arrangements. But its implementation in class-divided societies is premature and even dangerous. It becomes apt only after class divisions and therefore class dictatorships are superseded.

This conclusion is sound and important, but it is also misleading because it exaggerates the sense in which a proletarian class dictatorship must be illiberal. To see why, it is well to reflect again on the Millean rationale for tolerance, and on the hasty and unwarranted optimism evident in traditional Marxist formulations.

For Mill, neutrality in the political arena is justified because it promotes autonomy and self-realization. But these effects are contingent and, by Mill's account, historically variable. Were the facts of the matter different, as Mill believed they had been throughout most of human history and as they still were throughout much of the world, the implications for liberal tolerance would differ accordingly. Thus Mill expressly denies that tolerance, say, of speech is appropriate in societies in which institutions do not (yet) sufficiently cultivate individuals' capacities to allow them to function as competent consumers in the marketplace of ideas, in short, in most human societies. Neutrality, then, is not a matter of right, as in arguments based on equal respect, but a means for advancing "the permanent interests of man as a progressive being" under particular historical conditions. From this perspective, it follows that the Marxist complaint that universality in class-divided societies is a sham and a mechanism for reproducing class domination is more compatible with Mill's case for tolerance than first appears. If Marx was right, before communism, a state of "the whole people" is a dangerous illusion, and it may sometimes be justifiable to counteract the dangers of this illusion by acting in contravention of what strict universality requires. But it does not follow from this conviction that, this side of communism, tolerance must be systematically withheld or restricted or selectively applied. What follows is that "What is to be done?" is always an open question, to be addressed by considering the implications of alternative proposals on "the permanent interests of man as a progressive being." If there is a disagreement between Mill and Marx, it has to do with their respective views of what the evidence shows or is likely to show with respect to this question.

It is only because their empirical speculations differ that, in the final analysis, the liberal state on Mill's construal differs from the last state of Marxist theory. The liberal state institutionalizes immunities from state and societal interferences; the last state, like the state defended in *The Social Contract*, relies on transformative democracy to achieve a similar effect.[20] Ultimately, this difference follows from empirical speculations based on different views of human nature and therefore of human beings' potentialities.

In all its variants, liberalism is pessimistic about human beings' prospects for radically altering their forms of political association. The "permanent interests of man as a progressive being" can be advanced indefinitely and, in consequence, humankind can progress morally. But men and women will never advance qualitatively beyond their present condition in a way that would render states unnecessary. Human nature, though improvable, remains recalcitrant to "the great leaps forward" Marxists envision. Hence liberal safeguards, to save us from ourselves and from each other, are in order not just now and for the foreseeable future but forever. If these safeguards conflict with democratic values, then democracy must give way or be transformed beyond recognition. This was effectively Mill's view in *Considerations on Representative Government*, even as he marshaled what amounts to a brief in support of participatory democracy. The permanent interests of man as a progressive being sometimes support a fusion of democratic and liberal institutions, but wherever the one opposes the other, as they are bound to do, the trade-off is struck in liberalism's favor.

In contrast, the strain of Marxist theory that envisions a last state is democratic to a fault. Its faith in the transformative power of democratic institutions underwrites the conviction that something approximating the "state" Rousseau described in *The Social Contract* can be established on earth, "taking men as they are and laws as they might be," if only, *pace* Rousseau, *private property in alienable means of production is abolished*. I have already suggested that this view is not so much wrong-headed as naive; that it underestimates, at great cost to human well-being, the difficulties in the

---

20 Cf. Levine, *The Politics of Autonomy*, Chapter 2, for a discussion of Rousseau's attempt to realize liberal values without recourse to liberal institutional arrangements. It should be noted, however, that, no matter how successful transformative democracy may be in ensuring the outcomes that liberals seek to achieve "constitutionally," the state Rousseau envisions would remain illiberal – in content as well as in form – because it assumes a direct and unmediated relation between the individual and "the whole community," and because it construes group interests as *private* interests. Rousseau's de jure state would therefore proscribe rights of association, at least insofar as associations can be expected to lead to the establishment of groups – and group interests – that mediate between the individual and the state, infirming the *generality* of each individual's will.

way of transforming human nature. In consequence, and in contrast to the received understanding but not the spirit of Rousseauean and Marxist political theory, the last state should be liberal and should remain liberal – for as long as need be. Paradoxically, liberalism is indispensable for the dictatorship of the proletariat, the state in transition to communism. It is only after that state has succeeded in its mission, by undoing the conditions that make it necessary, that it is safe to allow liberal safeguards to wither away completely.

But if it is necessary to retain and even enhance liberal protections in order to prevent dictatorships of the proletariat from devolving into tyrannies, it is also necessary to retain a sense of what distinguishes the last state from the liberal state, in order to keep the former true to its mission. The last state must proscribe the *implementation* of conceptions of the good detrimental to the transition to communism. To this end, it may sometimes need to deny their advocacy too. In this respect, it is potentially illiberal from the start. But so is the state Mill proposes. If it is to reproduce the protections it accords its citizens, the liberal state must prevent the implementation of conceptions of the good that undermine political neutrality. Therefore it too may be obliged, when circumstances require, to proscribe the advocacy of views that can be expected to have this effect. A thoroughgoing liberalism is possible only in states whose institutions are secure enough to withstand unflinching tolerance. In less propitious conditions, the liberal state may have no choice but to save itself by illiberal means. If it is not to lose its soul, it must, of course, act in a measured way and err on the side of tolerance. But it cannot allow its liberalism to be its own undoing.[21]

In short, proponents of autonomy and self-realization cannot allow these aims to be subverted. This rationale for illiberal departures from liberal norms applies equally to the proscriptions the last state enforces. If it is true that communism carries the promotion of autonomy and self-realization to the limit of what is humanly possible, and if the Marxist account of the prehistory of communism is sound, then the use of state power to prevent the

21 Similarly, Rousseau maintained that, in the face of dire emergencies, the de jure state may find it necessary to suspend its usual institutional apparatus and install "dictators" to rule by decree; see *The Social Contract*, Book IV, Chapter 6. Rousseau's account draws on Macchiavelli's discussion of the dictatorship in ancient Rome in *The Discourses*, Book I, Chapter 34. I discuss Rousseau's view of emergency government in *The End of the State*, pp. 53–57.

restoration of capitalism is as justified as its use by a liberal state to prevent the imposition of, say, an intolerant religious orthodoxy. In other words, there are no principled, theoretical differences between the liberal state and the last state in this respect. At most, there are differing assessments of the likely consequences of different social practices.

So long as it is *securely* on track, the last state need be no less tolerant than the liberal state of the *advocacy* of views inimical to its existence or opposed to its historical tendency. But, in practice, the last state must, of course, proscribe capitalist social relations, a prospect Millean liberals can hardly endorse. In this sense, a genuine proletarian class dictatorship is indeed less tolerant than liberal states. But it is so in virtue of what its proponents suppose about the possible futures of existing and feasible social and political arrangements. I would therefore suggest that it is misleading to describe the differences between the last state and the liberal state in terms of a lesser or greater commitment to political neutrality. It is more apt to conclude that what distinguishes Millean from Marxian politics is the fact that, unlike Mill, Marx was committed to a theory of history that foresaw communism as a historical possibility and radical democracy under socialist conditions as the means for bringing it about. Having no commitment to communism and therefore no plan for its realization, Mill could, as it were, proscribe less and still remain faithful to the justificatory program he effectively shares with Marx. In short, Mill had no reason to propose that liberals not tolerate practical experiments incompatible with socialism and radical democracy; Marx did. Mill's state is therefore less restrictive than Marx's. But the two states are equally responsive to the exigencies that make neutrality desirable and in that sense equally neutral.

Which ideal is more appealing? Some purchase on this question and on related themes can be gained by reflecting more directly on the connection between liberalism and Marxism, or rather the Rousseauean strain of Marxism that envisions statelessness under communism.

Chapter 7

Rousseauean Marxism and/versus liberalism

Marxist theory is based in large part on the writings Karl Marx produced from the early 1840s until his death in 1883. But Marx*ism* did not become a discernible tendency until around the time of the Paris Commune (1871) and was not a fully consolidated current within the workers' movement until after Marx's death. In contrast, the origins of modern liberalism can be traced back at least to pleas for religious toleration occasioned by the Protestant Reformation and to theories of limited government that arose almost concurrently with the nation-state itself. By the mid-eighteenth century, more than a hundred years before Marxism's classical period, liberalism was a self-conscious intellectual and political tendency.

It is therefore only within the past century that Marxism and liberalism have stood as ostensibly rival positions. However, it might appear misleading to describe them as opposed, for throughout the past hundred years most Marxists have maintained that Marxism spurns the very idea of normative theory. If Marxists have principled reasons for assuming this posture, then, strictly speaking, there would be no Marxist normative theory to rival liberal claims. But at the same time that Marxists have disavowed normative theory in general – and moral discourse in particular – they have also evinced an inclination, evident in Marx's own writings and in the work of nearly all Marxists after him, to render moral judgments. They have also insisted that normative discourse is ideological and therefore "superstructural," constrained, though not strictly determined, by the "economic base" of the societies that produce and reproduce it. Throughout Marxism's history, it has remained fatally unclear how constraining the economic base is supposed to be. But it is compatible with even the strictest (plausible) construal that existing (capitalist) economic structures can be faulted by appealing to the normative standards they support. This position, like Marxists' penchant for moral condemnation of existing social, political, and economic arrangements, is perhaps consistent with the claim that Marxism has no normative theory. But it is plainly in tension with it.[1] We can therefore conclude that, whether or not Marx*ism* includes a normative theory, Marx*ists* have always taken a normative stance. It is widely assumed that their stance, insofar as it is distinctively Marxist, is at odds with views advanced by liberal social philosophers.

In the Second International and then under the aegis of official Communism, when orthodox historical materialism held sway, it could be safely concluded that normative discourse was, at best, an appendix to Marxist theory. For historical materialist orthodoxy predicted capitalism's demise and communism's triumph. Normative arguments might be useful for encouraging class actors to assume their historical destinies. They could hasten humanity's future. But, in the end, they could not alter the outcome of a class struggle driven by inexorable *material interests*, not moral considerations.

Needless to say, this conviction has lapsed as support has waned for the orthodox account of the inevitability of capitalism's demise and communism's triumph. First, Western Marxists[2] distanced themselves implicitly from historical materialist orthodoxy in large part because of its claims for historical inevitability and the devaluation of human agency that this claim was thought to

1 For accounts of Marx's view(s) of morality, see, among others, Lukes, *Marxism and Morality*; Richard Miller, *Analyzing Marx: Morality, Power, and History* (Princeton: Princeton University Press, 1984), pp. 15–97; and G. A. Cohen, "Review of *Karl Marx* by Allen W. Wood," *Mind*, vol. 92 (1983).
2 I use the term "Western Marxism" in the widely accepted sense made current by Merleau-Ponty and Perry Anderson. See Maurice Merleau-Ponty, *The Adventures of the Dialectic*, trans. Joseph Bien (Evanston, Ill.: Northwestern University Press, 1973), pp. 30–58; and Perry Anderson, *Considerations on Western Marxism* (London: NLB, 1976). Roughly, the term denotes that current of theorizing that runs through the work of Georg Lukács, Karl Korsch, Antonio Gramsci, the "critical theorists" of the Frankfurt School (Adorno, Horkheimer, Marcuse, et al.), existentialist Marxists (Sartre, Merleau-Ponty), structuralist Marxists (Althusser, Balibar), and so on. Politically, Western Marxism is oppositional with respect to the official Marxism of the Soviet Union and the Western European Communist parties – though, in some cases, only implicitly. Philosophically, Western Marxism is shaped in varying ways by "continental" philosophical currents – neo-Hegelianism, above all – and tends to focus programmatically on grand reconstructions of Marxian philosophy.

imply.[3] More recently, analytical Marxists have identified internal shortcomings of the orthodox theory.[4] In consequence, for anyone who shares Marx's political objectives, normative issues have come to take on a political urgency absent from classical Marxism.

Historically, liberalism – as a theory of principled limitations on the use of public, coercive force – has served to defend and even justify (capitalist) property relations and (capitalist) markets. As an evolving political current, it has therefore usually opposed Marxist political aspirations. However, liberals have long evinced a commitment to *equality* in at least some sense of that deeply contested term. By the time of the Enlightenment, if not before, liberal theorists were committed in theory – if not always in practice – not just to the idea that, in the respects that matter fundamentally from a normative point of view, "all men are created equal"[5] but also to the conviction that the moral equality of persons entails that they be treated equally by basic political and social institutions.[6] In

3 This inference can, however, be resisted. Cf. G. A. Cohen, "Historical Inevitability and Revolutionary Agency," in *History, Labour, and Freedom*, pp. 51–82. Nevertheless, for virtually all Western Marxists except the Althusserians, historical materialism – insofar as it proclaimed the inevitability of socialism and communism – was at fault for diminishing the role of human agents in epochal social transformations. The Althusserians were second to none in discounting the role of human agency. For them, historical materialism's flaw was its "evolutionism" – by which they seem to have meant its claim to have identified an endogenous dynamic internal to social structures. Thus, unlike most Western Marxists, what Althusserians opposed in historical materialism actually is central to the theory.
4 See Cohen, *History, Labour, and Freedom*, Chapters 6–9. For an extended discussion of orthodox historical materialism and some reasons to be wary of its explanatory pretensions, see Wright, Levine, and Sober, *Reconstructing Marxism*, Chapters 2–5.
5 Liberals have sometimes encouraged and seldom actively discouraged societal norms that relegated the laboring poor, women, and native peoples to an inferior standing. Also, liberals once were remarkably sanguine about the institution of slavery and, later, about institutionalized racism. Contemporary liberals are less blatantly hypocritical, but it can hardly be denied that a gulf between the theory and practice of existing liberal states persists to this day.
6 The (fundamental) moral equality of persons does not strictly entail equal treatment. Thus the medial church held all human beings equal "in the mind of God" – that is, with respect to the possibilities for salvation or damnation or other statuses deemed to matter fundamentally. But this conviction was never thought to entail that individuals be treated equally by social and political institutions.

practice, equal treatment was usually understood to imply only political equality – equality before the law, equality in rendering collective choices, in short, equality of citizenship. It was this idea that Marx inveighed against so vehemently as he moved "beyond" his own earlier liberal convictions.[7] However, Marx's objection was not to political equality per se but to the idea that it is sufficient for treating persons as equals. Today, political equality is almost everywhere endorsed. To be sure, inequalities of citizenship persist. But hardly anyone is so *reactionary* as to defend them in principle.

Most liberals are also committed to equality of opportunity. But the consensus around this idea is more deeply contested than the consensus around political equality: Everyone is *for* equality of opportunity, but what equality of opportunity *is* is very much a matter of dispute. At one extreme, some "right-wing" defenders of the idea maintain that equality of opportunity is achieved when legal and customary impedances are removed against individuals competing on a meritocratic basis for scarce and widely desired benefits. On this understanding, equality of opportunity is tantamount to political equality.[8] At the other, "left-wing" extreme, are those who think that to attain equal opportunity individuals must be provided with equal resources. On this understanding, equality of opportunity is more or less tantamount to resource equality.[9] Intermediate positions too can be imagined. But inasmuch as the right-wing view has come to seem increasingly hollow under real-

7 See, especially, *On the Jewish Question* (1843), in Marx and Engels, *Collected Works*, vol. 3. Marx argued that "political emancipation," establishing political equality, actually exacerbates inequalities in "civil society" – thereby enhancing overall human unfreedom.

8 In practice, many on the right oppose state interventions in support of equality of opportunity (for instance, state monitoring of private firms' employment policies and state remedies against discrimination) more vehemently and more openly than they oppose similar remedies employed to redress violations of ordinary citizenship rights. Typically, efficiency considerations are invoked in support of proscribing state interventions in the economic sphere, considerations that would be deemed inappropriate in the political arena. In this sense, equality of opportunity, construed in the right-wing way, is not quite equivalent to political equality.

9 On some analyses, for instance Ronald Dworkin's, resource equality entails that there be (ongoing) compensation for the (morally arbitrary) unequal distribution of talents across individuals. Then resource equality would differ from even the most left-wing construal of (meritocratic) equality of opportunity. See Ronald Dworkin, "What is Equality? Part Two: Equality of Resources," *Philosophy and Public Affairs*, vol. 19, no. 4 (1981), pp. 283–345, but cf. esp. pp. 310–311.

world conditions, liberal opinion has tended to converge toward the left-wing pole.[10]

It has also become characteristic of liberal political culture in recent years to acknowledge a presumption in favor of full material equality, albeit a presumption that is easily overridden.[11] Thus it is widely thought that, other things being equal, benefits and burdens should be equally distributed. But, of course, other things are seldom equal. In general, two kinds of considerations typically swamp the presumption for equal distribution: those that are internal to a theory of justice broadly construed, and those that are not. In the former category lie property rights and other "entitlements" and also merit, desert, effort, productive contribution, and any other substantive considerations that liberal writers might invoke to defend the justice of unequal distributions. Inasmuch as the boundaries distinguishing justice from other normative standards can be vague, it is not always clear what would count as an external reason for overcoming the presumption for equal distribution. Efficiency demands, on some construals, are good candidates;[12] perhaps freedom is too.[13]

In any case, it is plain that liberalism has evolved a strain that is unabashedly egalitarian, and therefore in tension with the liberal tradition's long-standing support for capitalism and hostility to radical politics. Needless to say, egalitarian liberalism is more

10 Cf. Rawls, *A Theory of Justice*, pp. 75–90; an earlier, still classic formulation of this position is given by Bernard Williams in "The Idea of Equality," in *Philosophy, Politics, Society*, 2nd series (New York: Barnes and Noble, 1962).
11 Cf. Rawls, *A Theory of Justice*, pp. 100–108. The Difference Principle, according to which inequalities are justified if and only if they work to the advantage of a "representative member of the least well-off group," illustrates this presumption perspicuously. It is, of course, controversial what full *material* equality means. Rawls's account is expressly *resourcist*. His concern is with the distribution of certain resources – those that are instrumental for the realization of particular conceptions of the good likely to be entertained in actual societies. Rawls calls these resources "primary goods"; they include income and wealth, powers and offices, and the bases for self-respect. The "basic liberties" are also primary goods, but, for reasons that need not detain us here, Rawls would have them distributed equally and to the greatest extent possible.
12 Cf. Arthur M. Okun, *Equality and Efficiency: The Big Trade-off* (Washington, D.C.: Brookings Institution, 1975). But see Julian Le Grand, "Equity versus Efficiency: The Elusive Trade-off," *Ethics*, vol. 100 (1990), pp. 554–568.
13 Strictly speaking, what freedom may offend are views of justice according to which a just distribution is one that conforms to – or approximates – a certain structure. Cf. Robert Nozick, *Anarchy, State, and Utopia* (New York: Basic Books, 1974), esp. pp. 160–164.

theoretical than practical. Few, if any, liberals are expressly *anti*capitalist, and even the most radically egalitarian liberal visions assume continuity with existing political and social arrangements. But, as a social philosophy, liberalism has developed in ways that render it more compatible with political positions traditionally held by radical egalitarians and Marxists than was previously believed.

Thus (some) liberals have moved closer to Marxists politically, just as (some) Marxists have become more engaged with liberal philosophical concerns. Given their respective histories, it is not surprising that the emerging liberal–Marxist "dialogue," on its philosophical side, has unfolded mostly in a context familiar from liberal political and moral philosophy. In consequence, the old issue about Marxist normative theory – whether it exists at all – has given way to a new problem: whether it can still be maintained that Marxism and liberalism are at all opposed. Marxism may not eschew normative theory in the way that Marxists used to claim, but it has lately become doubtful whether in the domain of normative theory anything distinctively Marxist actually exists – except perhaps as a wrinkle, among others, in a universe of discourse shaped by liberal concerns.

As remarked in Chapter 6, Marxists differ from liberals in their views about the nature of society and the structure and direction of historical change. Thus Marxists envision a possible communist future that liberalism implicitly denies. Nevertheless, liberalism or at least the version of it articulated by Mill is nearly of one mind with the strain of Marxist political theory that underwrites claims for the end of the state. But the two are not entirely in accord. Marxism bases its case for statelessness partly on faith in the transformative powers of genuinely democratic participation, a faith Mill does not fully share. We have seen how this difference has important consequences for political theory. It is the burden of this chapter to show that it also indicates an important *underlying* difference at the level of moral theory – a difference having to do with conceptions of the person and ultimately with autonomy itself.

WHAT DO LIBERALS WANT?

Since its inception, liberalism in political philosophy has been defended alternately by appeal to utilitarian, contractarian, or rights-based moral philosophical arguments or some mixture of these positions. Each kind of argument takes individuals' interests, conceived atomistically, as its point of departure. But each treats these interests differently. Utilitarians suppose that individuals' interests are properly served when well-being is maximized.[14] If an individual's well-being is well defined and representable quantitatively, such that it can be meaningfully added to the representations of other individuals' well-beings, then the utilitarian seeks to maximize the logical sum of these magnitudes. Social and political arrangements are justified, on this view, to the extent that they maximize this quantity.[15] Contractarians treat individuals' interests in a more complex way. In their view, social and political arrangements properly serve individuals' interests if and only if, in suitably characterized situations, rational individuals – aware of their own interests and capable of adapting means to ends – would choose them freely.[16] Usually, the choice is made from a state of nature or, to use Rawls's more apt expression, an "original position."[17] To imagine an original position is, as Rawls would have it, to discover an "Archimedian point" – neither so richly characterized as to bias the outcome of individuals' choices nor so impoverished as to render determinate choices impossible. The existence of such a vantage point is an indispensable – and disputable – condition for the deployment of this argumentative

14 Utility measures well-being. Insofar as utility functions can be constructed intrapersonally – and then made interpersonally comparable – the point of utilitarian calculations is to realize as much utility as possible in a given circumstance. As remarked in Chapter 6, Mill's principle of utility – with its focus on human flourishing – stands somewhat apart from the mainstream utilitarian tradition.

15 Historically, utilitarians have sought to maximize *aggregate* utility. Some utilitarians today favor maximizing *average* utility. The distinction can be of some moment, especially for debates on population policy. A very large number of people with very low levels of well-being might have greater aggregate utility than a smaller population with higher levels of well-being. But in the smaller population the average level of utility would be higher. Cf. J. J. C. Smart and Bernard Williams, *Utilitarianism: For and Against* (Cambridge: Cambridge University Press, 1973); and Parfit, *Reasons and Persons*, Chapters 17–19.

16 Cf. Russell Grice, *The Grounds of Moral Judgment* (Cambridge: Cambridge University Press, 1967), and T. M. Scanlon, "Contractualism and Utilitarianism," in Amartya Sen and Bernard Williams (eds.), *Utilitarianism and Beyond* (Cambridge: Cambridge University Press, 1982).

17 Cf. Rawls, *A Theory of Justice*, pp. 260–263. On differences between Rawls's "original position" and Rousseau's account of the state of nature, see Chapter 2 herein.

strategy.[18] Rights-based theories, finally, consider certain interests – those that rights claims express – to take precedence over all other considerations. Social and political arrangements are justified, for rights-based theorists, if and only if they accommodate to these antecedently acknowledged claims.

These argument types, though analytically distinct, are sometimes jointed together. Thus one might hold, as many rights theorists do, that utilitarian calculations ought indeed to govern public policy debates, except where rights considerations interfere. Then rights take precedence over utilitarian calculations, trumping what the principle of utility instructs.[19] Or one might argue, as Locke did in *The Second Treatise of Government*, that the state is founded by a social contract but that the nature and extent of the contract that founds the state are limited by the rights individuals antecedently hold in the state of nature. Each of these mixed positions should be distinguished from arguments that assign rights *in consequence of* utilitarian or contractarian principles.[20] Virtually all modern political philosophies ascribe rights to individuals in order to specify what they may or may not do, or what may or may not be done to them. However, in genuine rights-based theories or theories that fuse rights-based considerations with considerations of other kinds, rights are fundamental. They are part of the primitive moral landscape, not consequences of principles that are yet more basic.

Again, these arguments share the conviction that the individual, conceived atomistically, is a point of departure for thinking about social and political arrangements normatively. The atomic individual is also a point of departure in *The Second Discourse* and in the

18 Marx, for one, can be taken to deny its existence. On this issue, see Michael Teitelman, "The Limits of Individualism," *Journal of Philosophy*, vol 69 (1972), pp. 545–556.
19 Therefore what is rightful can diverge from what is good. Thus rights theorists who are also utilitarians could hold that distributions that maximize utility are required by their notions of the good but that it would be wrong to implement this good by means that violate rights. Imagine, for example, a rights theorist like Robert Nozick in *Anarchy, State, and Utopia*, who holds that (idealized) capitalist markets generate distributions in which everyone has a right to his or her distributive share. This (imaginary) Nozickian might also be a utilitarian who would have resources distributed in accord with the principle of utility. If this good could not be achieved except by violating (property) rights – say, by state-organized redistribution of market-generated distributions – then the good would have to give way, as it were, to the right.
20 Cf. Russell Hardin, *Morality within the Limits of Reason* (Chicago: University of Chicago Press, 1988).

opening pages of *The Social Contract*. But in the state Rousseau's social contract founds, the atomic individual, moved by a private will, gives way to the citizen, directed by a general will. For citizens, the atomistic metaphor is therefore inappropriate. The difference is particularly salient when the Rousseauean model of general will deliberation is contrasted with the deliberations utilitarians envision.

Both Rousseauean and utilitarian deliberations contrast with ordinary ways of understanding political processes. In the mainstream political culture, legislation is conceived as a way to combine the competing private interests of individuals and groups.[21] In the state of nature, according to Rousseau's story, at the point that culminates in the establishment of political communities, these interests are mortally opposed. But in settled political communities there is an overriding interest, on the part of nearly all individuals and groups, in maintaining the political community itself. There is therefore a common interest in supporting a framework within which everyone can compete. But within this overriding consensus, individuals and groups are typically at odds. Thus the legislative process is like bargaining. Usually, all sides in a negotiation have an interest in striking a bargain, but within that consensus everyone is in competition with everyone else. As such, there is no fact of the matter about where a bargain should be struck. The "right answer" is just whatever the parties agree upon. The outcome will be *fair* if all interests are represented and the bargaining reflects the relative strengths of the contending sides, but it cannot be right or wrong. In short, *justice* can be served in bargaining, but not *truth*. Insofar as legislation is conceived in this way, it can be more or less fair. But since there is no fact of the matter to discover, voting can never determine what we ought to do independently of what we decide.

For Rousseau, on the other hand, voting in the assembly of the people is precisely a way to discover a matter of fact – what the general interest is. It is not a way to combine private interests, even within a general consensus favoring maintaining the political community above all.[22] Thus voting is more like a debate among

21 What follows concerns *voting*. If political representation (or delegation) is unavoidable and if, as suggested in Chapter 5, representatives (or delegates) might better be chosen at random rather than by elections, then the selection of representatives (or delegates) would, of course, fall outside the scope of the ensuing discussion.

22 Cf. Levine, *The Politics of Autonomy*, pp. 59–72.

"disinterested" experts than like bargaining among self-interested economic agents. It is a truth-discovery procedure. Rousseauean voters are not asked whether they prefer that a particular law be enacted but "whether or not it conforms to the general will that is theirs. Each man, in giving his vote, states his opinion on the matter, and the declaration of the general will is drawn from the counting of the votes."[23]

For utilitarians, the aim is to maximize aggregate (or average) utility, where the utilitarian maximum is the logical sum of individuals' utilities. Therefore utilitarian individuals, when they deliberate about what they ought to do, express their opinion about what the principle of utility requires. But although Rousseauean and utilitarian deliberations each aim at discovering a matter of fact, the question utilitarians ask themselves is not the same as the question asked of citizens in a de jure state. For the utilitarian maximum is the logical sum of individuals' utilities. In this sense, it is reducible or decomposable into the utilities of the individuals who constitute the political community. The general interest, however, is *irreducible* to the (private) interests of the individuals who constitute the state. Each individual, in entering into the social contract, becomes an *indivisible* part of a "moral and collective body." When an individual makes the general will his own, he is not concerned with what is best for some aggregation of (atomic) individuals that includes himself but with what is best for himself *qua* citizen and subject of a "moral and collective body" of which he is an "indivisible" part.

Imagine, again, a voter confronting a piece of legislation concerning highway construction: It must be decided, say, whether two cities should be linked by a new highway and, if so, where the road should be built. On the mainstream view, the voters will have preferences for the alternatives in contention and will register these preferences by their votes. If all (relevant) preferences are counted and the voting is fair, the outcome will be just in the sense that its content will reflect the distribution of preferences within the voting community. For a utilitarian, on the other hand, there is one outcome (or set of outcomes) that, if realized, would maximize social utility, the logical sum of individuals' utilities. It is this outcome that voting aims to discover.[24] On this view, there is a right

23 *The Social Contract*, Book IV, Chapter 2.
24 If there is reason to believe that a good way – or perhaps the only way – to "discover" the utilitarian maximum is for individuals to make their own private maximizing choices, in disregard of their views about other individuals'

answer to the question "What ought we to do with respect to this highway?" But the answer is right in virtue of the nature of individuals' utility functions, not in virtue of any mind-independent facts of the matter. For Rousseau, in contrast, there is a right answer to this question that is mind-independent in principle.[25] There is, in other words, an outcome that is best for "the moral and collective body" individuals constitute; and these individuals could in principle fail to discover that outcome, even when their preferences are fully informed and adequately considered.

But is there, in fact, a right answer? Can we reasonably conclude, say, that it is in the general interest that the highway be built and that it be built through these fields rather than those? And, if so, is it desirable that private interests be excluded from a decision of this kind? I think that the answer to both of these questions is no. There is no reason in general why there must be a general interest on all questions and, still less, on all aspects of all questions or why, when a general interest does exist, it alone should determine what we ought to do. Especially where there are indeterminacies, there is no alternative, given Rousseau's exhaustive and mutually exclusive account of individuals' interests, but to accede to private will determinations. Nevertheless, on many questions that could arise in the popular assemblies, there may be a general interest that bears on aspects of the issues in contention. In other words, there is reason to suppose that *in some cases* these questions can be answered affirmatively.

Rousseau appears to hold that there always is a general interest and that it bears on all matters of legislation. But on this matter, as in so many others, he is equivocal. Thus it is suggested in *The Social Contract* that legislative assemblies should meet infrequently (though periodically) and that most questions of social policy –

utility payoffs, then there will be no *practical* difference between utilitarian voting and mainstream voting. Economists since Adam Smith have held a similar view with respect to markets. For them, the unintended consequence of individual maximizing choices in idealized market arrangements is socially optimal (i.e., Pareto-optimal, taking preferences, production technologies, and the prevailing distribution of resources as given), and there is no other way reliably to achieve this result. Thus they recommend reliance on the "invisible hand" of the market and fault economic agents who might be disposed to seek socially optimal outcomes by aiming for them directly.

25 Of course, there is likely to be a *causal* connection between what individuals want – or what they would want in ideal circumstances – and what is best for "the whole community" they constitute. There is, however, no *logical* connection.

perhaps including questions about highway construction and the like – would be relegated to the magistrates who execute the (popular) sovereign's will, rather than to the sovereign people themselves.[26] Perhaps even Rousseau can therefore be enlisted in support of the idea that the general will does not bear on all matters of collective choice and in support of the inference that follows from this position: that private volition cannot be eliminated entirely from the administration of the de jure state. This conclusion is plainly compatible with the assignment of an indispensable role for general will coordination. But Rousseau is only slightly helpful in ascertaining what this role might be. I would venture that, in order to advance beyond his vague and equivocal suggestions, we need to think more carefully about historically feasible approximations of Rousseau's ideal; in short, we need to think more about communism and the role of general will deliberations in communist societies. This issue will be resumed in Chapter 8.

What can be concluded at this point is that, by *introducing* the idea of general will deliberations into political philosophy, Rousseau poured new wine into the old atomic individualist bottle.[27] In *The Social Contract*, the individual, conceived atomistically, is and is not the fundamental constituent of the de jure state. On the one hand, the social contract is in the private interest of individuals with independent and antagonistic wills insofar as they aim to become the autonomous agents they potentially are. In this way, the de jure state is constituted by the wills of (atomic) individuals. On the other hand, the condition for realizing autonomy is membership in "a moral and collective body" in which individuals will the same end, the general interest, and are therefore directed by a single will, the general will. When these conditions pertain, individuals relate to one another internally; they are no longer atomic individuals but integral parts of "a common self" (*un moi commun*).[28] Then their interests can no longer even be conceived apart from the interests of the other individuals who compose this

---

26 See, for example, *The Social Contract*, Book III, Chapter 13.
27 This is not the only example of Rousseau's penchant for representing new thoughts in old, inherited forms. Even the social contract itself is not, strictly, a contract at all, for it is not an agreement among independently existing parties but, as Rousseau acknowledges (in Book I, Chapter 7, of *The Social Contract*), an agreement each individual "makes, so to speak, with himself." See Levine, *The Politics of Autonomy*, Chapter 1.
28 *The Social Contract*, Book I, Chapter 6.

"self." Thus Rousseau articulated two quite distinct conceptions at the same time – or rather weaved very different visions together into a single story. In proffering an atomistic account of the genesis of political associations, he intimated a nonatomistic picture of the social order and of the state that superintends it.

According to this picture, individuals and their interests are still fundamental. But individuals are not atomic individuals, and their interests are not conceived atomistically. This conception is foreign to utilitarianism, contractarianism, and rights theories. In brief, the general will – and the kind of person a general will directs – falls outside the conceptual horizons of the moral philosophies that undergird liberal political philosophy. In this crucial respect, liberalism and Rousseauean political philosophy part ways. Therefore, if I am right in insisting that Marxian communism is an essentially Rousseauean idea, liberalism and Marxism part ways too.

AUTONOMY

Both liberals and Rousseauean Marxists accord *autonomy* pride of place. But, in consequence of the difference just identified, liberal autonomy is not quite the same as Rousseauean-Marxist autonomy. The dissimilarity is easily overlooked, in part because liberal and Marxist conceptions have so much in common.[29] But it is real and can be made evident by focusing, again, on general will coordination.

It is sometimes said that liberals are partisans of "negative" liberty only; that the freedom liberals value is just the absence of coercive restraint. On this view, individuals are free to the extent that there exists an area in which they are able to do as they want without the deliberate interference of others. No doubt, liberal writers characteristically do emphasize this aspect of freedom, sometimes to the detriment of more "positive" conceptions that focus on the *source* of control. But, as argued in Chapter 6, it is unclear what the point of negative liberty is, except insofar as the absence of coercive restraints helps agents to *do* what they want. Thus even the most austerely negative conception of freedom suggests a more

29 Cf. Levine, *Arguing for Socialism*, Chapter 2. What follows corrects a misleading impression conveyed by the account I gave there of autonomy as a value about which procapitalists and prosocialists (including Marxists) agree.

positive view: that agents are free to the extent that they are able (so far as institutional arrangements affect their abilities) to do as they please. But then even more positive conceptions suggest themselves. The freedom to do as one pleases would hardly seem worth having if one's ends were instilled by others. Indeed, why should one value the ability to do as one desires except insofar as one values situations in which individuals are also the authors of their own ends? Thus a commitment to negative liberty, conceived as an absence of political and social interferences in the pursuit of one's ends, leads inexorably to a notion of *autonomy*, understood as the ability, again so far as this ability is socially conditioned, to set (achievable) ends before oneself. Despite what may sometimes appear, there is therefore no tension between liberals' characteristic focus on negative liberty and the recognition, on the part of most liberals, that autonomy is a fundamental value. The rationale for negative liberty, far from opposing autonomy, actually supports the latter conception.

Liberal autonomy admits of degrees. Since the ends individuals will are conditioned by causal determinations, there are perhaps no entirely free (autonomous) acts. But individuals' choices can be more or less autonomous; therefore social and political arrangements can be assessed according to how well they enhance or diminish autonomy in this sense.

The autonomy liberals invoke is the autonomy that makes negative liberty worth having. This autonomy bears the mark of its atomic individualist origins. For partisans of negative liberty, it is individuals, conceived atomistically, who are free if unrestrained socially in the pursuit of their ends. Similarly, for partisans of autonomy in the liberal sense, it is individuals, still conceived atomistically, who set ends before themselves. On this view, there is no internal relation between one individual's ends and another's and therefore no reason, coincidence apart, why individuals, as autonomous agents, should not find themselves at odds.

However, for Rousseau, since autonomy is maintained only if the citizen-subjects of a de jure state will the same thing, the general interest, autonomous agents cannot be at odds. Kant appropriated this idea of Rousseau's political philosophy and developed it into the doctrine that rationality itself establishes a strong consensus on ends, a "harmony of rational wills."[30] For Kant, reason does rule on the content of our ends – not directly but by proscrib-

---

30 Cf. Levine, *The Politics of Autonomy*, Chapters 1 and 2.

ing certain ends as un-universalizable or, what comes to the same thing, incompatible with respect for moral personality as an end-in-itself.[31] These proscriptions are stringent enough to preclude (antagonistic) oppositions. Thus practical reason by itself coordinates individuals' wills. To the degree that reason controls individuals' willing, individuals become part of a coherent, harmonious system. "The war of all against all," a consequence of unreason or rather of reason deformed and rendered *private*, gives way to an order constituted by reason itself.

It is this idea that liberal opponents of positive freedom find menacing. If freedom is identified with *rational* self-determination, with direction by a "rational self," it justifies control of the less rational masses by their more rational leaders. At the limit, rational self-determination underwrites "totalitarian" usurpations of freedom for the sake of freedom itself.[32] When the state or the party presents itself as the privileged oracle of reason or the agent of a destiny reason requires, it establishes a claim to control the fate of others in order to make them free.

This is not the place to rebut this *mis*understanding of Rousseau's and Kant's idea.[33] I would only register the observation that there are many, eminently avoidable steps on the way from a harmony of rational wills to totalitarian usurpations of freedom for freedom's sake and remark that the impetus for finding philosophical origins for totalitarian politics seems to have been driven more by Cold War preoccupations than by analytical exigencies. In any case, it is not necessary to defend the side of Rousseau's thought that Kant seized upon here because the aspect of general will coordination that is needed for defending communism as a normative ideal does not rely on a distinctively Kantian notion of rational agency. It is instead the non-(atomic)individualist side of Rousseau's position that matters for our purpose – specifically, Rousseau's conception of autonomy's social dimension.

31 Cf. Kant, *The Foundations for the Metaphysics of Morals*, Part 2.
32 Berlin, "Two Concepts of Liberty," comes perilously close to advancing this view. It is more commonly associated with Jacob Talmon in *The Rise of Totalitarian Democracy* (Boston: Beacon, 1952) and, of course, with Karl R. Popper in *The Open Society and Its Enemies*, 2 vols. (Princeton: Princeton University Press, 1962).
33 Some elements of a rebuttal can be found in Levine, *The Politics of Autonomy*, pp. 72–80, and *Liberal Democracy*, Chapter 10, and in an ancestor of that chapter, "The Political Theory of Social Democracy," *Canadian Journal of Philosophy*, vol. 6, no. 2 (1976). The relation between the position in question and Cold War preoccupations is addressed directly in that article.

HARMONY

A master's ability to set ends before himself owes in part to the labor performed by his slaves. Slaves relieve masters from burdensome toil, provide them with means for realizing their ends, and, most important, permit them to will ends that they could not feasibly entertain and might not even imagine were they bereft of these instruments of their will. At the same time, because they are slaves, the autonomy of these autonomy-enhancing agents is diminished. Of course, liberals abhor slavery. Egalitarian liberals even insist that basic rights and liberties be distributed equally (and to the greatest extent possible).[34] But equal distribution of basic rights and liberties is compatible with resource inequalities and inequalities of powers and offices that affect autonomy causally. In principle, therefore, one individual can become more autonomous and another less so as an unintended consequence of inequalities that even egalitarian liberals allow. This is not a conclusion liberals typically acknowledge. But it is an implication of the individualistic view of autonomy that they hold.

Should a liberal seek to deny that someone's autonomy might be enhanced in consequence of the diminution of someone else's, it could only be for reasons unconnected to autonomy itself. It *could* be that the world always or generally is such that, as Marx said of communism, "the condition for the free development of each" is "the free development of all." But it would be incumbent on those proposing this claim to show why it is so here and now. Their burden would be to identify mechanisms capable of ensuring that the enhancement of one individual's autonomy cannot or generally will not diminish anyone else's. It does not seem likely that such mechanisms exist. It is more likely, as in the case of the master and slave, that the autonomy of some individuals will sometimes be enhanced at the expense of the autonomy of others.

In any case, so long as individuals are conceived atomistically, as independent centers of volition, there can be no *intrinsic* reason why autonomous wills should be in harmony – unless, as Kant maintained, autonomous willing itself somehow guarantees harmonious outcomes. But there is little comfort for liberals in the Kantian conception, despite its individualism, because liberals es-

34 For Rawls's account of basic rights and liberties, see *A Theory of Justice*, passim, but esp. Chapter 4.

chew substantive notions of rational agency. For liberals, following Hobbes, reason rules not on the content of our ends but only on their consistency and appropriateness for the *extra*rational ends we seek to bring about. In consequence, no matter how autonomous individuals may become, their wills remain radically independent of one another's. Pending the discovery of extravolitional mechanisms capable of ensuring harmonious interactions among such utterly distinct beings, it will always remain possible – and even likely – that individuals' wills will be opposed. Then the condition for the free development of each will generally not be the free development of all. Liberals would surely want to deny this eventuality. But they lack principled reasons for doing so.

Autonomy is perhaps as fundamental a value for liberals as for Rousseau, and liberal egalitarians may be as committed as Marxists, perhaps more so, to advancing the autonomy of *everyone*.[35] But if the world is bereft of mechanisms for ensuring equal respect for the autonomy of all moral agents and if practical reason is too "thin" to secure a harmonious outcome, radically independent individuals cannot in general be counted on to enhance their own autonomy *in harmony with other rational agents*. Liberals find the (social) world insufficiently mutable to seek harmony by transforming it, and they are averse to thinking of practical reason as more than instrumental. They are also committed atomic individualists. Rousseauean Marxists differ from liberals on each of these counts. In Chapter 8, we will see how *qua* Marxists they envision a world in which there is indeed reason to think that individuals will mutually support each other's autonomy. But *qua* Rousseaueans they also have resources for *socializing* (liberal) autonomy. We have seen that one possibility, following Kant's example, would be to place the burden for doing so on (practical) reason itself. However, as remarked, this strategy, whatever its merits, raises a number of vexing questions that defenders of communism need not confront. This is why I have instead pursued a different strand of Rousseau's account of the general will and proposed, throughout these pages,

35 Marxists *are* committed to enhancing the autonomy of everyone under communism. But, as we have seen, the state Marxists envision as an indispensable means for arriving at communism is, like all preceding states, a *class* dictatorship. It may therefore allow and sometimes actually encourage the domination of the old ruling classes and also the economically dominant classes under socialism – to the detriment of the autonomy of the individuals who constitute these groups.

that we relinquish atomic individualism and the exclusive support for private volition that it sustains. There is, however, an objection to this strategy that must be addressed before we turn to communism itself.

Individuals directed by a general will, who privilege the interests of the "moral and collective bodies" of which they are indivisible parts over their own "private" interests, could be faulted for neglecting "the cartes they owe themselves" and also the cares they owe each other for the sake of "the whole community." For the interests of the whole community could sometimes require the diminution of the autonomy of some individuals, oneself or others, in violation of the "equal respect" that is everyone's due. Unless this possibility can be discounted, equal respect for the autonomy of others would seem ill served by general will coordination as by private willing.

But this conclusion is mistaken. To see why, it will be instructive, once again, to contrast Rousseau's position with utilitarianism or, more precisely, with welfarist versions of utilitarianism. Were individuals' interests only welfare interests and were these interests measurable, as utilitarians believe, then the interests of the whole community would be the largest possible sum of individuals' utilities. Schematically, if U_s, social utility, represents the welfare of the whole society and U_1, U_2, . . . , U_n represent the welfares of individuals 1, 2, . . . , n, respectively,

$$U_s = U_1 + U_2 + \ldots + U_n.$$

Circumstances might then be such that in order to increase the utilities of some individuals and thereby to maximize the value of U_s, it is necessary to lower the welfares of others. Critics of utilitarianism have long made much of this possibility. They have faulted utilitarianism for failing to treat individuals' interests correctly. According to their critics, utilitarians regard individuals' welfares – and therefore individuals too – only as means for maximizing social utility, U_s, not as intrinsically valuable in themselves. Those who would fault general will coordination for failing to respect the autonomy of each associate assume that general will coordination is like utilitarianism in this respect; that its concern for the interest of "the whole community" is at odds with respect for persons as ends in themselves.

But the individuals Rousseau envisions aim to maximize autonomy, not welfare. Does this difference cut against the claim that

Rousseauean political philosophy fails to accord individuals proper respect? I think it does – if autonomy is understood in the way that Rousseauean Marxists intend. There are two reasons why this is so: The first has to do with the nature of the community autonomous agents form; the second with its historical trajectory. The first reason, developed by Kant, follows from Rousseau's account of the social contract; since it is implicit in what has already been discussed, it can be briefly resumed. The second is a distinctively Marxist innovation that I shall only note here and develop in Chapter 8. Both suggest a notion of community genuinely at odds with liberal positions.

COMMUNITY

As remarked, Kant's notion of moral community was intended, in part, to draw out the moral philosophical implications of "the whole community" constituted by Rousseau's social contract. To this end, Kant deployed an account of practical reason richer than the instrumentalist conception liberals assume. But Rousseau's view and relevant aspects of Kant's elaboration of it can be reconstructed without directly engaging issues about rational agency. The core idea, identified by Kant, is that autonomy is *essentially social* because it can only be realized through interaction with others in a "community" of equals, a moral community.

This claim is implicit in the idea that human beings, "born free but everywhere in chains," only *become* the autonomous agents they potentially are in consequence of a social contract that establishes full equality of citizenship. Generalizing this idea, Kant maintained that individuals are equal *qua* moral agents precisely because they are (potentially) autonomous and that autonomy is therefore a necessary and sufficient condition for membership in the community of moral agents. But, at the same time, individuals cannot become autonomous outside the moral community. For what it is to stand outside this community – in a "state of nature" – is just to act in a way that fails to respect moral personality in oneself and others. It is to fail to respect the autonomy that renders everyone, including oneself, a (potentially) moral agent. Therefore the autonomy of our fellow human beings is indispensable for what matters supremely to each of us, and the enhancement of their autonomy, being necessary for the sustenance and development of the moral community that is our own first concern, must matter to us, just as our own autonomy does. For a flourishing moral community is a condition for the enhancement of each individual's autonomy. It is what we all supremely value.[36]

The ability to set ends before oneself is a universal human capacity. But the nature and limits of autonomy vary with levels of material and moral development. Very generally, with increasing material development, the horizons for autonomous choice expand. Marx's theory of history makes material development the fundamental structuring principle of human history. We have seen that Mill also assumed a tendency for continuous material progress, even if he did not have an elaborated theory of it, and that he maintained, more directly than Marx, that moral progress accompanies the growth of productive forces. It was suggested in Chapter 6 that this idea is congenial to Marx's theory of history as well. It is therefore fair to say, for Marx too, that moral progress consists in the enhancement of human autonomy, and that material progress is instrumental for its advance.

Does historical materialism provide special reason for thinking that moral progress involves the progressive *socialization* of (liberal) autonomy? This is not a question that Marx directly addresses. Nevertheless, historical materialism is relevant to it. Marx depicts a history of class struggles culminating in a proletarian class dictatorship and finally in classlessness under communism. Historical materialism describes, in short, the demise of class divisions, the very obstacle that, in Marx's view, made Rousseau's de jure state a utopian fantasy. Only when economic forces no longer draw people apart, according to Marx, can people finally treat each other as ends in themselves. At that point, real citizenship in a state truly based on Right (*Recht*) becomes possible. The moral

---

36 Readers who find the Kantian tone of these reflections off-putting may be persuaded by the more prosaic, Humean idea that, in a direct confrontation between moral agents and individuals pursuing their own self-interests, moral agents would not survive. In a word, they would be losers in a Prisoner's Dilemma game in which they "cooperate" while their opponents "defect." It follows from this consideration that those who value moral agency for themselves ought also to value it in others and ought therefore to do whatever is necessary to help moral agency survive and flourish. If we add to this conclusion the idea that morality supposes individual autonomy and then regard the collection of moral agents as a moral community, we have a good approximation of Kant's position. Cf. David Hume, *An Enquiry Concerning the Principles of Morals*, section 3, Part 1, p. 1987, in L. A. Selby-Bigge (ed.) *Enquiries Concerning Human Understanding and Concerning the Principles of Morals*, 3rd ed. (Oxford: Oxford University Press, 1975). The Prisoner's Dilemma is discussed in Chapter 2 herein.

community Rousseau envisioned and Kant described is then transformed from an ideological snare and delusion to a genuine human opportunity.

In short, the Marxist theory of history suggests that, at the end
of the trajectory it describes, communities can exist in which "the
condition for the free development of each" is indeed "the free development of all." How defensible is this view? This is not the
place, once again, to subject historical materialism itself to critical
scrutiny.[37] But it is apt to reflect on the plausibility of the (possible)
end of the process it depicts. It is therefore time finally to reflect
directly on communism and the conditions under which whole
communities can exemplify "the exercise of the general will."

37 Cf. Wright, Levine, and Sober, *Reconstructing Marxism*, Chapters 2–5.

Chapter 8

Communism

Marx was famously loath to provide "recipes to the cookshops of the future,"[1] and Marxists after him have generally followed his counsel. Of course all Marxists would agree that under communism class divisions will be overcome and the historical materialist dynamic will have finally run its course. But beyond these very general implications of Marx's theory of history, the Marxist corpus has little to say about the nature of communist societies. However, caution in the face of an unpredictable future has not always prevented Marxists from depicting communism in ways that today seem blatantly utopian. Revealingly, these descriptions are usually cast negatively; thus we are told that communism is a society *without* commodity production, *without* alienation, and, of course, *without* a state. Marxists have suggested too that at the end of the historical materialist trajectory lies a society beyond scarcity and therefore beyond justice. Marxists have also proposed that communist societies are populated by men and women of a radically different kind from those found in class societies, genuinely "social" human beings. Some of these characterizations are exaggerated, others flawed. But even were they entirely on target, they would provide, at most, only vague intimations of what a communist society might be like. In any case, despite their vagueness, there are few today, including dedicated Marxists, who would not find them misleading. If nothing else, in their exuberant optimism, they are too much at odds with that skepticism about human perfectibility that has come to pervade our intellectual culture. This skepticism is exemplified perspicuously by mainstream liberalism, the hegemonic political theory today.

1 Karl Marx, *Capital*, vol. 1, trans. Moore and Aveling (Moscow: Foreign Language Publishing House, 1959), Afterword, p. 17.

Marxists have generally paid scant attention to the affinities linking communism with the state Rousseau envisioned in *The Social Contract*. With few exceptions, Rousseau scholars have been similarly reluctant to join Rousseau with Marx.[2] However, in *The End of the State*, I argued that Marxian communism accords pride of place to the model of rational cooperation Rousseau imputed to the de jure state and that distinctively Marxist views about history and politics provide good, if inconclusive, reasons for thinking this ideal practicable. I maintained, in addition, that, despite Rousseau's deeply paradoxical and equivocal formulations, the de jure state is not strictly a state at all but an internally coordinated "republic of ends." So too, therefore, is Marxian communism. If these claims are on track, it follows that, in its political dimensions, communism is precisely what traditional formulations have claimed: a society without a state. It is so in just the way that the "state" of *The Social Contract* is.

It is time to elaborate on this contention and to investigate some of its implications. I shall begin by focusing on two claims sometimes made about communism – that it is a society *beyond* scarcity, and that it is populated by distinctively *social* individuals. A clearer understanding of these issues will help to clarify further the Rousseauean-Marxist idea of autonomy and the notion of personal responsibility it suggests. From that perspective, it will be feasible to broach questions about the nature and role of justice under communism. By pursuing this line of inquiry, a purchase on communism emerges that renders the idea normatively appealing and that shields it from charges of incoherence or utopianism.

BEYOND SCARCITY?

Distributive justice is morally compelling whenever *fairness* is of concern to those to whom benefits or burdens are distributed. A society *beyond* justice is therefore one in which fairness is of little or no concern. One way for fairness not to matter, for individuals who are disposed to care only (or mainly) about their own distributive shares, is in conditions of abundance. When air is abundant, as it normally is, it does not matter how it is distributed. In this

---

2 Conspicuous among the exceptions are Galvanno Della Volpe and Lucio Colletti. See for example, Della Volpe's *Rousseau and Marx*, trans. John Fraser (London: Lawrence and Wishart, 1978); and Colletti's *From Rousseau to Lenin: Studies in Ideology and Society*, trans. John Merrington and Judith White (London: New Left Books, 1972).

sense, even our society is "beyond justice" with respect to the distribution of air. When it is claimed that communist societies are "beyond justice," what is evidently meant is that, under communism, most of the things people want will be relevantly like air now is. Then scarcity would not be a fact of the human condition, and the fairness of distributions would not be a concern. In a world of abundance, justice would be of no normative significance.

The idea that communist societies will have overcome scarcity is suggested by Marx's theory of history. In the historical materialist scheme, modes of production rise and fall in order to accommodate to ever-increasing levels of development of productive forces. This movement is propelled, ultimately, by transhistorical aspects of human nature. As remarked, in Marx's view, human beings seek to realize themselves, to become what they (potentially) are, through productive activity. But scarcity frustrates this impulse. History is then propelled by an interest in removing this frustration, in making the world human beings confront more hospitable to the self-realization they seek. In a world of scarcity, an interest in self-realization is tantamount to an interest in developing productive forces. As scarcity gives way to abundance, this universal human interest is increasingly transformed into an interest in removing specifically human obstacles in the way of self-realization. Thus late capitalism is unstable not because it thwarts the expansion of productive capacities but because its way of developing productive forces is detrimental to this fundamental human concern.[3] The end of the historical materialist trajectory is reached precisely when scarcity no longer propels this movement and when an economic structure, communism in its "higher phases," is in place – permitting, to the greatest degree possible, the realization of that universal human interest that scarcity had previously thwarted.

3 See G. A. Cohen, *Karl Marx's Theory of History: A Defense* (Oxford: Oxford University Press, 1978), pp. 302–307. Cohen's account of historical materialism differs from more traditional formulations. In the standard view, capitalism is destined to "break down" in consequence of an endogenous tendency for the rate of profit to decline in capitalist economies. As this tendency works its course, investment possibilities dwindle and the economy, if capitalism has not already been overthrown, grinds to a halt. On this understanding, capitalism is doomed in just the way precapitalist economic structures are – because it is bound eventually to "fetter" the development of productive forces. In contrast, Cohen's account of "the distinctive contradiction of late capitalism" does not imply an inevitable capitalist breakdown, nor does it endorse the orthodox Marxist political economic analysis from which this prediction follows.

The core intuition underlying this rationale has been elaborated by philosophers in the liberal tradition for more than two hundred years. In consequence, the so-called circumstances of justice, the conditions under which the requirements of justice are morally compelling, are now widely understood.[4] They involve both a "subjective" and an "objective" side. The subjective component, the idea that individuals are generally self-interested, will be discussed in the next section. Objectively, justice matters whenever cooperative interactions are both possible and necessary for individuals concerned to maximize their own distributive shares. In conditions of *absolute* scarcity, where cooperation will not expand the supply of goods to be distributed and interactions therefore have a zero-sum character, awarding a benefit to one individual necessarily deprives another of it, so that there is no advantage to anyone in interacting cooperatively. Thus two individuals on a lifeboat with only enough water to assure the survival of one have nothing to gain from cooperation. These individuals have no stake in a *fair* distribution of the water; justice is not a (private) interest of theirs.[5] Were (nearly) everything absolutely scarce, like water on this lifeboat, the requirements of justice would pale in (normative) importance. A society of this kind would be, as it were, *beneath* justice, in contrast to a world of abundance which would be *beyond* it. In short, justice matters when most of the things people want are *relatively* scarce. But relative scarcity is not the only fact about the world that renders justice morally urgent. In addition, individuals must be sufficiently equal in natural endowments for cooperation to be mutually advantageous, and they must find themselves in circumstances where, in consequence of geographical proximity, they are obliged to interact.[6]

4 On "the circumstances of justice," see, among others, Hume, *A Treatise of Human Nature*, Book III, Part 2, Chapter 2, and *An Enquiry Concerning the Principles of Morals*, section 3, Part 1; H. L. A. Hart, *The Concept of Law* (Oxford: Clarendon Press, 1961), pp. 189–195; J. R. Lucas, *The Principles of Politics* (Oxford: Clarendon Press, 1966), pp. 1–10; and Rawls, *A Theory of Justice*.

5 Nevertheless, individuals whose sensibilities have been formed in the circumstances of justice, finding themselves on a lifeboat with only enough water for one, might feel that a good way to decide who gets the (absolutely) scarce water might be through some *fair* procedure – say, by drawing lots.

6 There is an evident connection between the circumstances of justice and traditional contractarian accounts of the state of nature. Thus relative equality in the distribution of natural endowments – in conjunction with geographical proximity – helps to explain why, in Hobbes's view, individuals in a state of nature are vulnerable to mortal assault from one another, a fact which helps explain, in turn, why the state of nature is, for Hobbes, a "war of all against all."

Of these circumstances, relative scarcity is surely the most alterable. Despite Rousseau's account of the early state of nature, it is implausible to think that human beings could ever live without coming into contact with one other. It is even less likely that individuals will ever become so unequal in natural endowments that persons with private wills would cease to find it in their interests to cooperate. Certainly Marxist theory offers no reason to imagine these eventualities, nor do any other theoretical traditions upon which defenders of communism might draw. But Marx's theory of history does seem to provide a reason for predicting the eventual elimination of scarcity as a fact of the human condition.

Strictly speaking, what historical materialism envisions is an economic surplus so massive that class struggles over it and ultimately class divisions themselves will expire for want of a sufficient reason. But, for its more orthodox adherents, historical materialism has, by force of suggestion, if not strict implication, underwritten an almost unlimited faith in the beneficent consequences of developing productive capacities. Perhaps at no time was this faith more evident than in the period when Stalinist orthodoxy held sway among Communist militants and their sympathizers among the intelligentsia of Western and Third World countries. It was this ideology that underwrote the Stalinists' subordination of all aspects of the revolutionary project, including the transformation of production relations, to the development of productive forces. It was this ideology too that helps explain the long-standing disregard of the norms of political morality that afflicted the Soviet polity for decades. The unhappy consequences of this political orientation are a matter of historical record: the brutal collectivization of agriculture; the imposition of a hierarchical structure and "productivist" ideology in the manufacturing sector; a selective, technocratic, and authoritarian educational system; a severe centralization of political power; and most damaging of all, an indefinite prolongation of police terror and the inexorable growth of bureaucratic domination. Today, of course, Stalinism is in total disrepute. But the idea that there can be a society *beyond justice* is partly a residue of this abandoned faith or, more precisely, of its one-sided exaggeration of historical materialist positions.

In any case, if the understanding of communism as a society beyond justice must be revised or abandoned, it should be on its merits, not to avoid guilt by association with Stalinist enthusiasms. There is surely much to fault in the received view. Nevertheless, the idea is not nearly so wrong-headed as may appear. So long as some goods, like being ranked first in an ordering, are "positional" such that not everyone who wants them can have them; so long as others will in fact remain scarce no matter how overwhelmingly developed productive capacities become; and so long as individuals' lifetimes remain finite so that time must always be budgeted and some desires are bound to go unfulfilled, scarcity will remain a fact of human life. But relative scarcity *can* cease to structure and direct human life in the way it heretofore has. The conviction that the requirements of justice diminish in moral importance as productive forces expand is eminently defensible, even if scarcity cannot be "overcome" entirely and altogether. Thus talk of a society beyond scarcity and, for that reason, beyond justice is misleading, but the intuition that motivates it is basically sound.

BEYOND SELF-INTEREST?

Another way that Marxists have envisioned moving beyond justice is by maintaining that, in the higher phases of communism, individuals will have "transcended" self-interested motivation. An example of this genre of theorizing is provided by the early Soviet legal scholar Pashukanis.[7] In contrast to a bourgeois order composed of individuals with wills in conflict, he envisioned "the social person of the future, who submerges his ego in the collective and finds the greatest satisfaction and meaning of life in this act." Employing the expression of Feuerbach and other Young Hegelians including Marx, Pashukanis foresaw "the development of higher forms of humanity as the transformation of man into a species-being."[8] If "species-being" is identified with membership in a "moral and collective body," Pashukanis might seem to be echoing Rousseau. But there is a more likely way to understand what Pashukanis and others like him had in mind. On this construal, under communism, individuals are altruists rather than egoists. Self-interest is not so much "transcended" as replaced by its opposite. Since this understanding challenges neither the received view of rational agency nor the reigning metaphor of

7 See E. B. Pashukanis, *Law and Marxism: A General Theory* (1924), trans. Barbara Einhorn, ed. Chris Arthur (London: Ink Links, 1978). See also Lukes, *Marxism and Morality*, pp. 35–36.
8 Pashukanis, *Law and Marxism*, pp. 159–160.

the atomic individual, it translates easily into the familiar liberal framework. Communism is a society "beyond" justice because one of the (subjective) circumstances of justice, self-interest, fails to pertain.

Liberals may find this position implausible, but they can hardly fault its intelligibility. We have seen how the Hobbesian–liberal account of rational agency is distinct from Hobbesian and liberal predictions about individuals' interests. Therefore those who identify rational agency with utility maximization have no grounds for insisting that individuals maximize utility by seeking to advance their own well-being.[9] Altruism is as rational as egoism is. Altruism is as individualist as egoism is too. Egoists are concerned with their own well-being conceived atomistically. Altruists are concerned with the well-being of one or more other atomic individuals. In each case, it is only the welfare interests of atomic individuals that matter.

In Chapter 2, I suggested that Hobbes's account of the state of nature provides an uncompromising picture of atomic individuals with interests of this sort. Moved by a fear of one another ("diffidence"), an unceasing desire to accumulate ("competition"), and a yearning to dominate others and stand high in their esteem ("vainglory"), each individual's utility function is utterly self-regarding. We also saw how, starting from very different assumptions, Rousseau arrived at a similar understanding of the motivations of his contemporaries and, we may extrapolate, our own. In his view, after the introduction of private property, the mentality Hobbes thought universal emerges. If he was right, rational egoism need not be the destiny of rational human beings;

9 However, on this view, once utility functions are formed, rational individuals must then be assumed to be disinterested in each others' interests. Individuals can rationally seek to advance (or diminish) the welfare of other individuals. But these desires, if they exist, are represented in their utility functions. In other words, the Hobbesian–liberal theory of rational agency takes utility functions as given, but once they are in place the theory stipulates that individuals care only about the utility payoffs to themselves. Egoism and mutual unconcern are therefore distinct ideas. When individuals are rational egoists, it is not only in virtue of their being (mutually unconcerned) utility maximizers but also because of the nature of their utility functions. In a word, their interests themselves are egoistic. On mutual unconcern, see Rawls, *A Theory of Justice*, p. 13. David Gauthier, following P. H. Wicksteed, has designated mutual unconcern "non-tuism" and asserted that it is a "dogma" of the prevailing conception of practical reason. See David Gauthier, *Morals by Agreement* (Oxford: Oxford University Press, 1986), p. 87, and "Reason and Maximization," pp. 413–415.

whatever Hobbes may have believed, it is not inscribed in human nature as such.

Hobbesian egoism, precisely because it is so stark and uncompromising, provides an unappealing and unrealistic basis for thinking about political association. But in consequence of its severity, it puts the subjective component of the circumstances of justice into clear focus. These circumstances pertain, however, even if more moderate accounts of self-interested motivation are assumed. It is enough, as writers after Hobbes have made clear, that, in assessing alternative courses of action, individuals generally adopt a self-regarding attitude. Their wills need not evince an exclusive or all-consuming desire to enhance their own well-being but only a significant desire to do so. Altruists evince a corresponding desire to enhance the welfare positions of others.

I argued in Chapter 3 that conditional altruism is at some remove from general will coordination. This conclusion holds with equal force for altruism generally. The social individual of Pashukanis's imagination differs from the egoist only in substituting altruism for egoism. But individuals moved by a general will are neither egoists nor altruists. They are indivisible parts of the moral and collective bodies whose interests they seek to advance. In short, they are creatures of a universe that the atomic-individualist metaphor denies. Therefore Pashukanis's social individual is more at home than the Rousseauean citizen in an intellectual culture governed by the image of the atomic individual. As remarked, his idea is perfectly intelligible from the standpoint of mainstream liberalism. But however compatible it may be with liberal theoretical positions, Pashukanis's vision is so demanding that, even were it feasible, it would be unappealing if not chilling to anyone moved by liberal sensibilities. Paradoxically, the Rousseauean-Marxist alternative fares a good deal better in this regard.

LIBERALISM AND THE GENERAL WILL

The parties to Rousseau's social contract do not deliberate as "citizens" all the time. In non- or extrapolitical contexts they are egoists and perhaps sometimes altruists too. In order to understand how general will coordination can coexist with forms of coordination underwritten by the metaphor of the atomic individual, it will be well to consider more carefully than we so far have why the citizens of a just state are not and ought not to be directed exclusively by the general will. Inasmuch as communism is a feasible approximation of this Rousseauean ideal, similar considerations will carry over to men and women living in communist societies.

/ According to Rousseau, when individuals place themselves under "the supreme direction of the general will" – in particular, when they deliberate as "indivisible" members of the "moral and collective bodies" they (freely) constitute – they are equal *qua* citizens. It is for this reason that each individual has one and only one vote, and that declarations of the general will are made by counting votes. Moreover, despite what citizens of liberal democracies have come to accept, equality of citizenship is not a strictly formal requirement. For majority rule voting to serve as a reliable means for discovering what the general will is, a condition absolutely necessary if the majority's decision is to obligate those whose positions were defeated in the popular assemblies, citizens must actually be equal or very nearly so with respect to everything that bears on the "rectitude" of their deliberations and choices. Voters in a de jure state do not express preferences for alternative outcomes in contention but express opinions on what the general will is; they register judgments about a matter of fact that they are presumed to be (equally) capable of ascertaining. As with jury voting or the statistical pooling of (disinterested) expert opinions on public policy questions, voting is a mechanism for aggregating judgments that, even if they are not in fact equally sound, are reasonably treated as if they were. General will coordination or at least the form of it that Rousseau expressly described cannot obtain in conditions that are detrimental to the development of rational and independent judgments by all the members of the whole community. Whatever detracts from real equality of citizenship is therefore inimical to general will coordination.

Ironically, general will coordination itself can have precisely this effect if it is allowed to supersede private will interactions completely. Recall, for example, the John and Mary of Chapter 1, deliberating now about the division of labor within their household. Suppose that in this matter too they are determined to advance the general interest of the couple John–Mary, rather than the private interests of the individuals John and Mary who constitute this "moral and collective body." Finally, imagine that they can somehow screen out particular interests that masquerade as general interests, so that John and Mary's general will deliberations have all the rectitude Rousseau ascribes to the popular assemblies of the de jure state. It could turn out, perhaps for reasons having to do with their respective life histories to that point, that it is the general interest of this couple that one of their members, say Mary, should do all and only housework, while the other, John, should participate actively in civil society and the state. By hypothesis, this division of labor, because it is in the general interest, in no way depends upon actual domination.[10] Nevertheless, in consequence of this choice, one member of the couple is consigned to menial and constricting tasks that, let us suppose, progressively undermine her abilities to engage actively and autonomously in collective decision making. At the same time, the other is able to cultivate these capacities at an accelerated rate thanks to the life opportunities he confronts. This result will, in turn, affect the outcomes of subsequent general will deliberations between John and Mary; the reasons that warranted the initial division of labor will pertain with increasingly greater force. At some point, if this process continues indefinitely, it may become impossible to continue to regard John and Mary as equal citizens. The factors that bear on their abilities to engage equally and independently in collective deliberations and collective decision making will have become too unequally distributed between them. This sad turn of events will not have come about in consequence of a contest of competing private wills; it will be a result of general will coordination itself. The exercise of the general will will have undermined the conditions for its own possibility.

In this sense, general will coordination can be self-defeating over time; it can also be undesirable, as even Rousseau recognized. Once the state of nature has become a war of all against all, the social contract is in each contracting party's interest. At that point, since general will coordination is indispensable for saving individual autonomy, it is best for each individual to "place himself under the supreme direction of the general will." But Rousseau's argument pertains only to the state itself. In civil society, especially in the commercial sphere, private interests continue to hold sway. Thus, in the economy that Rousseau imagined, individuals would be (largely) self-sufficient yeoman farmers or small-scale

10 Arguably, it does depend on residues of past domination. Those who would maintain that true general will deliberations should not countenance past domination even in this attenuated sense may suppose that the same division of labor is in the general interest solely in consequence of differences in (innate) aptitudes.

artisinal producers who exchange their surplus products through market transactions.[11] Outside the political arena, people remain paradigmatic private willers, just as they were in the state of nature. Were they not so moved, they would, in Rousseau's expression, "neglect the cares they owe themselves,"[12] precisely the fault that the social contract remedies in political life. Similar considerations apply to John and Mary in deliberations over their division of household labor. Even if general will deliberations in this case would not undermine the equality that is the condition for its possibility, there would have to be a compelling reason why Mary or John should make the interest of the John–Mary couple their own in this case. On any likely elaboration of their story, it is virtually certain that they would be better off pursuing their own private interests. For should they fail to make their private interests their own, they would put their own well-beings in jeopardy without obtaining adequate compensation in return. In contrast, the individuals who alienate all their rights to the whole community get back nothing less than essential autonomy, thereby saving their very humanity from mortal peril.

Nevertheless, as with the idea of a world beyond scarcity, there is something right-headed in the picture of communism as a society in which human beings have ceased to be generally self-interested. Communism surely does require something like the "transcendence" of the subjective component of the circumstances of justice – insofar as it involves general will coordination, of course, but also in those aspects of social life where private volition continues to be appropriate. Marxists have generally denied the possibility of a "third way" between rational egoism and whatever it is supposed to contrast with – whether it be "species-being" in Pashukanis's sense or the very different, Rousseauean alternative that I maintain Marxian communism presupposes. In depicting the private and the general will as mutually exclusive and eternally opposed, Rousseau too effectively denied the existence of a third way. But, in this case as in so many others, Rousseau's reflections on politics provide resources for rectifying the misapprehensions his political theory suggests. It will therefore be useful, again, to turn back to Rousseau, and to reflect on the character of the individuals who constitute the society the de jure state superintends.

11 See Levine, *The Politics of Autonomy*, Chapter 5, pp. 187–198.
12 *The Social Contract*, Book I, Chapter 6.

VIRTUE

Rousseau's citizens, in their commercial interactions and more generally in the sphere of civil society, are moved by private wills, but they are not, after the social contract, the untrammeled egoists whose Hobbesian dispositions make a social contract necessary. Like the public-minded citizens envisioned by other eighteenth-century political theorists, they are imbued with republican *virtue* – with a disposition toward moderation, simplicity of manners and morals (*moeurs*), and a powerful longing for equality itself.[13] To be sure, they are still generally self-regarding. But their egoism is moderate and gentle. They are more nearly creatures of Hume's *Treatise* than Hobbes's *Leviathan* or the concluding pages of *The Second Discourse*.

Virtue, for theorists in the republican tradition, is a disposition to accord precedence to communal over individual concerns. For Rousseau, it is this disposition that allows the state, directed by a general will, to superintend a society composed of small independent producers who own their own means of production – and therefore the products of their labor – and who, insofar as they are not self-sufficient, trade on markets. Private property and markets generate resource inequalities, and these inequalities, if they grow too large, put liberty and therefore general will coordination itself in jeopardy.[14] Individuals must therefore be made virtuous in order to counter the mentality markets encourage; otherwise, there is no hope of mitigating their effects. It is far from clear, however, that a virtuous disposition alone can suffice to stem the tide. But Rousseau, along with other republican theorists, imagines no alternatives to markets and private property. He is therefore unable to envision any more efficacious means for keeping inequality – and private volition – in bounds. Thus he proposes a host of "superstructural" measures – from schooling to public spectacles to the institution of a civil religion – for inculcating virtue in the face of an economic "base" that militates against it.[15]

13 Cf. Levine, *The Politics of Autonomy*, pp. 168–172.
14 Cf. *The Social Contract*, Book II, Chapter 11; and Levine, *The Politics of Autonomy*, pp. 188–192.
15 For discussion of some of the practical political measures Rousseau proposes, see Levine, *The Politics of Autonomy*, Chapter 4, and *The End of the State*, Chapter 2. Rousseau's reflections on political institutions are always sensitive to conjunctural factors and peculiarities of geographical and historical circumstance. Thus the institutional arrangements he endorses are not, strictly, technical manipulations deemed necessary for any de jure state, but measures that are

It is one thing to have a virtuous disposition and something else to subordinate one's private will to the general will. Rousseau esteemed virtue in its own right; he had only praise for the simplicity and equality of the yeoman society of his imagination. And his celebrated contempt for luxury and the vanities of life in the cities and great estates is evident throughout his writings. But in *The Social Contract*, Rousseau defended virtue mainly for its efficacy in promoting general will coordination. Virtuous people, he maintained, are more likely than unabashed egoists to subordinate their private wills to the general will. From this perspective, it is immaterial whether or not virtue is an end in itself. What matters is that it is instrumental for general will coordination. Virtue's domain is civil society; the proper arena for general will coordination is the state. In Rousseau's view, it is (partly) because men and women in civil society are virtuous that they are able to become citizens, indivisible parts of the sovereign, when they come together as legislators in the assemblies of the people.

It has been widely observed that revolutionaries from Cromwell through Lenin and beyond and, to a lesser degree, radicals generally share a common political style, and that this style is rooted in the republican tradition.[16] A modern revolutionary or militant radical is likely to be virtuous in roughly the republican sense, if only because anyone whose life is directed toward realizing fundamental political and social transformations, typically at considerable personal cost, almost certainly places public values above personal concerns. But there is an affinity too at the level of individual sensibilities. People who dedicate their lives to revolutionary objectives are characteristically inclined, as seventeenth- and eighteenth-century republicans were, to lead lives of personal austerity and strict discipline. Indeed, many revolutionary groups, since the seventeenth century, have gone so far as to model themselves on military organizations. To some degree, the latter phenomenon can be explained as a functional adaptation to the tasks revolutionaries confront. But it is probably also explainable by ap-

---

generally instrumental for rendering de jure institutions feasible in conditions likely to be confronted by the (contemporary) readership of *The Social Contract*. In this respect, they are like the measures advanced by Marx and Engels in *The Communist Manifesto* – programmatic policies appropriate for Germany in the prerevolutionary situation leading up to 1848 but not necessarily for communists in other times and places.

16 See, for example, Michael Walzer, *The Revolution of the Saints: A Study in the Origins of Radical Politics* (Cambridge, Mass.: Harvard University Press, 1965).

peal to the mentality of those disposed to become "professional revolutionaries," a cast of mind relevantly similar to the temperament republican theorists esteem.

Typically, revolutionaries do not just strive to be virtuous themselves; they seek to establish virtuous communities. In this respect, the more radical Jacobins like Robespierre and Saint-Just, like the Puritans before them, were exemplary.[17] But even the Bolsheviks and their successors, despite their official antipathy toward moralistic assessments, evince a similar sensibility. The classical Communist aversion to bourgeois excess and to that preoccupation with the self that bourgeois society fosters reflects this attitude.[18] These class hatreds stemmed, in part, from the same source as did Rousseau's abhorrence of luxury, his animosity toward city life, and his glorification of simple peasant ways.

Bolshevik attitudes reflect a similar sensibility in Marx himself. Marx was an ardent, though critical, admirer of the Jacobins, and his enthusiasm has been recognized and appropriated by his followers. To be sure, Rousseau's express declarations in behalf of virtue are foreign to Marx's immediate theoretical concerns, and Rousseau's use of virtue as a "corrective" within essentially capitalist societies must appear anachronistic to any defender of historical materialist positions. Rousseau could not conceive of alternatives to private property and markets; Marx could and did. Thus his liking for the mentality republicans sought to foster was not nearly so driven by theoretical exigencies as Rousseau's. It was more a matter of sentiment than intellectual conviction.

Nevertheless, there is something defenders of Marxian communism can learn from the use Rousseau made of virtue. By restricting general will coordination to the political sphere and then seeking to mitigate but not entirely eliminate private willing elsewhere, Rousseau's example suggests a way to save the idea of communism from the excesses of its Marxist defenders. Their communism seems utopian and unappealing because they depict it as a society *beyond* justice or, more precisely, beyond the circumstances of justice; because they insist that neither scarcity nor self-interest pertains under communist conditions. Taken literally,

---

17 I discuss the place of virtue in radical Jacobin politics in *The End of the State*, Chapter 3.

18 The fact that Communist leaders, the *nomenklatura* of the post-Stalinist period, came increasingly to adopt bourgeois life-styles themselves no doubt contributed, in part, to the "legitimation crisis" of Communist regimes and ultimately, therefore, to their demise.

these claims cannot be sustained. It is appropriate, therefore, to turn to the role of justice – and also virtue, especially the virtue of justice – under communism. With this focus, it will become possible to recognize what genuinely is insightful in traditional accounts of communism. We will find that the received doctrine can be reconstructed in a way that is faithful to its fundamental contentions but that does not burden communism with unrealistic and undesirable properties.

FROM VIRTUE TO JUSTICE

We have seen that the central objective component of the circumstances of justice, relative scarcity, can never be eliminated entirely – because some (generally desired) goods are likely to remain scarce, as a matter of fact, no matter how massively developed productive forces become, and because others, like honors or privileges, are necessarily scarce in the sense that they would be devalued the more generally available they become. In addition, the fact that people, even under communism, would be bound to budget their time, if only to decide which (virtually) free goods they will deploy at particular moments, implies that a preeminently important good, time itself, will always remain in short supply in any imaginable human future.

On the other hand, there is no reason in principle why the subjective component of the circumstances of justice, self-regard, cannot be entirely overcome. Human beings could become full-time altruists or general willers or even grow indifferent altogether to distributional concerns. However, such far-reaching changes in human beings' characters are unlikely. More importantly, the wholesale abandonment of private volition would be unappealing, even if it could somehow be achieved.

Thus a society entirely beyond the circumstances of justice is impossible and undesirable in any case. But if the historical materialist picture is sound, scarcity will diminish markedly before communism is established and then under its aegis, and human beings will become less egoistic – in roughly the way that republican theorists supposed. Thus it might seem that the moral urgency of justice will wither away, even if it will never disappear completely. However, this conclusion is importantly misleading. Paradoxically, the ever-receding salience of the circumstances of justice, far from making justice unimportant, will actually make justice paramount in communist societies.

With diminishing scarcity and egoism abating, struggles over distributive shares are likely to diminish in frequency and urgency. But if justice as a property of institutions withers away (without ever vanishing entirely) as a normative concern, justice as a property of persons is sure to become more important. As a disposition internalized in the men and women of communist societies, justice is indispensable for communism in just the way that Rousseau declared virtue indispensable for the de jure state. Allowing for differences in precision and discounting the eighteenth-century cast of Rousseau's republicanism, these contentions represent the same idea. In brief, communism presupposes the virtue of justice.[19]

In contrast to the political culture of bourgeois societies, politics in communism's higher phases will no longer be a contest of private wills, a struggle over who gets what. With diminishing scarcity and increasingly transformed individuals, people will be increasingly disposed to look to the general interest in making collective choices. They will be general willers in those aspects of their lives – the political sphere, above all – in which communal concerns are their true interests; otherwise, they will be *just* men and women. Similarly, Rousseau believed that in a state based on the social contract individuals would be citizens in the assemblies of the people and virtuous independent producers otherwise. The reason is plain: In order to achieve the uncoerced equality of communism, people must be disposed to do what just social institutions would compel them to do were private interests still driving them apart.

Formally, justice requires that like cases be treated alike. This principle is transhistorical and universal but without content because it says nothing about what constitutes like cases or equal treatments. In different times and places, different views of these matters have gained wide acceptance. The idea that human beings generally constitute a category that counts as a like case is a distinctly modern conception; more inegalitarian understandings were commonplace in earlier times. Even today, hardly anyone would place all individuals in the same category with respect to every distributive concern. Thus it is widely believed that some goods should be distributed for reasons of merit or need or productive contribution – in other words, that people can be sorted out into morally relevant categories with respect to how meritorious or

19 Cf. G. A. Cohen, "Self-Ownership, Equality, and Communism," *Supplementary Proceedings of the Aristotelian Society* (1990).

needy they are or how much they have contributed. The idea that all human beings merit equal treatment is only a *presumption*. As such, it is almost universally entertained. Inequalities may accord with justice, according to contemporary understandings, but when they do they must be justified; there must be defensible grounds for treating persons differently. If no acceptable case for unequal treatment can be made, everyone should be treated the same.[20]

The principle "to each the same" is therefore fundamental to modern conceptions of justice. But "to each the same" is not by itself equivalent to the modern conception. Thus, in monastic orders or in the radical sects of antiquity, egalitarian distributions served to foster a sense of in-group identification and difference from the outside world, not an awareness of unity with human beings generally. Historically, the egalitarian principle has probably functioned more often to foster differences among people than to unite them. It is only when joined with a belief in the moral equality of persons, a conviction liberals and Marxists share, that the prevailing sense of justice exhibits the egalitarian cast of contemporary liberalism and Marxism.

Understood as a character trait, justice denotes a disposition on the part of each individual to treat everyone in the same way – except insofar as a case can be made, compatible with a commitment to the moral equality of persons and to their equal treatment, for differentiating between them. A just disposition mitigates private volition without eliminating it, and it renders persons more capable of general willing in those instances in which it genuinely is in individuals' interests to place themselves under the supreme direction of a general will. But the virtue of justice does not function in quite the same way that virtue does in Rousseau's political philosophy. Rousseau's invocation of virtue was an act of desperation. He needed a "corrective" in the face of an economic system that threatened to generate social divisions inimical to the exercise of the general will. For want of an alternative to markets and private property, virtue was the straw he grasped. However, under communism, even in its earliest (socialist) phases, the economic order – because it works against the reproduction of class divisions –

---

20 Since human beings differ in their preferences for resources and in their situations, equal treatment does not entail providing everyone with exactly the same things. See Ronald Dworkin, "Equality of Resources," *Philosophy and Public Affairs*, vol. 10, no. 4 (1981), pp. 283–345.

promotes equality of citizenship. Therefore the virtue of justice is a complement, not a corrective, to the economic system of socialist and later communist societies.

EQUALITY AND "BOURGEOIS RIGHT"

Modern views of justice exhibit a tendency toward equality but allow for inequalities of various kinds. Thus there are accounts of justice, liberal in intention, that countenance inequalities for the sake of property rights; others that acknowledge claims on resources based on merit or effort or whatever else might render individuals deserving; and others that permit inequalities for reasons of efficiency (broadly conceived). Rawls's theory of justice is a theory of this sort. According to Rawls, unequal distributions are just if they satisfy the Difference Principle – that is, if they benefit representative members of the least well-off group. Inequalities can have this effect only if they help to improve productivity enough to make the worst position better than it would have been without those inequalities. Rawls's theory is among the most egalitarian of extant liberal conceptions and is certainly the most theoretically developed. It also bears on distributive principles that give expression to what Marx called "bourgeois right," the idea that distributions should correlate directly with (productive) contributions. This idea is pervasive in the political cultures of capitalist societies and appropriate, in Marx's view, for socialist societies too. It is worth reflecting on these interconnected issues in order to probe the implications for equality – and for the general will – of societies populated by individuals imbued with a sense of justice.

In *The Critique of the Gotha Program*, Marx maintained that under socialism, communism's lowest phase, what individuals get should be in proportion to their productive inputs, denominated in socially necessary labor time, after various "social deductions" have been exacted to support nonproductive sectors of the population and to provide revenue for the state.[21] This concession to "bourgeois right," like Rawls's Difference Principle, was plainly motivated by efficiency concerns. Individuals emerging from capitalist societies would not be inclined to develop their talents or to deploy them efficiently without material incentives for doing so. In consequence (nearly) everyone, including the least well-off, would

21 Cf. Karl Marx and Friedrich Engels, *Selected Works*, vol. 2 (Moscow: Foreign Languages Publishing House, 1962), pp. 13–48. Also, see Chapter 7, herein.

likely suffer. Hence the need to provide differential remunerations – based no longer on ownership of external things, as under capitalism, but on the quality of workers' skills and their expenditures of effort. It is only as socialism evolves into communism – in particular, after human beings have been weaned away from unabashed self-interest – that differential rewards for direct producers and other economic agents can be relegated to a superseded past and human communities can finally inscribe upon their banners "From each according to his ability, to each according to his need."

This well-known slogan of Marx's is easily misunderstood. By the time that human societies will have moved into the higher phases of communism, a truly massive economic surplus will exist. We can therefore assume that basic needs – insofar as they can be distinguished from wants – will have been met long before. Thus the "need" Marx speaks of comes to the same thing as "wants." The idea would then be that, under communism, individuals will take from the common stock as they please, regardless of their contributions to it, and contribute to the common stock according to their different abilities. Marx does not quite say so, but we can infer as well that, with productive capacities massively developed, contributions too will be provided more or less as producers please. In any case, under communism, it would no longer serve a purpose for distributive shares to be proportional to the duration or intensity of the labor power recipients expend. The Difference Principle would therefore be otiose too – inequalities never would enlarge the distributive share of the least well-off. In short, under communism, the Difference Principle would mandate equal distributions; the presumption for strict equality would generally prevail. Then if, following Rawls, rights-based or desert-based arguments for inequality are taken to have no normative force – if only the Difference Principle or, more generally, incentive-based arguments can justify inequalities – under communism there would be no way to defend inequalities on grounds of justice.

Since people do not value resources in the same way, a distribution of resources that implements the goal of treating persons equally can involve people getting very different things. It can therefore look inegalitarian.[22] In addition, production and trade

22 Despite their many differences, virtually all accounts of equal treatment agree
   on this point. See, among others, Dworkin, "Equality of Resources"; Richard

are bound to upset distributional patterns and therefore to perturb distributions that implement the (complex) ideal of resource equality. Finally, individuals' free choices or, more generally, their "option luck" will upset distributional patterns.[23] For egalitarian liberals, the resulting distributions would not violate the ideal of resource equality. Quite the contrary. For them, distributive shares that arise in consequence of individuals' free choices would actually *implement* resource equality – even if, as a result of these choices, individuals have very different holdings. Therefore, egalitarians can defend differences that arise for reasons distinct from the efficiency considerations the Difference Principle articulates and still maintain that only the Difference Principle justifies *inequalities*. They need only argue – in a principled way – that the differences they allow are not, in fact, inequalities. Thus, even if the Difference Principle, having become otiose, were to mandate strictly equal distributions, it would be compatible with its view of justice that people hold different goods.

I would venture that Rousseauean Marxists can accept the idea the Difference Principle articulates. They differ from liberals, I will suggest, only in the kinds of differences they would allow under the egalitarian ideal. Liberals want egalitarian distributions to be sensitive *both* to individuals' preferences for different resources and to their "ambitions," as registered in the choices they freely make. I shall argue presently that Rousseauean Marxists are even more radically egalitarian. They would have distributions be sensitive *only* to individuals' preferences and would therefore intervene to rectify (some) of the consequences of individuals' free choices. Before we turn to this contention, however, a few remarks on Rawlsian justice are in order.

The idea that motivates the Difference Principle, that inequalities are justified only if they work to the advantage of the least well-off, is congenial to both liberal and Rousseauean-Marxist positions. Marxists can also agree with Rawlsian liberals that material

Arneson, "Equality and Equality of Opportunity for Welfare," *Philosophical Studies*, vol. 55 (1989), pp. 77–93; and G. A. Cohen, "On the Currency of Egalitarian Justice," *Ethics*, vol. 99 (1989), pp. 906–944.
23 The term owes to Dworkin. It designates an individual's luck in deliberately undertaken gambles – that is, in choices made in conditions of uncertainty or risk. It is distinguished from "brute luck," which designates an individual's good or bad fortune in "the natural lottery."

rewards can be legitimately used as incentives to productivity. But Rousseauean Marxists need not accede to Rawls's way of introjecting the latter idea into the Difference Principle itself. The Difference Principle, as Rawls conceives it, accords normative standing to the advantages talented or industrious people are able to procure for themselves. Thus it incorporates incentive effects into the theory of justice itself. However, it is not at all clear how claims of justice can arise out of individuals' differential abilities to take advantage of their respective situations.[24] It is one thing to concede that effort and talent must be rewarded differentially under pre-communist conditions. It is something else to depict this concession as a requirement of justice. Thus the distributional principle proposed for socialism in *The Critique of the Gotha Program* has precisely the rationale Marx imputed; its justification depends on an appeal to efficiency (broadly conceived). In contrast to Rawls's express view, this rationale does not implicate justice directly. Marx was surely wrong to eschew justice as an evaluative category. However, this mistake may actually work to the advantage of his position in this case. For Marx, inequalities under socialism are unfortunate though unavoidable concessions to a human nature that only communism in its higher stages can sufficiently transform. They are not requirements of justice.

BASIC LIBERTIES

If distribution and contribution are dissociated, individuals cannot claim, as a matter of right, that they are entitled to the wealth their labor produces simply because they expended their own labor. If they are accorded such a right, it must be for other reasons. But if there are no entitlements to the revenues labor generates, must individuals also relinquish control over their labor itself? If so, radical egalitarianism would look less attractive than it otherwise might.

Fortunately, Rawlsians and Rousseauean Marxists, insofar as their position implicitly accords with Rawls's, need not draw this conclusion. But it is easy to see how it might suggest itself. In general, ownership is a combination of income rights and control rights, and claims on the income a resource generates typically do come bundled together with control rights over this resource. But

---

24 See G. A. Cohen, "Incentives, Inequality, and Community," *Tanner Lectures on Human Values*, May 1991, pp. 263–329.

it is plain that these rights can be distinguished conceptually and disaggregated normatively. Pooling income generated from labor does not entail pooling labor inputs and vice versa. If Rawls and Marx are right, justice tends to support the former, even if it does not strictly require it. But it is hard to imagine any normative principle that could justify the latter. So pervasive, however, is the prevailing view of ownership – joining income rights with control rights – that procommunists must nevertheless confront issues about labor pooling and labor conscription.

Arguably, under communism, the problem would solve itself automatically. If a society could reproduce itself with hardly any labor expenditures, it could safely rely on individuals to expend labor according to their uncoerced desires. Diminishing scarcity would therefore obviate any need for labor conscription. But before we resort to this "technological fix," it is well to recall the priority Rawls accords to the equal distribution of basic rights and liberties in all well-ordered and (moderately) developed societies.[25]

Rawls's principles of justice are intended to regulate the distribution of "primary goods" – basic rights and liberties, income and wealth, powers and offices, and "the bases for self-respect." In Rawls's view, justice requires that basic rights and liberties be distributed equally and to the greatest extent possible, and that all other primary goods be distributed as the Difference Principle requires (so long as opportunities for benefiting differentially are themselves equally distributed). These principles are lexically ordered; the first must be satisfied before the second goes into effect. It is, of course, a matter of controversy what the basic rights and liberties are. Rawls, like most liberals, understands the term to refer in the main to the political rights that liberal polities traditionally accord their subjects. Control rights over one's own body and powers are assumed and therefore not directly acknowledged. But

25 Rawls distinguishes the "general" from the "special" theory of justice: The former is given by the Difference Principle under conditions of equal opportunity; the special theory, in addition, accords lexical priority to basic rights and liberties. In Rawls's view, individuals in the "original position" would adopt the special theory whenever it would be "irrational [for them] to acknowledge a lesser liberty for the sake of greater material means and amenities of office." According to Rawls, this option would always be irrational except in conditions of extreme material deprivation. Rawls expressly holds that existing liberal (capitalist) societies exceed this threshold. Thus he thinks the special theory already applicable at levels of development vastly inferior to those Marx deemed necessary for socialism – and a fortiori communism; cf. *A Theory of Justice*, pp. 60–64 and esp. pp. 541–548.

it is well to be explicit – especially if prevailing views of property that join income rights with control rights are challenged. It is therefore fair to assert what Rawlsian liberalism implicitly understands: that, in specifying the basic rights and liberties they would distribute equally, parties in the original position would institute protections against the appropriation of their bodies and powers by the whole community. They would do so whether or not the community pools the wealth their bodies and powers generate.

Thus there is a "rational kernel" implicit in those (non-Rawlsian) strains of liberalism that endorse the idea of self-ownership.[26] Self-ownership confers rights against coerced deployments of individuals' bodies and powers. But the same result can be obtained without invoking a notion steeped in a form of discourse appropriate for neo-Lockean libertarians but hardly for liberal or radical egalitarians. We need only recognize that control rights over one's own body and powers, as distinct from rights to the income these "assets" generate, are basic rights in Rawls's sense and that, like other basic rights, they should be distributed equally and to the greatest extent possible. If, under communist conditions, the Difference Principle warrants income pooling, the lexical priority accorded these control rights continues to guard against labor conscription or other unsavory and unwarranted features that might be thought to afflict a social order in which contribution and distribution are radically dissociated.

JUSTICE INTERNALIZED

Under communist conditions, justice and equality converge, and a just – or equal – society can be sustained without a state, though not entirely without some public coercive force to overcome collective weaknesses of will. These claims capture most of what Marx envisioned for communism. Therefore communism is not quite *beyond* justice. It is, however, beyond the deleterious effects of the circumstances of justice.

When the conditions that make justice necessary and possible, relative scarcity and general self-regard, are most acute, justice is difficult to attain. Justice is then in tension with peoples' inclinations to treat others unfairly – in those all-too-common cases in

---

26 Cf. my "Capitalist Persons," in Ellen Frankel Paul, Fred D. Miller, Jr., Jeffrey Paul, and John Ahrens (eds.), *Capitalism* (Oxford: Basil Blackwell, 1989), pp. 39–59. See also Richard J. Arneson, "Lockean Self-Ownership: Towards a Demolition," *Political Studies*, vol. 29, no. 1 (1991), pp. 36–54.

which, by so doing, they can accrue a larger share of the relatively scarce resources they covet. Then it is all the more in each of our interests that institutions and practices be just. Therefore the struggle to make society conform to what justice requires is an urgent task. On the other hand, when scarcity and self-regard are less overwhelming, justice is more readily internalized. In those circumstances, just institutions would emerge as by-products of individuals spontaneously being just. Like the de jure state of *The Social Contract*, social justice will be realized fully only when it is no longer needed.

But why would people be disposed to achieve justice when they no longer need it? Because justice or, at least, modern egalitarian justice articulates a commitment to the moral equality of persons, a commitment that democratic participation under socialist and later communist conditions nurtures and expands. In material conditions this side of communism, equal treatment would not generally mandate equal provision. Justice and equality would frequently diverge. However, under communist conditions, the tendency toward equality implicit in all modern conceptions of justice would be realized almost perfectly; except for those (few) goods that in one way or another remain scarce, justice and equal provision would come to the same thing. People committed to equal treatment, as people nowadays already are and as they likely would be all the more under communism, would therefore seek to reproduce the social order that allows for its greatest possible realization. The disposition to be just would then be tantamount to a compelling preference, internalized in communist men and women, to reproduce the social order in which they live – and in which their most fundamental impulses toward self-realization and sociability are realized to a degree unprecedented in societies plagued by material scarcity and riven by class divisions.

RESPONSIBILITY

From an egalitarian liberal perspective, individuals ought not to be held responsible for their good or bad fortune in "the natural lottery" or for its consequences. Mental and physical endowments and other "accidents of birth" do not generate entitlements to distributive shares. However, it may be just to accommodate to differences that these contingencies help to produce. Thus even the most radically egalitarian liberals maintain that capitalist markets, in which outcomes depend in part on happenstance and other morally arbitrary factors including luck in the natural lottery, can be just. But no claims of justice arise from these factors themselves. No one has, as it were, a presocial entitlement to the assets that they own in consequence of their good or bad fortune. If capitalist markets are just, it is in spite of – not because of – the morally arbitrary factors that determine the outcomes they produce.

However, egalitarian liberals do not exclude the consequences of luck entirely from the requirements of justice. When individuals engage in production and trade, they typically make choices in conditions of risk or uncertainty. Then, whether they choose wisely or poorly, luck affects the outcomes of their choices significantly, perhaps even decisively. Characteristically, egalitarian liberals allow fortune its due in these cases. Thus no liberal endorses a theory of justice that nullifies the consequences of choices individuals freely make. Justice, in the liberal view, does not demand that there be compensation for freely made choices that turn out badly, or that individuals be deprived of benefits generated by "gambles" that turn out well.

Of course, for luck to accord with justice, choices must be genuinely free. Whenever they are, respect for autonomy requires that individuals be held responsible for what they autonomously choose. But individuals' choices are affected by their circumstances and their psychological propensities – including their attitudes toward risk – and these factors would seem to be morally arbitrary too. Nevertheless, I shall, without argument, accept the idea, defended by Kant, that autonomy can coexist with an empirical order governed by strict causality.[27] Following Kant, let us therefore suppose that genuinely autonomous choices do exist – because they involve some further *volitional* fact beyond empirical and morally arbitrary contingencies – and concede as well that the acts of will that make autonomous choices autonomous sustain claims of justice. Even so, actual choices are so confounded with what is unequivocally arbitrary that their outcomes, even when consonant with justice, can hardly be defended solely on the grounds that they are just.

It would therefore follow that the distinction liberals draw between "option luck" and "brute" fortune, whatever its analytical cogency, cannot generally be made in practice. But if it cannot,

27 Cf. Immanuel Kant, *The Critique of Pure Reason*, trans. Norman Kemp Smith (London: Macmillan, 1963), pp. 409–415.

how can the idea that institutions ought to hold individuals responsible for the choices they (freely) make be defended? Autonomy may be real at the level of abstraction that Kant intended, but actual choices would seem to be too confounded by morally arbitrary factors to count as autonomous in a way that could sustain claims of justice.

What is at issue is not the reality of autonomous choice but its implications for social justice. Liberals defend distributions generated by the use individuals make of the resources they control, insofar as they result from free choices made in conditions of uncertainty, but their doing so seems to be in conflict with their principled determination to discount – and wherever possible to nullify – the effects of morally arbitrary contingencies. In other words, two core liberal intuitions about justice – that luck does not generate morally binding entitlements, and that individuals must bear the fruits of the choices they freely make – are, to say the least, in tension. To what extent do similar tensions afflict the positions of other partisans of autonomy who, like Rousseau and Marx, eschew the idea, dear to liberals and nearly everyone else, that all interests are private? To pursue this question is to rethink the connection between justice and autonomy and, in so doing, to elaborate some implications of general will coordination.

JUSTICE AND THE GENERAL WILL

It has been recognized at least since Aristotle that the core idea that justice articulates is that "like cases be treated alike." Then different substantive principles – for instance, "to each according to need" – supply content to the underlying formal principle.[28] I have suggested that, under communism, with the circumstances of justice severely mitigated, the principle "to each according to need" is not strictly a substantive principle of justice at all. It does not hold that, under communism, differences of need are morally relevant and therefore provide grounds for identifying like cases deserving of like treatment. It is instead a (speculative) descriptive principle, an account of how distributions under communism will occur. Under communism, on this understanding, individuals will add to social wealth according to their abilities, and take from it as they please, according to their needs.

28 Cf. Chaim Perleman *The Idea of Justice and the Problem of Argument*, trans. John Petrie (New York: Humanities Press, 1963), Chapter 1.

When scarcity is salient, it is of paramount importance that individuals be treated fairly. But what counts as fair treatment, according to intuitions nearly universally entertained, depends upon facts about these same individuals – on what they have done or, on some accounts, on what is true of them regardless of what they have done. In other words, it is supposed that there exists an intrinsic connection between facts about individuals and their defensible claims on societal benefits and burdens. That some relation of this sort should exist is to be expected. If the individual, conceived atomistically, is the proper point of departure for justifying social and political arrangements, facts about individuals should determine the justice of distributions to these individuals.

However, insofar as individuals are not radically independent "atoms" bearing private wills but indivisible members of "whole communities" bearing general wills, the facts that determine their distributive shares will not be facts about atomic individuals. Proponents of one or another substantive principle of justice do effectively conceive individuals and their properties atomistically. These principles do not therefore lend themselves to articulating a notion of justice for societies of the kind Rousseau and Marx envisioned. The sense of justice they express can coexist with the new order, but it is not peculiar to it. It is the old justice that has not and, in all likelihood, cannot entirely "wither away." If there is a distinctive notion of justice associated with general will coordination, the properties of individuals that will be pertinent for determining their distributive shares must concern individuals *qua* members of the "moral and collective bodies" they constitute. But the only pertinent fact of this kind is that individuals are free, that they are autonomous beings.

Insofar as equality in autonomy is all that matters for justice – as it is when individuals appropriately "place themselves under the supreme direction of the general will" – justice entails equality *tout court*, not *inequality* in consequence of the choices individuals (autonomously) make. As essentially autonomous beings, individuals are equal *qua* constituents of the moral and collective bodies they constitute. Therefore considerations of justice, to the extent that they remain normatively pertinent, become considerations of equality. It remains problematic how societies coordinated through a general will, communist societies, would implement this ideal at any given moment and over time – since production, trade, and the vagaries of fortune will occur under communism as well as in precommunist economies. It is likely that, even under communism, equality cannot be realized perfectly. It is also likely, as we shall see presently, that, for reasons extrinsic to but not incompatible with justice, inequalities of various kinds might persist indefinitely. But "the tendency towards equality," to borrow an expression of Rawls's, would be vastly more pronounced under communism than in even the most egalitarian liberal societies.[29] Where the general will is in control, justice requires that, so far as possible, individuals ought at all times to have equal shares – irrespective of their option luck.[30]

Liberal conceptions of justice will probably remain appropriate in some contexts for an indefinite period if not forever. As we have seen, the role of general will coordination in communist societies is anything but exclusive. And even in those circumstances where it is appropriate for individuals to be governed by the general will, there will probably remain efficiency reasons, even as scarcity radically diminishes, for rewarding individuals differentially according to their good or bad fortune in gambles they have freely undertaken. Thus, under communism, competing intuitions about what justice requires are likely to coexist – and so too are competing practices. Exactly how this tension will be resolved cannot be specified in advance. All we can say for now is that, as the circumstances of justice "wither away" and the moral urgency of justice pales, the tensions will become less acute. There may always be a tendency to countenance inequalities that arise in consequence of individuals' free choices. But the balance will surely shift in the direction of equality irrespective of option luck. Liberal egalitarians have put the link between what individuals do or are and what they get into question. Under communism, the severance of this link will be carried to its limit. If merit or contribution or *needs* are to be rewarded differentially, it will not be for reasons of justice.

Marx himself was famously ambivalent about radical egalitarianism. In large part, he was drawn to non- and even antiegalitarian

29 For Rawls's very different construal of the tendency he named, see *A Theory of Justice*, pp. 100–108.
30 The idea that option luck should be countered rather than embraced, as in liberal egalitarian theories, does not imply that there should be compensation for literally anything individuals do with the resources they control. For example, individuals who squander their resources outright will usually be acting in opposition to the general will. There is therefore no reason of Rousseauean (or Marxist) provenance to seek to equalize outcomes that have been produced in this way.

positions for polemical reasons – to distinguish his views of social-ism and communism from those of other socialist and anarchist thinkers. But it also seems that he was insufficiently sensitive to some of the implications of the model of rational cooperation that he effectively deployed. But, as generations of Marx's followers have believed, sometimes despite express pronouncements to the contrary, the struggle for communism is a struggle for equality. It is, in fact, a struggle for an equality more radical than most of Marx's opponents envisioned. Equality under communism would disconcert anyone still in the thrall of atomic individualism. For the egalitarianism that would reign under communism tends to obliterate individual responsibility in the domain of distributive justice.[31] In contrast to the liberal view, for partisans of general will coordination, no fact about anyone except membership in the moral community itself matters, so far as justice is concerned, for determining an individual's distributive share.

THE EXERCISE OF THE GENERAL WILL

In Rousseau's de jure state, virtue facilitates general will coordi-nation even as it exemplifies a volitional principle at odds with it. This tension is evident in the difference Rousseau's political phi-losophy implicitly identified between the just state and civil soci-ety, the difference that led Marx to fault "political emancipation" for intensifying unfreedom (in some respects) at the same that it advanced it (in others). Under communism, this tension would be severely mitigated. Just individuals (in the liberal sense) would still be private willers. But, under communist conditions, private volition would no longer work to undermine uncoerced coopera-tion between individuals. It would instead work in tandem with general will coordination. Then, necessarily in cases where the general will directs individuals and tendentially in cases where

31 Absolution from responsibility in this sense in no way mitigates an individual's moral responsibility for freely chosen actions. It has been recognized, at least since Aristotle, that distributive and "retributive" or "rectificatory" justice constitute distinct domains, linked only by the formal principle that "like cases be treated alike." Thus the circumstances that make distributive justice morally urgent can pale without in any way lessening the urgency of retributive justice. And the criteria for counting as a like case can differ markedly from one do-main to another. For Aristotle, retributive justice was largely an affair of insti-tutions, tantamount to a (normative) theory of punishment. But similar considerations pertain beyond institutional "retribution" to moral judgments generally. Cf. Aristotle, *Nicomachean Ethics*, Book V, section H, Part 1.

private volition remains in force, the freedom and self-realization of everyone would be everyone's concern.

It would be foolish, from the vantage point of a world in which untrammeled capitalism seems (temporarily) triumphant, to try to surmise which aspects of communist societies would be regulated by an internalized sense of justice and which by general will co-ordination. However, some very general speculations are feasible even now. In this instance, as in so many others, Rousseau's lead is instructive – to a point.

For Rousseau, the general will was to be exercised in the domain of collective choice – that is, in individuals' capacities as components of the sovereign power. Sovereignty, on his construal, is "the exercise of the general will" because, for (potentially) autonomous agents, the existence of a moral community is the preeminent concern and general will coordination is indispensable for the realization of this end. This contention is insightful and crucial for conceiving collective decision making under communism. But Rousseau's idea can be understood in a number of ways, and Rousseau himself provides little help in adjudicating among these understandings.

At the very least, the claim might be that autonomy can only be realized within communities that recognize and implement the moral equality of persons. Then, insofar as each individual's principal interest is the maintenance and enhancement of his or her own autonomy, individuals have an overriding interest in attending to the interests of the community that make autonomy possible. For matters in which the community itself is directly implicated, therefore, it would be reasonable for individuals to deliberate as indivisible members of it. But in a well-functioning communist polity, as in a de jure state, it is unlikely that issues will arise very often in which the interests of the whole community are at stake. General will deliberation would then seldom impinge on collective decision making. On this understanding, communist men and women would be like the Rousseauean citizens who, according to one plausible reading of Rousseau's intention, delegate virtually all political tasks to "magistrates," while themselves coming together to legislate as indivisible components of "the whole community" only at periodic intervals – and then only to reconfirm (or deny) that the government is executing the sovereign's will. At the other extreme, it could be held that there is a general interest on a wide range of issues and that, as a matter of fact, these general interests advance the autonomy of the individuals who constitute the whole community. On this view, "the whole people would legislate concerning the whole people" regularly and extensively.[32] This claim is plausible to the extent that there is a determinate general interest on many of the issues – or on many aspects of the issues – that arise for collective choice. This is the most likely understanding of Rousseau's view. Whether or not it is correct is of course an empirical question that philosophical speculation is helpless to decide.

In any case, the claim is that, under communist conditions (or in their unworldly anticipation, the state of *The Social Contract*) whenever individuals do appropriately legislate as indivisible parts of the whole communities they constitute, they ought to choose options that maximize overall autonomy. This position is not so implausible as may at first appear. To be sure, there are interests besides autonomy that in general voters ought to heed – welfare interests, in particular. However, under communism, welfare interests are already largely (though not entirely) addressed. With scarcity substantially overcome and self-interest rendered benign, people can therefore set about to become the free (autonomous) beings that, according to Rousseau's vision, they always essentially were. They can make the enhancement of autonomy their overwhelmingly preeminent concern.

AGGREGATING AUTONOMY

Insofar as the virtue of (liberal) justice is instilled in communist men and women, they will contend with each other fairly whenever their (private) interests put them at odds. Then the likelihood that they might seek to advance their own autonomy at the expense of the autonomy of others will be severely mitigated. But it will still be appropriate to regard aggregate autonomy as the logical sum of individuals' autonomies. Whoever would propose the maximization of autonomy would therefore hold a view analogous to the position of utilitarians – provided, of course, that degrees of autonomy can be regarded quantitatively the way utility is.[33] Util-

32 Cf. *The Social Contract*, Book II, Chapter 6.
33 It is not necessary to suppose that there is actually an autonomy metric but only that, in a very general sense, autonomy can be conceived as if it could be represented as an additive magnitude. Despite all the attention paid to measuring utility intra- and interpersonally, most utilitarians and their critics effectively assume a similar position on utility. It is enough, for them, in

itarians would maximize social utility, U_s, where U_s is the logical sum of the utilities of individuals $1, \ldots, n$.

(1) $$U_s = U_1 + U_2, \ldots, + U_n.$$

Autonomy maximizers would maximize social autonomy, A_s, where A_s is the logical sum of the autonomies of individuals $1, \ldots, n$.

(2) $$A_s = A_1 + A_2, \ldots, + A_n.$$

Therefore the possibility that some individuals' autonomy may be diminished in order to maximize A_s remains at least a theoretical possibility.

On the other hand, when individuals' interests are internally related, as they are when their actions are directed by a general will, the general interest, G – insofar as it is tantamount to an interest in enhancing individual autonomy – is not the logical sum of individuals' autonomies but more nearly the effect of their interactions. Rousseau's idea does not lend itself well to formal representation, but a reasonable approximation would be:

(3) $$G = A_1 \times A_2 \times \ldots \times A_n.$$

Whoever is concerned to maximize autonomy and who acknowledges a place for both justice and general will coordination would therefore aim to combine (2) and (3). The global maximind, total autonomy, A_t, would then be the sum of individual autonomies plus their interactive effects.

(4) $$A_t = A_s + G,$$

or equivalently,

(5) $$A_t = A_1 + A_2 + \ldots + A_n + (A_1 \times A_2 \times \ldots A_n).$$

In these terms, Rousseau and Marx after him, insofar as his view of communism is Rousseauean, implicitly claimed: (a) that, in a de jure state or under communist conditions, A_t is indeed the proper maximind, and (b) that the way to maximize A_t is to be just in *private* interactions and *In the public arena* to seek to maximize G directly. The rationale for (a) has already been discussed. In order to

assessing utilitarianism, that we can think of utility as an additive magnitude whether or not there is a good way – in practice or even in principle – to construct an appropriate metric.

defend (*b*), an additional claim, also of Rousseauean provenance, must be brought to bear.

As noted, a very weak construal of Rousseau's core idea would have autonomy be realized only within communities that recognize and implement the moral equality of persons, and would then conclude that, since autonomy enhancement is everyone's principal interest, individuals have an overriding interest in maintaining the viability of the community that makes autonomy possible. But since the existence of the political community itself is seldom likely to be implicated in collective decision making, the preeminence of general will coordination would properly become manifest only in rare instances. I have suggested that Rousseau probably intended more than this in grounding the de jure state on "the exercise of the general will" but that the reasonableness of this claim cannot be settled a priori. The issue can however be represented perspicuously.

Schematically, what Rousseau can be taken to have claimed is that individual autonomy itself is a function, at least in part, of total social autonomy. Then, if A_i designates the autonomy of the *i*th individual and x designates causal factors distinct from total social autonomy that affect *i*'s autonomy,

$$(6) \qquad A_i = f(A_t) + g(x).$$

Rousseau provides scarce help in specifying the form of the functions f and g, although it is evident that he does assume them to increase monotonically. In these terms, questions about the scope of general will coordination are questions about the importance of the function $g(x)$. At one extreme, it could be held that the value of A_i is mainly determined by this function; at the other, that $g(x)$ is set at zero or nearly zero. As remarked, the relative importance of A_t and x respectively is ultimately an empirical question.

From the timeless perspective of *The Social Contract*, Rousseau appears to be committed to the view that in a de jure state individual autonomy, A_i, is largely a function of total social autonomy, A_t. Rousseauean Marxists, equipped with a theory of history's trajectory, would draw the same conclusion, but relativized to a particular historical context. For reasons already marshaled, their conviction is that in the radically egalitarian world of communism the enhancement of individual autonomy would increasingly become a collective endeavor in which "the condition for the free development of each" is indeed "the free development of all." Insofar as individuals imbued with the virtue of justice and living in a world with massive economic surpluses would need to render collective choices, and insofar as there is a determinate general interest implicated in the choices they must make, they would be inclined, increasingly, to make this general interest their own and to place themselves, accordingly, "under the supreme direction of the general will."

It should be noted, finally, that although the diminution of some individuals' autonomies will seldom, if ever, be required for the enhancement of total autonomy under communist conditions it is likely, even under communism, that in order to maximize A_t some individuals' autonomies will be enhanced more than others. Undertaking some public work – constructing a new highway, for instance – will almost certainly affect individuals differently, with different implications for their autonomy. But insofar as formula (6), joined with formula (4) or (5), captures a sound idea, whenever anyone's autonomy is enhanced, everyone becomes, to some degree, more free. Egalitarians cannot hope for more. Inasmuch as autonomy depends on access to resources, and since even socialized resources are bound to be differentially available to individuals, it is unlikely that autonomy can ever be equally distributed. But under communism – a society without compelling scarcities, directed by a general will, populated by just individuals, and with distributive shares equalized to a degree uncontemplated even by liberal egalitarians – autonomy will be, as it were, sufficiently abundant that, like most other things, its distribution will no longer be of particular normative concern.

As remarked in Chapter 1, the most likely arena for general will coordination this side of communism is in small groups and intimate associations. There is no reason to doubt that this situation will remain true after communism too. If anything, a multiplication of "moral and collective bodies," of various sizes and (overlapping) constituencies, will be a likely feature of communist societies. In the (decentralized) administrative organs through which individuals' behaviors will be coordinated, institutions for "the administration of things," people may often find it reasonable to subordinate their private wills to the general will of these collective entities for just the reason Rousseau identified: in order to further their own most fundamental concerns.

Will "the exercise of the general will" then supplant its complement, the virtue of justice? Not entirely, since justice internalized will continue to coordinate individuals' behaviors in those spheres of life in which they set about to discover and realize their own distinctive potentialities, and since "the realm of freedom" is the best imaginable, materially feasible social order conducive to this end. Paradoxically, the recognition and implementation of the social dimension of autonomy are the conditions for the fullest possible realization of the core values, autonomy and self-realization, that liberals share with Rousseauean Marxists. The difference is that liberal construals of these ideas are flawed by their allegiance to the governing metaphor of the atomic individual. Following Rousseau, Marxists can overcome this allegiance as they grope, bereft of "recipes for the cookshops of the future," toward discovering what can now only be grasped schematically: the precise role of general will coordination under communism, the earthly – that is, materially possible – "form of association" in which, following Rousseau's prescription, "each one, while uniting with all, nevertheless obeys only himself."[34]

34 *The Social Contract*, Book I, Chapter 6.

Chapter 9

After Communism, communism?

We are still too close to a yet unfolding story to draw more than tentative conclusions about (big-C) Communism's demise. But even without the benefit of a long historical perspective, it is plain that 1989, the year Communism ended in Eastern Europe and imploded dramatically in the Soviet Union itself, and 1991, when Communism officially ended even in the land of its origin, were watershed years for socialist theory and practice. They marked the end of the historical project begun in 1917 and prepared, in part, in the three or four decades preceding the Bolshevik Revolution – during Marxism's classical phase, the Age of the Second International. As of this writing, China remains officially Communist, accounting for nearly a quarter of the world's population, and there are other survivors too at the peripheries of the old Communist system – in North Korea, Vietnam, and, of course, Cuba. But the exceptional status of these regimes is unlikely to last. Already in the Chinese case, it is mainly the political system that remains Communist (and even Stalinist). Vast sections of China have been opened up to infusions of capital and technology from Japan, East Asia, and the West – a fact that helps explain the persistence of the regime in power. Even if China remains officially Communist for some time, it is rapidly becoming transformed from an economic system built on the Soviet model into a source of cheap labor for foreign capital, a workshop for industries developed and organized elsewhere.

The causes and significance of these transformations will be debated for years. It has become commonplace for celebrants of capitalism in the West to gloat over the poor economic performance of the erstwhile socialist countries and to take their demise as proof of capitalism's superiority. But, in fact, the Soviet Union and Eastern Europe, before *glasnost* and *perestroika*, had been doing rather well by their own historical standards and in comparison with most Third World countries. In any case, it does not appear that any precipitous economic crisis brought the Second World to its demise. It is true that, for more than twenty years, the Eastern bloc countries had performed poorly when measured against levels of economic growth in the West and in some newly industrialized countries in the Third World.[1] No doubt, the perception of (comparative) stagnation, the sense that the gap in economic performance between the East and the West was no longer closing but actually intensifying, delegitimated Communist economic systems and helped lead to their eventual unraveling. More important, however, were the accumulated effects of the chronic shortcomings that had plagued the Soviet system from its inception: notorious inefficiencies in production and distribution, a general failure to meet consumer demands, and a glaring inability to produce at international standards, to innovate, or to marshal entrepreneurial forces.

But Communism almost certainly declined and fell more for social and political than strictly economic reasons. The rise of a highly educated, technocratic class and increasing cultural levels throughout the general population came into conflict with the old command system of economic management and its political superstructure. Ironically, in light of the future classical Marxism imputed to capitalism, the very success of the state bureaucratic system in the Eastern countries undid the conditions for its own reproducibility; the Soviet model of socialism dug its own grave. It has been famously argued by Herbert Marcuse that, despite the best intentions of liberal social philosophers, free speech and tolerance generally – in conditions of economic inequality and in the presence of mechanisms that militate against critical thinking – can work to ensure conformity and even function "repressively."[2] In the Soviet Union and Eastern Europe, the phenomenon of repressive tolerance seems hardly to have existed. There only repression functioned repressively. Thus *glasnost*, however necessary it might have been for economic development, was deadly for the political order of the erstwhile socialist countries.

It is impossible, after only a few years, to assess these changes. It is plain, however, that the optimism of 1989 has quickly soured

1 They had also done remarkably well in comparison with most of the Third World, a not insignificant sector of the world capitalist system.
2 See Chapter 3, note 15, herein.

and that the short- and middle-term prospects for the countries of the former Soviet bloc seem bleak – particularly on the economic front where the introduction of "free markets" was supposed to work magic. Perhaps someday parts of Eastern Europe will reach Western European standards of economic performance. However, for the foreseeable future, unemployment, stagnation, and continuing environmental hazards lie ahead. And devastating economic consequences for third parties are already evident too. Thus, in even the most optimistic of scenarios, Western and Japanese investments will be channeled away from Third World countries, especially from Africa and Latin America, exacerbating the already severe hardships the peoples of those continents face. With the end of Communism, the worst-off will therefore become worse off still, even allowing, as is far from assured, that the lot of the majority of people in what was once the Second World will eventually improve.

It is also plain that the end of Communism has unleashed long repressed nationalist and chauvinist passions along with religious and other reactionary and obscurantist convictions. By 1992, the consequences of political and moral regression have already caused incalculable harm. In addition, the collapse of the Soviet Union has removed the one constraint on the exercise of American military power in the Third World – with devastating consequences evident in the Gulf War, in the "moderation" of states that might otherwise seek a measure of national independence from the world capitalist system, and in the diminished programs and expectations of the remaining national liberation movements. Finally, even assuming economic success and discounting geopolitical consequences, the populations of the formerly socialist countries will have succeeded merely in trading one set of evils for another. The trade-off will seem appealing only to those too lacking in imagination to realize that the systems in place prior to 1989 hardly exhaust the historical possibilities.

If the experience of liberal democracies in the West provides an indication, the regimes likely to succeed the formerly Communist states will enjoy a greater measure of de facto legitimacy if they provide a (largely illusory) measure of popular control over public officials and if they are able to offer historically high standards of living to some significant portion of the population and the hope of higher standards of living to another significant portion. Some Western countries – the United States, for example – have attained extraordinary levels of political stability in so doing, even as nearly a third of the population is left politically and economically marginalized. It is far from clear, however, that this sense of legitimacy will continue indefinitely. In time, as in all the Western countries, even the relatively well-off will come to wonder whether a consumer society, with its perils to human well-being and to the world in which human beings live, is a prize worth struggling for after all.[3]

But this is not the place to speculate on the future of the erstwhile Second World or even on the causes of the fall of the system in place there. The question instead is what, if anything, the end of Communism has to do with small-*c* communism. The immediate but too easy answer is Nothing at all. This response cannot stand without modification, but there is substantial merit to it nonetheless. It is therefore worth exploring this answer before broaching the more subtle issues that make it too facile.

SMALL-C COMMUNISM

The idea of communism arose within radical and revolutionary currents in late-eighteenth- and early-nineteenth-century French politics. But its connection – or lack of it – with Communism has to do with the appropriation of that idea by Marx and Marxists after him. The too facile reason why the end of Communism has nothing to do with communism is that Communism has nothing – or only very little – to do with the communism of Marxist theory.

The term "Marxist theory" actually designates a constellation of theories that are not nearly so tightly integrated as was once assumed. Two components of this constellation are of particular relevance: historical materialism (Marx's theory of history) and Marxist political theory.

Historical materialism is a theory of history's structure and direction. It purports to provide an account of necessary and sufficient conditions for epochal historical change. In the historical materialist scheme, Communism is the final epochal stage, the historical successor of capitalism. However, communism admits of

3 Twenty-five years ago, this consciousness was sufficiently widespread in France and then in Italy to promote a sense of impending social revolution. Elsewhere, at least among students and youth generally, it became the basis for a large and insurgent social movement. Today, social movements inspired by a genuinely oppositional political vision are in eclipse, but awareness of the evils of (late) capitalism persists unabated.

phases. Socialism, still a form of class society in which the working class is politically dominant, is its lowest phase. It has become clear in recent years that the orthodox theory can be weakened and still remain "Marxist"; it can even be recast as an account only of necessary *material* conditions for the historical transformations the orthodox theory describes.[4] But any account of history's structure and direction that remains continuous conceptually with Marx's theory would maintain that socialism, communism's lowest phase, can only come about after capitalism has exhausted its potential for developing productive forces.[5] In other words, capitalism must first be "mature," even rotten (or rotting), before the socialist project can hope to succeed.

Now Communism was launched not where capitalism was already rotting but in one of Europe's least developed regions. Thus the Bolsheviks, because they were historical materialists, assumed, at the outset, that they were only attacking capitalism at its "weakest link" – the first step in a revolution of global or at least European dimensions. The idea that socialism could be built in one country was a later innovation – still framed, significantly, within a theoretical perspective shaped by classical historical materialist conceptions. But the doctrine of "socialism in one country," introduced under Stalin's aegis, represented a desperate – and barely coherent – attempt to legitimate Soviet reality in Marxist terms. Classical Marxists have always been wary of it, if not implacably opposed.

From a historical materialist vantage point, then, Communism was bound to fail. If anything, what embarrasses the theory is not 1989 or 1991 but the fact that it took more than seventy years after the Bolshevik project began for it to run its course in defeat.

It is also plain that Communism had little, if anything, to do with the strain of Marxist political theory or practice sketched in Chapter 5. Far from undermining the conditions for the reproducibility of the state form of political governance, the Communists permanently installed a repressive and ideological state apparatus – varying, over the years, in severity but not in form – that

---

4 See Wright, Levine, and Sober, *Reconstructing Marxism*, Chapter 5.
5 In this respect, the theory and practice of Communism after Communist power became entrenched in the Soviet Union are not conceptually continuous with Marx's theory. In view of the enormous influence of Communism on Marxist and socialist thought throughout most of this century, especially in the Third World, a similar conclusion would have to be drawn for many, if not most, twentieth-century Marxists.

worked, as ought to have been anticipated, to reinforce aspects of class society. For decades, socialists in the West and elsewhere pondered over the nature of Soviet society and shaped their political orientations around competing analyses of it. Many socialists have argued, with some plausibility, that the Soviet state even brought a "new class" of state and party bureaucrats to power. But whatever the true nature of Soviet and Eastern European societies before 1989, the one hypothesis that seems least defensible to all but the most ideologically blinded is the idea that the political system in place in those countries represented a form of workers' power. Again, in the Marxist scheme, it is precisely workers' power that socialist societies in transition to communism are supposed to implement.

Insofar as there was a Marxist warrant for neglecting to transform political institutions – to "smash" the old forms, as Lenin would have it, and introduce political structures of a new kind in their stead – it was drawn ironically from a crude historical materialist world view. Historical materialism invests the dynamic of historical change in the development of productive forces. The Bolsheviks accordingly took it upon themselves to develop productive forces by any means necessary – above all, by brutally enforced hierarchical controls and the subordination of all social struggles to the paramount task of increasing productivity. Social relations and their political and ideological superstructures could then take care of themselves – evolving into appropriate forms as productive forces advanced. It need hardly be said that this attitude is not consonant with Marx's express views, nor is it implied by historical materialist positions, properly understood.

In short, Communism neglected historical materialism when it should have taken it seriously and then misappropriated it, turning it into an excuse for not attempting the radical transformation of the social order Communists ruled.[6] One cannot help thinking that this manifest misuse of historical materialist positions was motivated, at least in part, by an attempt to reinforce the already

6 Without successful revolutionary endeavors in more advanced capitalist countries, it is unclear that the Bolsheviks or their successors could have done much better. Nor is it clear, except perhaps retrospectively, that they ought to have abstained from taking power in 1917. What is clear is just that historical materialism provides strong grounds for predicting the deformation and eventual demise of their revolutionary project – so long as socialism remained in place *only* in (relatively) undeveloped parts of the globe.

considerable power of state and party bureaucracies.[7] Thus, insofar as communism is an idea proper to Marxist theories, Communism had nothing to do with it. Therefore it would appear that the end of Communism does not in any way challenge procommunist convictions. But, of course, this response is too quick.

SOCIALISM

Since even a meretricious link between Communism and communism long ago dropped out of Communist thinking, and since communism has played little role of late either in the popular imagination or in political theory, the implosion of Communism and then its hasty termination in Eastern Europe and the Soviet Union and its decline and transformation in Western Europe and in most of the Third World have not done much harm to communism as an idea. But these events plainly have damaged the idea of socialism.

The damage has been exacerbated and perhaps even impelled by a parallel decline and transformation of social democracy. This phenomenon, which has been more subtle but nevertheless significant for the socialist project, stems from different causes: among others, the decline of labor movements in the advanced capitalist countries and a general inability on the part of the older Social Democratic parties to join forces constructively with ecologists, with feminists, or indeed with any of "the new social movements." In consequence, Social Democrats have become increasingly disinclined to imagine alternatives to capitalism or to propose even modest "structural reforms" of the regimes they manage or serve as "loyal oppositions."

In the First and Third Worlds, socialism has been hurt too by the apparent economic successes of capitalism in the 1980s. Self-representations to the contrary, the advanced capitalist countries have hardly succeeded in solving their fundamental social problems. But they have succeeded in enriching larger segments of their populations than heretofore, without too seriously diminishing

7   In this regard, it is well to recall that an important and compelling (partial) explanation for Communism's demise is that a large number of the new generation of state and party functionaries thought that they could do even better for themselves if they could take advantage of their expertise by becoming capitalists or at least by modifying the old command structures of the economies they governed.

the consumption possibilities of many – but by no means all – of those who have become worse off. The even more distorted economic successes registered by export-driven capitalist development in a few Third World countries in Asia have also redounded to socialism's disrepute.

Why these phenomena should be taken to justify traditional (nonegalitarian) economic liberalism is something for historians of the future, with the advantages of hindsight, to try to explain. But there can be no doubt that even laissez-faire capitalism is now widely thought to have been vindicated. Until quite recently, it seemed politically appropriate to debate the relative merits of capitalism and socialism. I have argued that, in that debate, socialism had the upper hand.[8] Nothing of substance has changed, but so abruptly has the political and intellectual climate been transformed that nowadays the idea that socialism might triumph over or even rival capitalism seems anachronistic even in academic discussions. Indeed, in many circles, the very idea of socialism has come to seem increasingly quaint.

To account for this turn of events fully, these and other vicissitudes of Communism, social democracy, and (late) capitalism would have to be taken into account. I would venture that it is Communism's fate that has had the greatest effect. But I will not pursue the issue further here. Instead, I shall turn to a problem that this change in intellectual fashion betokens. This problem is best approached not by reacting to the situations of political movements that in varying degrees identified with or opposed Marxism but by considering the vicissitudes of Marxism itself. Small-*c* communism is an idea proper to Marxist theory. If there is something about the end of Communism that has made it (more) problematic, we can best see what it is by focusing on the theory in which it is embedded.

MARXISM TODAY

For more than two decades, "analytical" Marxists have pursued the reconstruction, defense, and criticism of distinctively Marxist positions – in a way that has finally made many Marxist claims amenable to rational adjudication and revision.[9] The result has

8 See Levine, *Arguing for Socialism*, passim; on the political urgency of the capitalism–socialism debate, see esp. pp. 1–4.
9 Cf. Wright, Levine, and Sober, *Reconstructing Marxism*, Chapter 1.

been damaging to traditional understandings, but not nearly so devastating as is widely believed. It will be instructive to sketch how matters now stand before returning to communism in light of that understanding.

Historically, there were three kinds of projects that Marxists effectively combined – either because they recognized them as distinct and asserted a connection between them or because they failed even to acknowledge their differences.[10] There was first of all "scientific socialism," an account of "the laws of motion" of modes of production generally and, in particular, of the capitalist mode of production. Then there was class analysis, a view about what is explanatory of a range of phenomena of special interest to scientific socialists. Finally, there was the theory and practice of class emancipation, an attempt to identify and alleviate a particular form of oppression. Marxism as a theory of class emancipation identified the disease afflicting the existing world; Marxism as class analysis provided a diagnosis of its (rectifiable) causes; Marxism as scientific socialism identified the cure. Without class analysis and scientific socialism, the emancipatory critique would only be a moral condemnation; without the emancipatory objective, class analysis and scientific socialism would be of scientific interest only.

Until recently, the appeal of Marxism came, in large part, from the purported unity of these elements. Together they provided a basis for thinking that the principal oppressions of the existing order could be overcome; that human miseries could be understood scientifically and that their elimination could become the target of a feasible – indeed, of an ongoing – political project.

But in light of recent work, Marxism as scientific socialism and Marxism as class analysis have had their explanatory pretensions reduced. I have already suggested that, at best, historical materialism explains much less than was thought. It almost certainly does not explain the real course of historical change. At most, it identifies an endogenous process that establishes a historical agenda, an account of the economic structures that become materially possible or impossible as productive forces develop. It is also an open question how explanatory class analysis is. There is reason to think that it explains more than many people nowadays, including some who once thought it explained (nearly) everything, would be inclined to suppose. But it surely does not explain all

10 Many of the claims that follow are elaborated and defended in ibid., Chapter 8.

that Marxists used to think. More importantly, it may not connect with scientific socialism as tightly as was formerly thought. Thus class analysis may not figure as prominently as was once assumed in accounting for capitalism and its futures – or socialism and its possibilities.

Even more tellingly, the link between class emancipation and Marx's explanatory objectives is now less clear than it once seemed to be. The problem is not just that new social movements have brought to the fore the idea that there are oppressions that are not class oppressions. Then we would only be left with a diffuse pluralist emancipatory project – as some "post-Marxists," including many feminists, keep suggesting. The problem is rather that socialism itself, or at least its role in *any* emancipatory project, no longer seems as obvious as it formerly did. It is at least evident that not just *any* socialism is preferable to *any* capitalism. The wholesale rejection of Communism by the masses of people living under Communist regimes makes this conclusion indisputable.

An autobiographical digression will illustrate what I have in mind. In *Arguing for Socialism*, written less than a decade ago when the socialism–capitalism debate still seemed timely, I posed the following question: Given prevailing views of such values as freedom, justice, welfare, and democracy, can we say that socialism is better (for realizing these values) than capitalism or vice versa? Not surprisingly, I found that nothing very sure could be concluded without more specification of the particular institutional arrangements through which these economic structures were maintained. What was then called "actually existing socialism" was plainly less satisfactory with respect to many of the values in consideration than some existing (capitalist) liberal democracies. But I argued that many of the procapitalist arguments floated at the time carried little force and that, even at the level of abstraction at which my question was posed, a weak case could be made for socialism over capitalism with respect to all of the values in question, except perhaps welfare (or more exactly economic efficiency).

Since the terms "socialism" and "capitalism" are used very loosely in our political culture, it was a desideratum to define them, for my purpose, in a way that encompassed a wide range of legitimate uses. I also wanted definitions that were not tendentious – that did not, for instance, make socialism win the democracy competition by definition, as many prosocialist writers do. Finally, I wanted my definitions to concur with the historical materialist purchase on the subject. I therefore defined capitalism minimally, in the historical materialist way, as an economic structure without private ownership of other persons but with private property in external productive assets. Then socialism (or, better, postcapitalism) would, like capitalism, deny ownership of (other) persons but also exclude private property in (productively significant) external things. This is not the place to resume why, despite massive indeterminacies, socialism, so defined, fares better than capitalism. But it should be noted that this conclusion, and the problem it addresses, reflected precisely what the received Marxist view assumed: that the deprivatization of external things was instrumental for realizing fundamental normative objectives. It then followed that actually existing socialism, for all its faults and for all the respects in which it was worse (by consensus standards) than some existing capitalist regimes, was nevertheless a better or more advanced social system, *because* of its economic structure.

Strictly speaking, this position is not incompatible with what happened in 1989 and 1991. Nor is it a view that I would now repudiate. But it can no longer be assumed, in light of recent events, that socialism (postcapitalism) and capitalism are the right categories for comparison in light of the overwhelming popular repudiation of the (allegedly) more advanced form of society by the masses of people living in its grip.

To be sure, Communism and communism have little in common. But there is one powerful understanding they share inasmuch as both arose within the socialist movement and both, even Communism, have roots in the Marxist tradition. For both Communists and communists, capitalism's (likely) future is socialism, and socialism (and eventually communism) is indispensable for human emancipation. The events of 1989 and 1991 in no way prove these views wrong. But the massive popular rejection of "actually existing socialism" does show that even the most dedicated proponent of communism cannot simply assume them any longer. The relation among capitalism, socialism, and human emancipation must be rethought, even if, as I believe, the old understandings will finally be vindicated.

Of course one could argue that the Soviet Union and the regimes modeled on it, their laws and self-representations notwithstanding, were not genuinely socialist (postcapitalist). This view may seem disingenuous, but it is worth taking seriously as a theoretical claim. It has been advanced in different ways since the

1930s by dissident Trotskyists[11] and since the 1960s also by some Maoists.[12] In the final analysis, the nature of these societies is an empirical question. I will not pursue the issue here except to register the opinion that the popular perception of the socialist countries as socialist is almost certainly correct in the sense that their principal productive resources were in fact deprivatized. Of course, the means of production in these countries were not in any meaningful way "socialized." Nothing that has happened in recent years therefore impugns the idea that the socialization – indeed, the democratization – of society's principal means of production is instrumental for communism. But the more fundamental Marxist idea – that deprivatization is in itself emancipatory – has indeed been put in question.

Specifically, what needs to be reassessed is the connection between socialism, in the historical materialist sense, and the emancipatory interests that have made socialism and communism attractive to those with more to lose than their chains. The challenge is to rethink the connection between Marxism as scientific socialism and Marxism as a theory of human emancipation. The events of 1989 and 1991 are relevant to efforts to address this challenge if only because they put historical materialism in question in previously unforeseen ways.

HISTORICAL MATERIALISM

Historical materialism, the theoretical basis for scientific socialism, postulates the existence of discrete economic structures and of an endogenous dynamic connection between them. In its orthodox version, it proposes, as it were, a map of historical possibilities and an account of necessary movements along that map. Its weaker version, which only purports to show what economic structures are materially possible, retains the orthodox theory's map and even its notion of directionality. It only denies the inexorability of movement along the depicted trajectory. The difference in historical materialisms therefore does not touch on the features of the map. Historical materialists, however, have disagreed on what epochal structures the theory recognizes. Marx sometimes populated

11 See, for example, James Burnham, *The Managerial Revolution* (London, 1942).
12 See, for example, Charles Bettelheim, *Calcul économique et formes de propriété* (Paris: Maspero, 1971), *La transition vers l'économie socialiste* (Paris: Maspero, 1970), and *Class Struggles in the USSR*, vol. 1 (New York: Monthly Review Press, 1976), vol. 2 (New York: Monthly Review Press, 1978).

the historical trajectory with a host of precapitalist economic formations.[13] G. A. Cohen, in reconstructing Marx's theory with a view of defending it, identified only four epochal structures.[14] But all historical materialists agree that capitalism and socialism are on the list and that, at the level of abstraction at which the theory is pitched, these modes of production are mutually exclusive historical alternatives.

At that level of abstraction, Cohen's or Marx's periodization of history is as defensible (or indefensible) as it ever was. However, what has become more clear is that this level of abstraction is less useful for plotting the course of real history than even proponents of weak historical materialism used to think. Again, an autobiographical digression will illustrate the point.

In *Arguing for Socialism*, I supposed, following Marx, that political, ideological, and cultural factors were of secondary importance for understanding and assessing historical transformations of an epochal stature; what mainly mattered was "the economic base." I did maintain that forms of the state and even ideology could be decisive for understanding the future(s) of existing socialist and capitalist societies. But I assumed that what was most important – for implementing the normative values in consideration – was the underlying set of production relations. Again, this position is not refuted by recent events. But these events suggest that the historical materialist scheme, at most, charts only very long-range structural possibilities. Recent history forces theoreticians to question whether these possibilities may not be too remote for the political (and emancipatory) tasks to which they had been previously put.

According to the traditional historical materialist understanding, particular events, no matter how they are individuated, can be explained causally at least in principle, and historical trends can also be explained. However, these *explananda* are distinct; hence the frequently remarked observation that Marx's historical writings bear little evident connection to his theorizing about history. In any case, for Marxist politics, the account of historical trends is central. For Marxism since its inception, the struggle to advance to the next epochal stage – to socialism – has been the paramount emancipatory objective.

13 See, for example, *The German Ideology,* Part 1; and, more in point, the portions of the *Grundrisse* published in Karl Marx, *Pre-Capitalist Economic Formations,* ed. E. J. Hobsbawm (New York: International Publishers, 1964).
14 Cohen, *Karl Marx's Theory of History,* pp. 197–201.

However, it is now beginning to appear, especially after 1989, that the Marxist emancipatory project – whether or not it is continued in a Marxist idiom[15] – will need to identify economic structures at lower levels of abstraction than those historical materialism acknowledges. It may therefore be necessary to rethink the notions of capitalism and socialism that have for so long shaped Marxist political practice. I am not suggesting that the traditional focus on economic structures, on sets of production relations, be abandoned in favor of a theoretical and political program that treats "superstructural" phenomena on a par with the "economic base." The suggestion rather is that, for the Marxist emancipatory project, the capitalism–socialism distinction may be too abstract, that *intermediate* economic structures may be more politically pertinent.

In other words, the historical materialist "map," even if it does represent a materially possible course for human history, may be too abstract to illuminate emancipatory possibilities. If this suggestion is sound, it is not enough to know, in general, where we are coming from and where we are going. We also need a clear account of the shape of the land in order to know how to get from here to there. Socialism and ultimately communism may be humanity's (possible) future, but to reach that destination we may need to think more carefully about the feasibility and desirability of economic structures at lower levels of abstraction or, in more traditional terms, about "mixed" economic systems.

Historical materialism will be altered, but not overthrown, if it turns out that there are "intermediate" economic structures, neither capitalist nor socialist, that are in some sense "transitional" to the economic structures Marxists have traditionally acknowledged and that have a role to play in advancing class and general human emancipation. On the other hand, if it becomes clear, in light of sufficient evidence, that the deprivatization of alienable productive assets is irrelevant to the emancipatory interests it was supposed to serve, or even that it is detrimental, then the link between Marxism as scientific socialism and Marxism as class analysis will have been so profoundly severed that "Marxism" will indeed have come to an end.

15 I discuss the possibility that Marxism might be continued without allegiance to the traditional trappings of Marxist discourse in "What Is a Marxist Today?" *Canadian Journal of Philosophy*, supp. vol. 15, *Analyzing Marxism* (1989), pp. 29–58.

After Communism, communism?

MUST WE BRING SOCIAL DEMOCRACY BACK IN?

Neither recent events nor recent work in Marxist theory necessitate this conclusion. But in the present theoretical and political conjuncture it is prudent nevertheless for procommunists to look beyond Marxist sources. This conviction has motivated the attention paid to egalitarian liberalism in preceding chapters. If the central argument of those chapters is sound, liberal social philosophy is indispensable for forging a defensible normative theory of communism. At a more practical political level, the ecumenical attitude I am suggesting should also motivate taking non-Marxist socialism and the anarchist tradition seriously. It is worth recalling that in many European countries, and even in the United States, there once existed strains of socialist theory and practice distinct from Marxism that aimed at overcoming capitalism, not at humanizing it or managing it more efficiently. In recent decades, non-Marxist revolutionary socialism has all but disappeared. However, at a time when Marxism's core theoretical intuitions are in doubt, it is well for those who would continue the emancipatory project Marx undertook to look more carefully at these alternative traditions.

Perhaps the most pressing set of questions underscored by the events of 1989 and 1991 have to do with the role of markets in the organization of national and world economies. After Communism, it seems to many commentators in both the East and the West that the once raging contest between markets and plans has been won decisively by the former. Needless to say, it has been known in the capitalist West for decades that pure market economies are not sustainable. Existing capitalisms, even at the Thatcherite–Reaganite extremes, are state-regulated market exchange economies, not market economies in the strict sense. Nevertheless, there is now a virtual consensus – probably temporary, possibly not – that market incentives are indispensable for promoting the efficient utilization of productive capacities (including labor power). In addition, some measure of market competition or its functional equivalent now seems useful too for rendering bureaucrats and other state functionaries accountable. For many years, a number of socialist opponents of Communism, many of them declared Marxists, have insisted on the viability of *market socialism*[16] – that is, on

16 See, among others, Oskar Lange and Fred M. Taylor, *On the Economic Theory of Socialism*, ed. Benjamin Lippincott (Minneapolis: University of Minnesota

the possibility and desirability of market or marketlike arrangements without private ownership of (external) productive assets.[17] But no defender of market socialism committed to a view of socialism even remotely connected with Marx's can coherently propose that there be (substantial) capital markets in a socialist economy. Private control over investments and claims on the revenues that investments generate define private ownership. In the historical materialist scheme, therefore, the private control of investment effectively marks an economy as capitalist.[18]

If capital markets turn out to be indispensable for efficiency and therefore for creating the massive economic surpluses necessary for communism, then *pace* Marx and Marxism, it may be necessary for procommunists to propose roads to communism that bypass socialism (ostensibly, communism's lowest phase) and even to wonder if capitalism itself, suitably reformed, may not be a viable – perhaps the only viable – path to this end.[19] These are questions that, to date, have barely been broached – in large part thanks to the influence of Communism and the perceived need of non-Communist socialists to contrast their positions with Communist views.[20] But if these issues are to be raised and explored, as now seems urgent, strains of socialist theory and practice that have

Press, 1938); David Schweickart, *Capitalism or Worker Control? An Ethical and Economic Appraisal* (New York: Praeger, 1980); and John Roemer, "The Morality and Efficiency of Market Socialism," *Ethics*, vol. 102, no. 3 (1992), pp. 448–464.

17 A major shortcoming of the market socialist literature – and, more generally, of all attempts to conceive alternatives to capitalism distinct from the Soviet model – is a deep unclarity about "public ownership," the system of property rights that would supersede private ownership. For the beginnings of a theory of public ownership, see John Roemer, *Free to Lose* (Cambridge, Mass.: Harvard University Press, 1988), Chapter 10.

18 More precisely, individuals in societies that Marxists would regard as socialist probably can capitalize some of their assets and even introduce markets in these capitalized assets without destabilizing the basic economic structure. What socialism proscribes therefore is not capital markets per se, but capital markets that control the general contours of social investment.

19 Cf. Philippe Van Parijs and Robert Van der Veen, "The Capitalist Road to Communism," *Theory and Society*, vol. 15 (1986), pp. 635–655; and Philippe Van Parijs, "Basic Income Capitalism," *Ethics*, vol. 102, no. 3 (1992), pp. 465–484.

20 In so doing, Social Democrats have staked out a place for themselves to the right of the Communists, tending therefore to relinquish even a tenuous connection with socialism and communism. Those who have opposed the Communists from the left, particularly in the 1960s and 1970s, tended to wrap themselves even more resolutely than the Communists in the mantle of Marxist and Leninist orthodoxy, much to the detriment of the kind of rethinking that is now so plainly needed.

evinced more tolerance than Communism has for market arrangements – including tendencies that are identified with the Social Democratic tradition – are likely to be valuable resources.

There is also a Social Democratic political legacy that procommunists used to despise but that now appears more worth taking seriously. For decades, Communists played a generally conservative role in the maintenance of world order, their support for some Third World liberation movements notwithstanding. But the Communists, in view of their historical link with Bolshevism, were at least officially committed to the revolutionary overthrow of capitalist societies. Social Democrats, in contrast, favored more gradual structural transformations and continuity with liberal democratic political forms. If, as I have argued, liberal constraints are crucial for societies in transition to communism, political continuity with liberal democracy, wherever possible, may be the soundest way to achieve this desideratum. In the face of current economic and political realities, gradual structural transformations may be the only way fundamentally to alter the system in place.

I do not mean to suggest that, in the long-standing dispute between Social Democrats and Communists, the Social Democratic position has been vindicated. My point is rather that, with the end of Communism and the devolution of social democracy into a centrist, procapitalist political formation, the old debate has been superseded by events in a way that finally makes it possible for communists to look to both sides – and elsewhere too – for whatever guidance past theory and practice can afford. In a very different time and place, Lenin insisted on drawing "lines of demarcation" in theory and practice, even on abstruse matters of philosophical doctrine.[21] Now, in contrast, a broad ecumenicism, drawing even on theoretical currents traditionally opposed to Marxism and therefore ostensibly to communism, seems much the wiser stance.

What remains of the Left after "the crisis of Marxism" and the collapse of Communism is a motley of good causes, free of any coherent social vision. Good will and energetic social activism abide. But in all too many cases what has replaced the old Marxist project, grounded in scientific socialism, is a moralizing politics bereft of any guiding principle. The idea of communism, of a re-

---

21 See, for example, *Materialism and Empirio-Criticism* (1908), in Lenin, *Collected Works*, vol. 14.

public of ends directed by the *general* will of each individual, was a lodestar pointing in a different direction. Perhaps it can serve this function again; perhaps communism genuinely can be the end of history. In any case, I hope to have shown that the idea is not nearly so utopian or indefensible as many, including many on the left, nowadays assume.

But, in the end, theoretical speculation by itself can never establish the possibility or desirability of moving from "the realm of necessity" into "the realm of freedom." Therefore, insofar as I have been able to make a case for communism, my conclusions are tentative and provisional. What is beyond serious dispute is just that the traditional resources in the communist arsenal are not adequate to the task of again making communism a viable political ideal. For anyone who would take communism seriously – indeed, for anyone concerned with the emancipatory objectives that have spurred Marxist theory since its inception – now is a time in which many things that once seemed secure must be rethought.

It is fair to suppose that the end of Communism, harmful as it has been for this endeavor in the short run, can only help eventually in this increasingly urgent project. It is far from assured that a genuine communism will result from Communism's demise. But, with Communism daily discrediting communism, it could hardly be expected to emerge without it. In any case, after Communism, communism is not defunct. Indeed, the communist project remains much as it has always been. The principle difference after the events of recent years, surely a change for the better, is that communists must now face the future with fewer illusions, and with a sharper determination to rethink the convictions that sustain them.

Index of names

Adorno, Theodor, 148n
Althusser, Louis, xii, 33n, 115–122, 148n
Anderson, Perry, 148n
Aristotle, 128, 131–132, 136, 139, 142, 193, 196n
Arneson, Richard, 187n, 190n
Arrow, Kenneth, 78n, 84–85
Augustine, St., 48n
Axelrod, Robert, 64n

Balibar, Etienne, 148n
Bayle, Pierre, 9
Bentham, Jeremy, 137n
Berlin, Isaiah, 133n, 161n
Bettelheim, Charles, 214n
Bossanquet, Bernard, 33
Bossuet, Jacques Bénigne, 9
Bradley, Francis Herbert, 33
Brandt, Richard, 22n
Burnheim, James, 214n
Burnheim, John, 82n, 99n

Cohen, G. A., 104n, 148n, 149n, 170n, 183n, 187n, 188n, 215
Cohen, Joshua, 57n
Colletti, Lucio, 169n
Cromwell, Oliver, 180

Della Volpe, Galvanno, 169n
Diderot, Dennis, 9
Dworkin, Ronald, 150n, 184n, 187n

Elster, Jon, 64n, 128n
Engels, Friedrich 5, 135n

Fannon, Frantz, 72n
Fénelon, François de Salignac de la Mothe, 9
Feuerbach, Ludwig, 129
Fralin, Richard, 90–91n

Gauthier, David, 37n, 50n, 174n
Gilbert, Alan, 119n
Gramsci, Antonio, 115–120, 148n
Grice, Russell, 153n
Gutman, Amy, 124n

Hacking, Ian, 10n
Hampton, Jean, 50n
Hardin, Russell, 154n
Hart, Herbert L. A., 171n
Hartman, Heidi, 13n
Hegel, Georg Wilhelm Friedrich, 105, 110, 129, 135
Hillel, Rabbi, 60–63, 74
Hindess, Barry, 13n
Hirst, Paul Q. 13n
Hobbes, Thomas, 7, 9, 11, 19, 27, 36–59, passim, 66–68, 69n, 75, 103, 105, 163, 171n, 174–175, 179
Horkheimer, Max, 148n
Hume, David, 115n, 166n, 171n

Kant, Immanuel, 5, 21n, 32, 55n, 68–72, 160–167, 192–193
Kavka, Gregory S., 50n
Korsch, Karl, 148n

Lange, Oskar, 217n
Larmore, Charles E., 125n
Lenin, Vladimir Illyich, 93, 101–122 passim, 137, 180, 208, 219
Locke, John, 7, 9, 154, 190
Lukacs, Georg, 148n
Lukes, Steven, 71n, 148n, 173n

MacCallum, Gerald, 133n
Macchiavelli, Nicolo, 145n
Macpherson, Charles B., 133n
Malebranche, Nicolas de, 9

221

Index of names

Mao Ze-dong, 120–122
Marcuse, Herbert, 72–73, 148n, 204
Merleau-Ponty, Maurice, 148n
Mill, John Stuart 7, 9, 11, 112, 123–146
    passim, 152
Miller, Richard, 148n
Montesquieu, Charles Louis de
    Secondat, 9, 98n

Nozick, Robert, 151n

Okin Susan Moller, 130n
Okun, Arthur M., 151n
Ollman, Bertell, 33

Parfit, Derek, 57n
Pascal, Blaise, 9, 66–68
Pashukanis, E. B., 173–175, 178
Peffer, Rodney G., 135n
Perelman, Chaim, 193n
Plato, 113
Popper, Karl R., 161n

Rawls, John, 38n, 125–126,
    132, 151n, 153, 162n, 174n,
    185–190, 195
Resnick, Stephen, 13n
Riley, Patrick, 9n
Robespierre, Maxmillien, 181
Roemer, John, 218n
Royce, Josiah, 33

Saint-Just, Louis Antoine, 181
Saint-Simon, Claude Henri, 5
Sandel, Michael J., 124n
Sartre, Jean-Paul, 72–73, 148n
Scanlon, Thomas M., 153n
Schofield, Norman J., 78n
Schumpeter, Joseph, 77n
Schwartz, Thomas, 78n
Schweikart, David, 218n
Sen, Amartya K., 22n
Shklar, Judith N., 9n, 103n
Smith, Adam, 157n
Stalin, Joseph, 172

Talmon, Jacob, 161n
Taylor, Fred M., 217n
Taylor, Michael, 64n
Teitelman, Michael, 154n
Thompson, Dennis F., 112n, 134n
Trotsky, Leon, 214
Tucker, Robert, 135n

Van der Veen, Robert, 218n
Van Parijs, Philippe, 218n

Walzer, Michael, 92n, 124n, 180n
Weber, Max, 71–72
Wilde, Oscar, 92
Williams, Bernard, 153n
Wolff, Richard, 13n
Wolff, Robert Paul, xi–xii, 126n